W9-BKK-348

RIVERSIDE PUBLIC LIBRARY

3 1403 00273 7624

12/09

THE
DIFFERENCE
GOD MAKES

THE DIFFERENCE GOD MAKES

A Catholic Vision of Faith, Communion, and Culture

Francis Cardinal George, O.M.I.

Riverside Public Library —
Thanks!
Franc Cardil George om.

Riverside Public Library
One Burling Road
Riverside, Illinois 60546

A Herder & Herder Book
The Crossroad Publishing Company
New York

The Crossroad Publishing Company
www.CrossroadPublishing.com

© 2009 by Francis Cardinal George, O.M.I.

All rights reserved. No part of this book may be reproduced, stored in a retrieval system, or transmitted, in any form or by any means, electronic, mechanical, photocopying, recording, or otherwise, without the written permission of The Crossroad Publishing Company.

Permissions appear on page 353, which is a continuation of this copyright page.

In continuation of our 200-year tradition of independent publishing, The Crossroad Publishing Company proudly offers a variety of books with strong, original voices and diverse perspectives. The viewpoints expressed in our books are not necessarily those of The Crossroad Publishing Company, any of its imprints or of its employees. No claims are made or responsibility assumed for any health or other benefit.

Printed in the United States of America.

The text of this book is set in 12.5/15.5 Adobe Garamond.
The display face is Mrs. Eaves.

Library of Congress Cataloging-in-Publication Data

George, Francis E. (Francis Eugene), 1937-
    The difference God makes : a Catholic vision of faith, communion, and culture / Francis George.
        p. cm.
    "A Herder & Herder book."
    Includes bibliographical references (p.   ) and index.
    ISBN-13: 978-0-8245-2582-8 (cloth)
    ISBN-10: 0-8245-2582-5 (cloth)
    1. Catholic Church—Doctrines.   I. Title.
BX1751.3.G46 2009
230′.2—dc22
                                                        2009032348

2   3   4   5   6   7   8   9   10   14   13   12   11   10   09

Contents

Living through Others

WHEN I WAS A VERY SMALL BOY, I learned a lot about how one person can absorb another's self-consciousness by observing my mother buying clothes for my father. She knew what he wanted better than he did, and her choices were always correct. He would wear what she bought for him because her decisions made a man not interested in fashion look good, and making him look good made her feel good.

Growing up means sometimes testing what your mother knew was good for you in order to find out if you have a mind of your own. Even when we make our own way, however, our mother and father's words come back, their attitudes and admonitions create a world always with us, for it is the world in which we first learned to love. We live through them and they through us. If their parental care is effective, we learn how to live both freely and lovingly.

Catholics call the Church "mother." We call her that truly because St. Paul tells us she is the bride of Christ (Eph. 5:21–33) and has the mind of Christ (1 Cor. 2:16). Christ is the difference that God makes in this world he so loves; and through the Church we are able to live in Christ here and with him and all the saints for all eternity. As children, we see things through our mother's eyes; but how do we see our mother? We discover her when we self-consciously examine our selves, our lives, and our actions in the family and in society.

The Second Vatican Council (1962–65) was a call from the Church for her children to think anew about the life from Christ she has given us and about how it should be lived in the world. The Council was missionary. It was called so that the Church, from the sources of her own internal unity, could bind up the wounds of a severely divided world. The theology of Church and mission that underlay the Council's documents was based on communion, understood as a network of relationships that are formed when the gifts of Christ are shared with others.

Exclusive nationalism, racism, cultural chauvinism, denial of human rights, economic oppression and other sources of disunity break communion. Less often is individualism as an ideology identified as an obstacle to relationships, to common life and common good. In the United States, individualism is so closely associated with creativity and personal freedom that the Gospel's injunction to surrender oneself to Christ and to others in order to be free has become largely incomprehensible. There is historic irony in our creating social polity on the basis of individualism. We have created a society that both needs numerous instruments to protect individuals from the consequences, for themselves and others, of their own desires and that also encourages individuals to act out their "dreams" without counting the consequences. In the clash of individualistic claims, courts sort out the winners and the losers. The major loser in this often arbitrary system is society as a whole.

At the time of the Council, many assumed that the proper realm of freedom was not the Church but the world then coming to be with the help of new technology and expanding democracy. Today, that world has lost much of its claim to be the protector of freedom, and the Church must again press her case, preaching the truth about human nature and destiny, presenting the mind of Christ in new ways. The essays assembled in this collection address the relationships that are the means and the goal of a new evangelization, a deepening of our life with Christ that makes all the difference in the world, for us and for the world itself.

The beginning and end of all relationships is our relation to God. Communion with God poses the question of "which" God is true, for surrender to a false God leads to death. In a vision based on communion, the search for objective truth is communal and inter-subjective in both its basis and its method. Methods of philosophy and theology are, however, less evident in these pages than is the delineation of the relational context in which the search for truth has to be nurtured.

The Church is always situated in history and, as catholic, the Church finds herself in the history of the entire human race. The mysteries of faith are themselves social, from the doctrine of the Trinity to St. Paul's understanding of the Church as body. The con-viction that we are all related not only in one race or one family but also in one body brings with it the realization that everything any-one does affects in some way everyone else. This assertion about the life of the spirit, paradoxically, should gain new credibility with the development of ecological consciousness. The classical dilem-mas of the relationship between mind and body or between grace and nature now play themselves out in a new theater of action, but all the answers point to the primacy of relationship in establishing identity. That is the basic thesis of these reflections.

If every facet of our existence is related, then spiritual growth entails coming to full consciousness of what participation in being, in humanity, in voluntary associations of all types and in the Church calls us to become. Growth qualifies all the relationships, so a phenomenology of human experience can become a kaleidoscope of changes nearly impossible to detail. But a difficulty in seeing the whole in detail does not mean we cannot see it at all. Reducing knowledge to specializations and life to a series of disparate details or unrelated events is a formula for despair or, worse, manipulation.

The Church, which is the primary subject of the relationships discussed in this book, is a communion of diverse relations. Some are ontological, rooted in the Trinity. Some are juridical, either based on divine institution or on ecclesiastical law. Some relations are invisible, some are external, and some are both. Some relations unite only those in visible ecclesial communion and some connect Christians with those who are not even believers. Some relations are adventitious, unnecessary for the constitution of the Church but still part of her lived experience in various cultures. Some relations are themselves symbols, extending the Church's communion beyond our space and time, making objectively present the divine goal that the relations point us toward and enable us to experience now.

Reading a book establishes a relationship of some sort between author and reader. The reader sees things through the author's mind and words. It's a somewhat lopsided relationship, similar to that between God and the world; God doesn't change but the world does. I hope, however, that in this case any changes in the reader will eventually further hone the thought and actions of the author. Producing a book also creates a relationship between author and editor and deepens the relationship among friends who thought the publication a good idea and gave needed encouragement and helpful advice.

I am particularly grateful to Thomas Levergood, the director of the Lumen Christi Institute at the University of Chicago, and to Robert Royal, president of the Faith and Reason Institute in Washington, D.C. John Jones edited the pieces for the Crossroad Publishing Company and was always patient with my impatience. The people with whom I live and work in Chicago, especially the vicar general of the archdiocese, Fr. John Canary, and the chancellor, Mr. Jimmy Lago, made it possible for me to find time to devote to this project. Ms. Marie Knoll arranges and puts order into my manuscripts. Ms. Mary Hallan FioRito, along with Fr. Dan Flens, try to put order into my life. All these and many others are integral to the relationships to which this book is witness, and I thank them.

Finally, the thought and example of Pope John Paul II are everywhere in this book. It was a great privilege to be a bishop of the Catholic Church during the pontificate of John Paul II. He was a father and a mentor. In the communion of saints, we believe that such relationships are stronger than death.

Francis Cardinal George, O.M.I.
Feast of St. Martin I, Pope and Martyr
April 13, 2009

Part One

THE CHURCH'S MISSION
Universal Communion

Chapter 1

Of God and Man

The Two Cities in the Third Millennium

HISTORY IS WHAT GOD REMEMBERS. No calendar is neutral, as the French revolutionaries and various fascist dictators well understood.[1] To mark a Christian millennium is to claim that we remember what God knows to be of central importance in human history. The millennium's importance is determined by the decisive and momentous influence of the person of Jesus Christ. Out of our understanding of who Christ is, the relationship between an incarnational metaphysics and the political/social sphere can be explored, demonstrating how the former ought to be the permanent, though freely offered, structuring element of the latter.

St. Augustine's understanding of this relationship is more helpful than the various views that have flowed from the characteristically modern construal of the world. This Augustinian perspective has shaped not only the Catholic community, but most Protestant and some other Christian groups as well. It has been a continuous point of reference throughout the past sixteen hundred years for analyzing the relationships between faith and society, and it continues to be a point of reference in understanding the relationship between faith and the modern nation state.

Philosophy of Incarnation

At the heart of Christianity is a provocative claim: *In Jesus Christ, God has become a creature, without ceasing to be God and without compromising the integrity of the creature he becomes.* Many pre-Christian myths and legends spoke of God or the gods "becoming" creaturely, but such incarnations always resulted in uneasy mixtures of the divine and the nondivine. Thus Achilles and Hercules are quasi-godly and quasi-mortal, their divinity compromised by their humanity and vice versa. But as the Greek and Latin theologians of the patristic period struggled to express their incarnational faith, they consciously abandoned this mythological construal. The Council of Chalcedon in 451 expressed the radicality of Christian belief when it said that in the divine person of Jesus Christ, two natures—divine and human—come together in a hypostatic union, without mixing, mingling, or confusion. This means that in Jesus the divine and the human unite without competition or compromise. Christ is not quasi-divine and quasi-human; in fact, just such a mythological reading was rejected in 325 at the Council of Nicea during the struggle against Arianism. Rather, Jesus is fully divine and fully human, the proximity of the divine enhancing and not weakening the integrity of the human.

But the condition for the possibility of such a claim is a new understanding of the nature of God. Finite things exist necessarily in a sort of mutual exclusivity: the being of one is predicated, at least in part, on its *not* being the other. Hence, when one finite thing "becomes" another, it does so through ontological aggression and surrender: the desk becomes a pile of ashes through being destroyed by fire, and the lion assimilates the antelope by devouring it. Competition characterizes the play between conditional realities. Therefore, when the Church proclaims that in Jesus Christ the divine and the human have come together without competition and compromise, she is saying something of extraordinary novelty. She is claiming that God is not a worldly nature, not *a* being, not one thing alongside others. God is not in competition with nature because God does not belong to created nature; God does not overwhelm finite being, because God is not a finite being.[2]

When Christian theologians, inspired by their faith in the Incarnation, attempted to name God, they accordingly reached for language that evoked this distinctiveness. Thus St. Anselm said that God is not so much the supreme being as "that than which no greater can be thought," implying, paradoxically, that God plus the world is not greater than God alone.[3] And when St. Thomas Aquinas named God, he avoided the term *ens summum* (highest being) and opted for *ipsum esse subsistens* (the subsistent act of to-be itself).[4]

Both of these theologians thought of God as noncompetitively transcendent to the realm of finite things and therefore totally immanent to all things as the cause of their being. God is *transcendent* cause, and therefore Christianity is not a form of pantheism or Emersonian panentheism; but God is therefore closer to his creatures than they are to themselves. God is not related to the world, for that would create too great a division between God and the world, but neither is God identified with the world. The transcendent God is within his creation as the cause of its very being.

It is from this understanding of God, rooted in but developed from Jewish faith, that the peculiarly Christian sense of creation flows. Because God is not one being among others but rather the sheer energy of to-be itself, God does not make the world through manipulation, change, or violence, as the gods of philosophy and mythology do. Since there is literally nothing outside of God, he makes the entirety of the finite realm *ex nihilo,* through an act of purest and gentlest generosity.[5] God's is a nonpossessive love. And since God is the act of to-be, all creaturely things exist in and through God, "participating" in the power of his being and the graciousness of his love. And we can draw a final implication: because all of nature and the cosmos are, likewise, creatures participating in the divine generosity, they are all related to one another by bonds of ontological intimacy.

When St. Francis of Assisi spoke of "brother sun and sister moon," he was making both a poetically evocative and metaphysically precise remark. All things in the cosmos exist in a *communio* with one another precisely because they are rooted in a more primordial *communio* with the creator God. This view of reality as a communion based on love is the worldview that proceeds from the Incarnation.

Augustine's Two Cities

Whatever Christians say about the social, political, and economic realm must flow from this grounding metaphysical vision. Or better put, there is an unavoidably social dimension to the Christian ontology of *communio* and participation. This can be discerned clearly in one of the most remarkable and influential presentations of the Christian worldview ever written: the *De Civitate Dei* — *On the City of God* — of St. Augustine. What strikes the modern reader perhaps most immediately is St. Augustine's adamant refusal to dialogue with the representatives of the polity of Rome who had challenged the legitimacy of Christianity. He is interested in neither accommodating nor compromising with the Roman system, which he sees as fallen. Rather, he boldly proposes the Christian way as being, in all regards, preferable. He does not turn to Rome to find a social theory or political arrangement compatible with a privatized and interiorized Christian spirituality; on the contrary, he excoriates Rome as an unjust society and holds up Christianity itself as the only valid basis for a just form of social arrangement.[6]

Augustine's hermeneutical key is well known. He distinguishes sharply between the City of Man (a collectivity based upon self-love) and the City of God (a collectivity whose foundation is the shared love of God). The former is not so much an inadequate society; it is rather like a group of thieves or marauders masquerading as a body politic. Much of the first part of *De Civitate Dei* is a spirited demonstration that what looks like a paragon of justice—the Roman Empire—is in fact a manifestation of the City of Man.

Augustine's argument has a "theological" and a "political" phase. First, he shows, over hundreds of pages, that the multiple gods of Rome are in fact demons because they engage in and encourage various forms of immorality, including and especially rivalry, jealousy, and warfare.[7] Then he paints a vivid picture of the political life that has followed from the worship of such gods. What has characterized Rome, from its founding in the fratricidal struggle between Romulus and Remus to the chaos of Augustine's day, is unremitting violence. The door of Janus, supposed to be closed during times of peace, has remained stubbornly open for almost the entirety of Roman history. The regnant spirit of Rome is what Augustine refers to as the *libido dominandi,* the lust for mastery, and it is this spirit that has sent conquering armies around the world. At the heart of Augustine's analysis of Rome is the correlation between a faulty metaphysics (the worship of finite and self-assertive gods) and a faulty polity of violence and domination. A denial of a metaphysic of participation and *communio* leads to the false imitation of justice in the City of Man.

But Christians believe in the God who is Father of Jesus Christ, a God of nonviolent and creative love who brings the whole of the world into being from nothing. Such a God, unlike the false gods of Rome, enters into competitive relation with no one or no thing. The worship of such a God leads to a society based not on the *libido dominandi* but on the love, compassion, nonviolence, and forgiveness preached and embodied by Jesus. What Augustine proposes, therefore, is an *altera civitas* that has "no logical or causal connection to the city of violence," requiring the repudiation of worldly *dominium* and worldly peace.[8] It is a city based upon the consensus that mirrors the community of the saints and angels in heaven, an icon of the heavenly *ordo*. This *communio* conception of society corresponds to God's original and deepest intention toward the world.

If one seeks to know the origins of the City of Man — the corruption of this original intention of God — one has to look to the rebellion of Adam and Eve. In the original sin, Augustine sees the first human decision to sever the relationship with God, to deny the implications of creation and *communio* and to establish a kind of "secular" realm apart from God. The violence and injustice of Rome is, for Augustine, simply the latest and most virulent consequence of this original rebellion.

Again, what is surprising for moderns is Augustine's refusal to place this analysis in anything even vaguely resembling a "church/state" context. It is not the case that the secular state ought to order public life while the Church cares for the spiritual good of the people. There is no such easy distinction in Augustine. There is, rather, the dramatic difference between the false worship (and hence flawed social arrangement) of the City of Man and the proper worship (and hence life-giving social arrangement) of the City of God. The problem is not how to reconcile the competing concerns of the spiritual and the secular; the problem is orthodoxy, that is to say, getting our metaphysics and our praise of God in order, so that we can live in a just, rightly ordered society.

It is impossible to trace in a brief chapter the complex development (and corruption) of this Augustinian notion through late antiquity and the Middle Ages. But one can see its perdurance in the remarkable relationship between medieval worship and social life. At the center of the medieval town — both physically and psychologically — was the church or cathedral, where the drama of the paschal mystery and its communal implications were played out in a sacramental rhythm. This visual display of the Christian faith shaped the consciousness of worshipers and in turn influenced economic, agricultural, and political life, as had the Temple in Jerusalem. The activity of medieval guilds, the labors of farmers, the ordering of the economy — all were predicated upon and shaped by the sacramental life, especially baptism and the Eucharist.[9] There was a keen sense that the heavenly liturgy (God's *ordo*), iconically displayed in the earthly liturgy, worked its way into all of those social and political realities that today we would misleadingly refer to as entirely "secular." In the medieval consciousness, a sacred/secular chasm would have seemed anomalous, since politics, economics, and social order existed as a sort of extension of the sacramental life of the Church.

As the civil society became more explicitly shaped by faith, it came to be treated as good in itself because it had the same ultimate goals as the Church: the incorporation of each citizen into communion with God. Thomas Aquinas, using Aristotle's reflections on man as essentially political and social, admitted real distinctions between church and state according to their respective functions, but he saw them united in a single goal — the common good of all on earth and a common life in God for all eternity.

The Emergence of the Modern: A Compromise with the City of Man

The dark underside of this ideal unity of the social order informed by religious faith was the use of state power, often uninfluenced by moral considerations of its limits, to enforce religious conformity — a conformity more often used for political than for genuinely religious ends. The reaction to this misuse of power justified modernity's understanding of religious freedom. What created modern consciousness is a breakdown of classical Christian participation metaphysics and the consequent emergence of a secular arena at best only incidentally related to God. It is this modern, nonparticipatory, ideological context that impoverishes most of our discussions of religion and politics. It is most evident, perhaps, not in the loss of visual symbols to integrate space but in the creation of rival calendars to shape the rhythm of public life. In the modern era, national feasts and ceremonies replaced the liturgical calendar of the Church, whose feasts become private observances. The end of the modern era, however, is signaled by the inability of the secular calendar to call people out of their private concerns into the rhythm of a shared public life. National holidays have become primarily occasions for private recreation. Time itself becomes a field to be personally scheduled, a function of private purposes. A rigorously secularized society is less and less able to call people to any kind of participation.

The loss of the *communio* ontology in Western thought begins, perhaps surprisingly, just after Aquinas, in the writings of Duns Scotus. Scotus consciously repudiates the Thomistic analogy of being — predicated upon participation — and adopts a univocal conception of being. Though it was perhaps Scotus's intention to draw the world and God into closer connection, this epistemological and ontological shift had the opposite effect. In maintaining that God and the world can be described with a univocal concept of being, Scotus implied that the divine and the nondivine are both instances of some greater and commonly shared power of existence.[10] But in so doing, he radically separated God from the world, rendering the former a supreme being (however infinite) and the latter a collectivity of beings. In opting for the univocity of the idea of existence, Scotus set God and world alongside each other, thereby separating "nature" and "grace" far more definitively than Aquinas or Augustine ever had and effectively undermining a metaphysics of creation and participation. God is no longer that generous power in which all things exist but rather that supreme being next to whom or apart from whom all other beings exist.

The distancing of God from creation and the defining of the world as profane, made possible by this univocal concept of being, can be seen in the voluntarism and nominalism of William of Ockham, which in turn had a decisive influence on Martin Luther. Scotus's compromised sense of analogy shaped the later and more decadent scholasticism, finally giving rise to Francisco Suarez's awkward rendering of Thomas's doctrine of analogy.[11] Some have argued that this Jesuit Renaissance version of Aquinas — with its sharp delineation of nature and grace — came to form modern consciousness, especially through the work of the Jesuit-trained René Descartes.[12] In both its Lutheran and Cartesian manifestations, modernity assumes a fundamental split between the divine and the nondivine and hence implicitly denies the participation/*communio* metaphysics that had shaped the Christian world through the ancient and medieval periods.

What does this modern worldview produce in the arena of the social and political? Thomas Hobbes made the political implications of modernity most evident. In his famous description of the natural (prepolitical) state of human beings as "solitary, poor, nasty, brutish, and short," Hobbes assumes the primacy of antagonism.[13] Void of a religious, and therefore communitarian, sensibility, natural man is engaged in a desperate attempt to keep himself alive, fighting a "war of all against all." Responding only to his most elemental passions, man in the state of nature lives a thoroughly individualist and "secular" existence, and any link to an englobing and transcendent context is lost.

Given this framework, the role of government — Hobbes's Leviathan — becomes what it was in ancient Rome: the maintenance of a temporary and ersatz peace on the basis of coercion and violent control. The only way to curb the relentless violence of the state of nature, Hobbes assumes, is to accept the mitigated violence of the commonwealth. Because debates over ultimate ends and especially over theology tend to be disruptive of the peace, Hobbes places the Church under the tight control of the Leviathan, the sovereign who determines and enforces what is to be believed. To be sure, this adoption of a particular religious policy has nothing to do with a correlation to an objective truth; it is simply adopted as political expediency. It is this stipulation that constitutes the core of the modern "theological" vision. The natural state of human beings is irreligious, unrelated to a transcendent God and his purposes, thoroughly secular. Whatever role religion plays in the structuring of life is artificial and totally subordinate to political ends.

This Hobbesianism is softened a bit but preserved in its essential structures in the political thought of John Locke. Though he allows a rudimentary moral sense to remain even in the state of nature, Locke follows Hobbes in deriving individual rights from irresistible and antagonizing passions and in defining government's role as basically protective of those individualist prerogatives. Government's only task is to ensure one man's legitimate claim to life, liberty, and property over and against the encroachments of others. The loss of a sense of man's nature as deeply social leaves unchallenged the assumption that antagonism, disassociation, and suspicion are the natural condition of human beings. Here, the metaphysics of participation and *communio* has become a distant cultural memory.

This Hobbes/Locke tradition profoundly shaped the minds of the founding fathers of the United States. In the prologue to the Declaration of Independence, we hear of "self-evident truths" concerning "inalienable rights" to life, liberty, and the pursuit of happiness. As in Hobbes and Locke, these rights are individualistic — my liberty and life over and against yours. These rights are somewhat correlated to moral ends outside of themselves by the greater or lesser religious sense of common destiny and purpose in the minds and beliefs of many of the founders; but it is, tellingly, the *pursuit* of happiness — unguided, unanchored, unfocused by truth — that is guaranteed as a right. And government is "instituted among men" in order to protect these prerogatives and hence assure some level of peace and order in a still primarily antagonistic community. In what appears to be a departure from Hobbes, the framers of our Constitution insisted that no single religion be officially established but that the state should remain separated from religion, neither sanctioning nor prohibiting its exercise. This approach to religion, however, is still essentially Hobbesian, since it proceeds from the distinctively modern creation of a thoroughly secular space, untouched by religious questions, concerns, and finalities.

Much more could be said about the subtle differences in emphasis and accent between the pure Hobbesian, Lockean, and American construals of political reality. For example, Alexis de Tocqueville's still provocative analysis of the play between the American "secular" state and the vibrant, though officially privatized, religiousness of the American people continues to yield insights into the actual experience of generations of Americans. But despite certain nuanced differences, all three perspectives remain recognizably secular and modern in form and content. All three are possible only after the breakdown of the *communio* metaphysics characteristic of authentic Christianity. And therefore, all three amount to an embrace — whether relatively enthusiastic or relatively cautious — of what Augustine would describe as the City of Man.

Protestantism and Modernity in the American Context

What was the Christian response to the challenge of modernity in its American form? The full answer is obviously complex, and it varies according to whether one begins from a Protestant or from a Catholic perspective. After Walter Rauschenbusch's theology of the Social Gospel in the beginning decades of the twentieth century, the two most influential American Protestant social thinkers of the last century were the prolific Niebuhr brothers, Reinhold and H. Richard. What makes these figures particularly interesting from our perspective is their Augustinianism, expressed in and for the peculiarly American context.

Reinhold Niebuhr began his career as a liberal in the tradition of Rauschenbusch and the Social Gospel, but soon he became disillusioned with what he took to be the ineffectuality and uncritical idealism of this position. Through his pastoral practice and his reading of the Hebrew prophets, he was in time converted to a stance that his commentators are nearly unanimous in referring to as "Christian realism." By this they mean that, despite (or perhaps because of) his religiosity, there was nothing dreamily idealist about Niebuhr's political analysis. He was willing to take human beings as they are — with all of their duplicity, violence, selfishness, rancor, and sin — and not as he would like them to be. "In political and moral theory, 'realism' denotes the disposition to take all factors in a social and political situation, which offer resistance to established norms, into account, particularly the factors of self-interest and power."[14]

Niebuhrean realism manifested itself in the distinction between a personal ethic of love and a social ethic of justice. Whereas the demands of radical love contained in the Sermon on the Mount could be justifiably applied to the personal realm, they would have to be set aside in favor of the more mitigated form of love that is justice when applied to the properly social or political arena. Given the fact of original sin, it is simply asking too much, thinks Niebuhr, to expect a body politic to behave according to the absolute moral demands of the Gospel. The more appropriate and "realistic" criterion for evaluation of the moral quality of a society is that of justice, that "rendering to each his due" which is a qualified mode of love.[15] This clarification, with its deepest roots in Max Weber's distinction between an "ethic of ends" and an "ethic of means," enabled Niebuhr to accept and affirm, for example, both a personal embrace of pacifism on the part of the saint and a social acceptance of warfare as a tragic necessity on the part of the body politic.

For our purposes, it is interesting to note that Niebuhr saw Augustine as a major influence in the development of his social ethic. Presumably it was Augustine's honest assessment of the City of Man and his qualified acceptance of certain social practices (such as warfare) that shaped Niebuhr's position. It seems, however, that Niebuhr's solution bears only a passing resemblance to Augustine's treatment of the two cities. For St. Augustine, the Niebuhrean distinction between love and justice would be highly problematic, precisely because what determines the justice of the City of God is finally the quality of its love. The City of God is just only in the measure that it remains a collectivity that loves God (and hence human beings) according to the pattern of Jesus. Furthermore, the privatization of love would have struck Augustine as untenable. As Henri de Lubac pointed out in his *Catholicism,* one of the defining marks of the Church Fathers as a whole is the passionate conviction that no dogma is to be construed individualistically, that every Christian claim has a social range and implication. That there is a private and interior dimension that can be cleanly distinguished from the public seems to be a conviction far more Lutheran than Augustinian, and it would certainly fly in the face of the *communio* metaphysic we have been describing.

A form of Protestant Augustinianism perhaps more congenial to this analysis is that of Reinhold Niebuhr's brother, H[elmut] Richard Niebuhr. In his classic text *Christ and Culture,* H. Richard Niebuhr distinguished several paradigms for the relationship of Christian faith to the culture in which it finds itself.[16] Christ has been envisioned over the centuries as, variously, *against, over, of,* and *in paradoxical relation to* the culture. Each of these positions has advantages and disadvantages, but Niebuhr seems to favor the paradigm that he articulates last, namely, Christ as the *transformer of culture.*

According to this model, the culture is fallen and hence in need of transformation, but it is also capable of conversion through the influence of Christ's way of being. The "transformation" paradigm is sufficiently "realistic" in its honest assessment of sin, but it is also spiritually alert to the possibility of a real and thorough conversion of a culture through Christ. Intriguingly, H. Richard Niebuhr, claims St. Augustine — especially in the *City of God* — as the best advocate of this position, and here we can agree. There is no artificial distinction between public and private and no pessimistic resignation to the intractability of the public realm. But rather, in the spirit of Augustine, the whole of the public *ordo* is seen as fallen through false love but redeemable through the authentic love of the *communio* opened up by Christ. This position, unlike Reinhold Niebuhr's, allows for a more robust Christian critique of the assumptions and practices of a political culture flowing from Hobbesian individualism.

Catholicism and Modernity in the American Context

What is the Catholic attitude to the distinctively modern polity that is the United States? Catholics have had, it seems fair to say, a complex relationship to American society. When they arrived in great numbers starting in the early nineteenth century, they were met with fierce opposition from a Protestant establishment fearing a "foreign" and despotic takeover. The Egyptians seemed to have managed to cross the Red Sea of the Atlantic Ocean and now threatened to corrupt the almost chosen people, to use Abraham Lincoln's phrase, of this American promised land. In the face of anti-Catholic propaganda, the burning of convents and monasteries, and the rise of the Know-Nothing party, American Catholics tended to lie low, muting the "political" dimension of their faith and preferring to build a Catholic culture under the protection of the religious freedom guaranteed by the First Amendment. And they did so with a passion, establishing by the beginning of the twentieth century a vibrant and institutionally powerful subculture in the still predominantly Protestant United States.

So favorable did this American environment seem that influential Catholic bishops such as James Cardinal Gibbons of Baltimore and Archbishop John Ireland of St. Paul actively promoted American-style separation of church and state. At the same time, some American Catholics—and Vatican observers—worried that the nonestablishment clause of the First Amendment would conduce to a secularized, or at least Protestantized, understanding of the relation between faith and society. At the end of the nineteenth century, this concern led to Pope Leo XIII's official ecclesial condemnation of the heresy called "Americanism."

John Courtney Murray—Reconciling the Catholic and the Modern

It is against this complex background that the thought of John Courtney Murray, S.J., emerged. Murray is undoubtedly the most persuasive voice advocating the reconciliation of the Catholic faith with a characteristically modern political experiment. Murray's proposal needs to be analyzed with some care in order to gauge the degree of success he achieved.

A fundamental and guiding assumption of the Murray project is that a civil society is characterized by constructive and disciplined argument, the working-out of consensus in a rational manner. The conditions for the possibility of this civil conversation are two: an agreement that there is "a heritage of an essential truth... [that] furnishes the substance of civil life," and a respect for the rights, freedom, and dignity of the individual.[17] If the former is missing, the conversation becomes unfocused; and if the latter is absent, the conversation devolves into power plays. When the founding fathers of this country embraced certain self-evident truths and placed their political efforts under the authority of a transcendent God, they fulfilled the first condition; and when they insisted that basic rights and freedoms — especially with regard to religion — are to be guaranteed, they fulfilled the second. Murray believed that, in their acceptance of both a form of natural law and the authority of the divine, the American founders differ radically from the Jacobin and laicist revolutionaries of Europe, whose convictions were marked by a fierce anticlericalism and a sort of uncritical rationalism.[18]

Though they were not antireligious, the American founders saw the necessity of eliminating a consideration of *ultimate* ends from the political conversation. Precisely because there was, in colonial America, such an irreconcilable pluralism of Protestant theological views, they saw that the consensus required for civil conversation would dissolve if any religious viewpoint were officially sanctioned or allowed to determine secular policy. Therefore, according to Murray, the framers declared the state incompetent in matters of religion and restricted its interests to the political sphere. The "truths" that are held in common and that undergird the civil conversation are thus not final or theological truths but are rather basic convictions and intuitions in principle available to all people of intelligence and good will. It is here that Murray senses a link to the Catholic tradition of the natural law, a universal moral sensibility distinguishable from the specific precepts of the revealed law.

In this context, one can begin to understand Murray's insistence that the two articles of the First Amendment should be interpreted, not as "articles of faith" but as "articles of peace."[19] Behind the separation of church and state in the American constitution is neither a secularist ideology that would simply drive religion from the public square nor a Calvinist theology placing exclusive stress on the divine transcendence. Rather, Murray claims, there is no ideological commitment — no faith — of any kind behind these purely legal decisions to restrict the range and sanction of the civil conversation. Their purpose is not to make claims regarding ultimate ends, but only to provide the conditions necessary for a peaceful and therefore civil dialogue.

Murray exults in the fact that the First Amendment is the product not of theologians but of lawyers. If it were otherwise, Catholics would be obliged, he thinks, to dissent from the American proposition. It is the very ideological agnosticism of the First Amendment that renders it palatable to people of various religious and philosophical persuasions. Under the protection, and within the confines, of these ideologically "neutral" articles, Catholics can feel free to develop their particular spiritual and faith-based culture while insisting that the original Protestant flavor of early American culture not be normative. Against a perceived Protestant hegemony, Catholics, along with Jews, have often acted as "secularizers" in American society.

The Price of Reconciliation

It appears as though we have found, in Murray's balanced argumentation, a philosophical justification for the pro-American sentiments of Archbishop Ireland and Cardinal Gibbons. It seems that a reconciliation of the Catholic and the modern is not only possible but welcome. With the benefit of a longer historical experience, however, this reconciliation seems less certain. If we look more closely, we uncover some of the distinctively modern ideological content of Murray's ostensibly agnostic solution.

It is no secret that John Courtney Murray's thought was shaped by a neo-Scholastic two-tiered conception of nature and grace, a view that he inherited from his Suarezian Jesuit tradition.[20] This sharp delineation between the natural and the supernatural is, as discussed above, a departure from the *communio* and participation metaphysics of the patristic and medieval periods. It is congruent with the typically modern carving out of a distinctively profane realm untouched by ultimate finalities or direct religious influence. Given this distinction, Murray could easily enough establish two realms, a "political" one where questions of ultimate ends are bracketed and a "religious" one where those ends can be proclaimed and sought.

Such a demarcation is impossible, however, within the context of a participation metaphysics, which sees all of finitude as grounded in and touched by the divine. It was, of course, John Courtney Murray's contemporary and fellow Jesuit Henri de Lubac who, in a series of groundbreaking texts, vigorously attacked the two-tiered conception of nature and grace and attempted a recovery of a *communio* metaphysics. According to de Lubac, nature is not a self-contained realm with its own finalities, but rather one that is permeated by and oriented toward the supernatural from the beginning. But if this is the case, then the separation that Murray tolerates — the bracketing of ultimate ends in the political context — is exposed as simply a pragmatic and religiously inadequate ploy.

Father Murray's separation assumes as well the implicit acceptance of a relentlessly modern view of the person. If the political or social dimension is essentially untouched by the sacred, then the human being who is naturally social is also by nature agnostic, perhaps even atheist. Whatever is religious in him is added as an extrinsic superstructure to a religiously neutral substructure. Any "truth" suggested by religion regarding humanity and its ends remains adventitious if not alien to this secularized natural man. To be sure, American liberalism is not, like continental Jacobinism, overtly atheist; but it is, one could argue, implicitly or covertly so. The "peace" gained by the articles of the First Amendment is bought at the price of a secularized understanding of the world and the loss of *communio*.

Communio

None of this relativizes the important contribution made by John Courtney Murray, for in Murray state neutrality in religion is not so much the condition for social peace as the necessary means for protecting personal religious liberty in a pluralistic society. In fact, his insistence on the centrality of religious liberty was affirmed at Vatican II, although the Council's defense of religious liberty owes at least as much to French Christian personalism as to Murray's historical and social analyses. Nevertheless, the anthropology of the Council's document *Dignitatis humanae* now shapes Catholic social teaching and has been consistently emphasized in the writings of John Paul II.

The pope's construal of this liberty, however, flows from the thought world of *communio* metaphysics rather than from a modern political framework. What is central to John Paul's interpretation is that freedom and truth belong together from the beginning, that the latter is in fact an essential component of the former. Without correlation to truths rooted in nature and in God, human freedom becomes license or, alternatively, acquiesces in state tyranny. In Augustinian terms, it becomes an improperly directed love, a mere "pursuit of happiness" rather than a structured spiritual activity. John Paul II consistently criticized in the Western democracies born of the Enlightenment this divorce of freedom from truth, this tendency to think that liberty can be unquestioningly affirmed while consideration of ultimate truth is bracketed or privatized. Such a bifurcation — allowed for by Murray in the interest of peace — was, for John Paul II, an undermining of the very structure of freedom itself.

And what indeed are the fruits of this great divorce? When we look at the moral landscape of America at the dawn of the millennium, what do we see? We see, again to invoke the Augustinian hermeneutic, ample evidence of the flourishing of the City of Man. In the millions of abortions annually, the divorce of human reproduction from the embrace of human love, the increased application of the death penalty, the practice of euthanasia, the conviction that hopelessly handicapped people are better off dead, the seemingly indiscriminate and sometimes disproportionate use of the military, the gun violence in the streets of our cities and the corridors of our schools — in all of this we see the fruits of what Pope John Paul II called "the culture of death," a society that allows for the destruction of its weakest members according to the simple will of the strong. The culture of death is none other than that "world" generated by the separation between freedom and truth; it is a result of the poorly conceived compromise between the City of God and the City of Man which stands at the heart of the modern experiment.

Conclusion

What follows from this faith-based critique of modernity? One might assume that, given the line of argument presented here, the only alternative is some sort of theocracy or confessional state. Nothing could be further from the truth. Having lived through late antiquity, the medieval period, and the modern era, the Church is opposed to "theocracy" on two basic grounds. First, as Murray argued and Vatican II clearly stated, faith is never to be pressed on anyone through coercive means of any kind. A coerced faith is not personal faith, and the development of doctrine in Vatican II has moved the Church from simply standing the modern problematic on its head and accepting a purely public faith as an article of peace in a contemporary version of medieval society.[21] Second, the Church should not seek to establish itself officially or juridically outside its own structures. A communion on its own terms, the Church cannot set up a "political" arm or expression without betraying its integrity. If churchmen over the centuries have sometimes embraced the theocratic model, they have done so without sufficient attention to the demands of the Gospel and the nature of the Church herself.

The community of Jesus Christ does not seek to take over the reins of political power; rather it seeks to create a culture. The debate on the institutional relationship between church and state has become now a conversation on the relationship between faith and culture. Provided the political order respects human dignity, *communio* can be visible in a culture open to transcendence. The faith creates such a culture by being simply, boldly, and unapologetically itself. At the heart of the Church is the sacred liturgy, what Vatican II called "the source and summit" of the Christian life. The liturgy on earth is an iconic display of the heavenly liturgy of the angels and saints, that community gathered together around the throne of God and united in praise. In the way we gather, the way we pray, the way we behave liturgically, we act out the paradigm of the heavenly *communio,* seeking to remake ourselves in its image. Then, as a liturgical people, we endeavor to shape the world according to this icon, bringing love where there is hatred, forgiveness where there is resentment, compassion where there is animosity, and peace where there is warfare. By the power of the Eucharist and through a kind of osmosis, we transform the culture, gently but subversively, from within.

In his text on the role of the laity, *Christifideles laici,* Pope John Paul II articulated several dimensions of this culture-creating work. First, the family must be remade as an expression of *communio.* Then, starting from that foundation, Eucharistic people must refashion the social, economic, and political realms; next, they should influence the arenas of education, entertainment, literature, and the arts. Finally, they ought to concern themselves with the environment and ecology, caring, in a spirit of *communio,* for the planet itself.[22] There is nothing coercive or violent about this process; but, at the same time, there is nothing "private" or self-effacing about it either. Its ambition is the total transformation of the world in all its dimensions. In the Lord's Prayer we ask that God's kingdom come, that his will be done on earth as in heaven. We are petitioning, in a word, that God's *ordo,* God's way of thinking and being, become, in the richest sense, our *ordo,* that the City of Man might be transformed by the City of God.

This transformation will not be easy. Personal conversion challenges individuals; cultures and entire societies also resist being evangelized. The history of tensions between the community of faith and the political order shifts according to what element of the faith seems the greatest challenge to the civil powers at any particular time. Emperors and feudal lords, during the many years of the controversy over the investiture of bishops, tried to take to themselves the government of the Church. Josephism[23] and the Napoleonic conventions tried to take to the state the control of the worship and ministry of the Church. Modern states founded in revolutions with universalist pretensions, such as the French, the American, and the Russian, have tried to arrogate to themselves the mission of the Church. Co-opting the faith's sense of purpose in order to create a secularist universal culture sets up tensions difficult to dispel. The Church resists being reduced to a department of state, a particular denomination, or a private club.

The deepest truth that Catholics proclaim is that of *communio:* all things and all people are ordered to God and hence ordered in love to one another. This truth informs everything we say about the political, social, economic, and cultural realms. If we surrender this truth — either through ideological compromise or even out of concern for civility — we succumb to the culture of death. At the beginning of the third millennium, the mission of the community that looks to Jesus as Lord is to create a culture of life and to do this within social structures that are more and more global in outreach. For the second time in two thousand years, the Church finds herself in social, economic, and some political structures that are increasingly universal. In such a situation, the Catholic Church is an agent of transformation that is, paradoxically, completely at home.

Chapter 2

Evangelizing American Culture

A Practical Project

"E VERYBODY'S DOING IT" has long been a refrain of youngsters who want to persuade their parents to permit something that family rules do not allow. It is also a phrase that shows how culture, like faith, shapes our lives. Both culture and faith tell us how to behave and what to believe. Both give us norms for acting and thinking and loving. Bringing people to know and love and accept Christ is easier or harder depending on what their culture tells them is good to know and love and accept. Recognizing the importance of culture's interaction with faith, Pope Paul VI wrote that the split between Gospel and culture is the drama of our times. He added, however, that it was the drama of other ages as well. The dialogue between faith and modernity is as old as the history of God's self-revelation and the human response to it in faith. The dialogue between faith and modernity finds its most persuasive expression in the experiment in democracy that is the United States of America.

Inculturating the Faith and Evangelizing the Culture

The dialogue between faith and culture is called "inculturation of the faith" when a particular culture's symbols, institutions, and values become vehicles for expressing the universal faith. Missiologists invented the term "inculturation" because it recalls the mystery of the Incarnation. Somewhat as the word of God became man, the faith of the Church becomes Nigerian, Chinese, or American as Nigerians, Chinese, and Americans come to know, love, and accept Christ. In you, Pope John Paul II tells the citizens of China, Christ has become Chinese; so in us Americans, Christ has become American.

What does this mean, and how does it happen? Between a transcendent gift (the faith) and an immanent construction (a culture), there will almost always be some tension. Sometimes a given culture will not possess the resources for expressing the faith in its fullness. A culture might be unable to make sense of God's self-revelation, unable to understand a merciful Father, an obedient Son, a self-effacing Spirit.

Beyond the inevitable tensions that arise when a culture is stretched to express Catholic faith, more positive resistance might develop. A culture can resist the faith as a sinner resists grace. The culture might enshrine customs opposed to evangelical life: polygamy, ritual murder, sexual promiscuity, abortion, exploitative business practices. The culture might attempt to reduce religion to a purely private affair, unrelated to the public social contract. When believers recognize demonic elements in their culture and work to diminish or eradicate them, the dialogue between faith and culture turns into "evangelization of culture."

To form Gospel-shaped people, the Church must work to create Gospel-friendly cultures. A faith that demands that culture change is sometimes called "countercultural." The adjective is unfortunate if it leads believers to see themselves on one side and their culture on another. Our culture is as much in us as we are in it. Religious critics of a culture can imagine a bad system opposed by good people, but the distinction is too facile. If our social system and culture are, at least in part, evangelically deficient or even corrupt, so are we all.

The evangelizer begins by taking responsibility for the culture to be evangelized.

Catholic Concern for Culture: Loving What You Evangelize

Separating good from bad in a culture's values and way of life, its institutional patterns, goals, and accomplishments, demands a principle of discernment. When the Catholic evangelizer looks for such a principle, he or she reaches for the Gospel as interpreted by the Church.

The Church tells us that our culture, despite its deficiencies and the positive obstacles it might place to belief, is salvageable. The Catholic Church teaches that grace builds on nature, for human nature, while wounded by sin, is not hopelessly corrupt. As grace builds on nature, so faith builds on culture, which is second nature. Culture is damaged by human sinfulness, but it is not hopelessly corrupt. Culture is the world before it becomes St. Augustine's City of Man, a society totally closed in on itself. Rather, human culture is a field that offers plants from native seeds for grafting onto the tree of faith.

Are there such seeds in American culture? Pope John Paul II, speaking in Chicago on October 5, 1979, found a seed of God's word in the history of different peoples coming to the United States to form a new union. Our bringing many rich cultural heritages together to create a new people reminded the pope of St. Paul's description of the Church: "We, though many, are one people in Christ" (Rom. 12:5). The Church is enriched by the diversity of her members, who make up the one body of Christ. All are united in one apostolic faith; all live through the action of one Spirit. Thus united, the Church can be active in evangelizing, much as a nation's strength and ability to act depend on its internal unity. U.S. history and American efforts to form a nation are, in some sense, an analogue of

the unity that is given believers in the Church. American evangelizers can build on our collective experience to form here an indigenous
Catholic Church. Like the pope, we can search for *semina verbi,*
seeds of God's word, in American history and cultural patterns, even
as we struggle with our social sin and anti-evangelical proclivities.

More than any previous pope, John Paul II moved culture to the
center of evangelization. Perhaps his own experience as a bishop
in communist Poland convinced him that culture is more important than institutions in preserving and spreading the faith. In his
country, as in other Marxist lands, the Church lost almost all her
public institutions; but even as the schools, newspapers, and social
organizations were taken over by a hostile state, the faith remained
strong in the hearts of many Poles because their culture had been
shaped by the Catholic faith.

In an evangelized culture, turns of phrase and cherished customs, habitual attitudes and daily activities serve to remind people
of the Gospel. Pope John Paul II said many times that faith must
"become culture." A faith that does not become culture, the pope
explained, is not fully received, not entirely thought through, not
faithfully lived. Faith is not true to its nature unless it transforms
everything human.

Faith becomes culture, however, as culture is opened to the ultimate truth about human nature and destiny. While the Church in
the United States enjoys a certain institutional freedom, she exists
in a culture that, in often surprising ways, resists Catholicism. Are
there clues to this American pattern of resistance to Catholic faith?

Awareness of American Culture:
Knowing What to Evangelize

Perhaps Americans have greater difficulty than others in understanding their own culture. The United States, while too small
to be the world, is big enough to be a world. Unlike the people

of Denmark or Zimbabwe or Uruguay, Americans can interpret what happens elsewhere in terms of their own experience. Since American popular culture influences the world, we can be led into thinking that all peoples are more like us than they really are. Further, to safeguard a national unity forged across great distances from peoples of different races, national origins, religions, and cultures, Americans often relegate differences to the private sphere, explaining that all peoples are really alike, at least under the skin. Awareness of American cultural peculiarity is suppressed by American culture itself.

In any society, however, the evangelizer is hard put to analyze his or her own culture. Culture is so all-inclusive that hundreds of definitions have been crafted to capture it. Pope John Paul II offered one of the broadest: culture is the realm of the human as such. Avery Cardinal Dulles, S.J., gave more details:

> By a culture we normally understand a system of meanings and values, historically transmitted, embodied in symbols, and instilled into the members of a sociological group so that they are spontaneously inclined to feel, think, judge, and behave in certain characteristic ways.[1]

Cultural analysis includes, therefore, a way of uncovering the meanings and values that are implicit in a people's behavior; a sense of the historical influences in a society; and a notion of how cultures interact, develop, and are transmitted.

Anthropology

From cultural anthropology, the evangelizer learns methods of questioning that tease out meanings and values hidden in collective behavior.[2] Take, for example, a family picnic on the Fourth of July. A cultural anthropologist preparing to evangelize American picnickers begins by asking *who* they are (people related by blood and marriage), *what* they are doing (eating hot dogs, playing a ball game, talking), *when* they are doing it (on a summer day), *where* they are doing it (in the open air), *how* they are doing it (some cooking, some cleaning, some organizing games, but all cooperating), and *what kind* of activity this picnic really is (a family coming together to relax in the context of a larger civic holiday).

Each of these questions enables the evangelizer to know the forms by which a culture organizes itself, but the more important question remains to be asked: *Why* is the family celebrating? On one level, "why" is answered functionally: the family eats hot dogs in order to satisfy their hunger without preparing an elaborate meal; the family plays games in order to exercise; the family spends time together because they love each other. If the evangelizer continues to question why a whole nation engages in this kind of behavior on the fourth day of the month of July each year, a deeper level of meaning unfolds. A story of the Fourth of July in the year 1776 is told; bits of multicolored bunting are displayed and the evangelizer recognizes the flag of the country; hot dogs are not just energy sources but "typical" food of the country; the ball game turns out to be the country's national pastime. Participating in the event is a way of reaffirming values—national independence and personal freedom—and the event itself is a symbol of the family's participation in the life and purposes of the nation. The family picnic, in short, displays meanings and values that define the cultural context. Questions should continue to be pressed until the evangelizer recognizes an order of importance among the meanings and values discovered. This hierarchy explains a culture's distinctive character and will indicate how the evangelizer might foster the culture's dialogue with faith.

History

Observation and questioning uncover meanings and values, but study of a group's history explains why a culture transmits only certain meanings and cherishes particular values more than others.

In the case of the United States, our culture's historical roots are traced to the Pilgrims and English Puritan dissenters; to the Deists of the American enlightenment; to the founders of the republic, who created the forms of American democracy; and to the activists and pragmatists of the last three and a half centuries, whose work generated economic growth and the cult of successful results. Each of these strains, sometimes existing in the same historical personage, has interacted with the others to create the distinctive system of values and meanings that is American culture.

No matter what our culture's roots, we live now in a society no longer integrated by religious faith. Most Americans might believe in some sort of God, but faith is compartmentalized, set apart, unrelated to much of contemporary experience and life. Of the historical shapers of culture in this country, Puritanism would seem to have most clearly lost ground. Yet attitudes and values can perdure even when separated from the historical movements that gave them birth. America is different from other modern, secularized societies because it is a secularized Puritan society rather than a culture that has replaced the Puritan ethos with something else.[3]

To speak of Puritan attitudes and habits, meanings and values surviving in a modern society may seem strange, but the conflict can hide a deeper continuity. The Puritan conversion narratives of colonial Massachusetts show a pattern of behavior that remains familiar today.[4] In Puritan New England, proof of internal conversion to Christ was required in order to be admitted to Church membership, so the candidate testified before the local congregation's representatives to the workings of grace in his or her soul. The congregation, for its part, had to listen carefully and respectfully to this recital of personal experience. Attention to feelings was of particular importance in establishing one's right to belong to the local church, for they were subjective testimony to the inner workings of God's grace. Personal experience and the public recital of it thus became the rhetoric of American identity. Americans claim a right to belong by reason of a personal experience that they choose to disclose and that demands the respect of others. Contemporary phenomena as diverse as civil rights movements and client-centered therapies find legitimation in this cultural pattern.

Beyond a local congregation, Puritans belonged to the New Israel, the kingdom of God in America. The Puritan Sabbath was a symbol of Christ's entry into his Father's kingdom after the work of redemption; and weekly Sabbath observance made the American Puritan community the church in new and purified form, without the baggage of Catholic history that encumbered even Protestant lands in once-Catholic Europe. The United States has no medieval memories; America was a new dispensation. Here the kingdom of God was at hand, and its coming was presaged in a series of revivals, beginning with the great awakening of the 1740s and renewed periodically to this day.

When the nation's purpose became the spread of democracy rather than the spread of the Gospel, Americans still thought of their land as a light to other nations and themselves as people with a mission. American public discourse remains millennialist. Puritan eschatology is echoed in predictions of nuclear warfare or ecological disaster. The end is always near, and we must change our ways. Even if we no longer believe in an angry God, a wounded earth will punish us.

The secularization of Puritan rhetoric and behavior began early. Alexis de Tocqueville, who visited the United States early in the nineteenth century to see how democratic political structures influenced character development, noted that Americans were "individualists."[5] Is individualism a help or hindrance to the Catholic evangelizer? Like many cultural phenomena, it is evangelically ambiguous. To the extent it means that each person is regarded as unique and even sacred, individualism is fertile soil for planting the faith. To the extent it means that persons are valuable because they are justified, whether by grace of the Puritan God or, more recently, by declaring themselves estimable, individualism is an unreliable base for Catholic ecclesial communion, whatever merits it might possess as a foundation for civic life.[6]

De Tocqueville's complement to individualism was something else he discovered in America: the voluntary association. This bridged the gap between self and society. American individuals do not isolate themselves. They form and join groups for social purposes, just as Puritan believers, individually converted, joined the local congregation. Voluntary associations conform also to the enlightenment vision of rational individuals forming a social contract that respects the rights of each while providing common security and the means for all to advance economically and politically. Americans belong: to the Red Cross, Greenpeace, the Moose and the Elks, the ACLU, Holy Name Societies, mutual funds, Gay Pride movements, the volunteer army. Americans have a right to belong, provided only that they want to and that they have had the experience that the rules demand for membership. Once in, of course, members have the right to change the rules.

The Catholic Church in America

This deeply ingrained pattern of individualism and voluntary association is an inadequate analogue for the Catholic Church's self-understanding as a hierarchical and participatory communion. American culture understands two ways of being religious: liberal and evangelical. How do these differ? To oversimplify to the point of distortion, liberal religion treats God as an ideal, a goal expressing all that is best in human experience, while the real agents of change in the world are human persons. Religious language is important poetry, agnostic about who God is but expressive of our experience of wholeness. The traditional sacraments are signs of our own interior dispositions and intentions. Worship might be structured, but, at its heart, religion is ethical and the social agenda central.

By contrast, and again to indulge in gross simplification, evangelicals have a keen sense of God's agency. God is real, independent, powerful, active. They know God in their emotional experience at prayer and from the reading of God's word in Holy Scripture. Religious language, at least among many fundamentalists, is literal, and the Bible is read much like a news report. Sacraments are signs of the interior faith given us before we receive them. The social agenda tends to be peripheral, because God will change things at the Armageddon or at the apocalyptic rapture or at some other moment we can only wait for.

This liberal/conservative split in the American Calvinist religious heritage occurred in the last century, during the controversies over Charles Darwin's theory of the evolution of species and the legitimacy of historical-critical approaches to Bible study. Some denominational lines were redrawn on the basis of liberal and evangelical tendencies. Left out of each is the Catholic sense of the Church as mediator of God's life and teacher of God's truth, the Church as a body one is joined to in order to be converted.

Culturally assimilated American Catholics who no longer belong to subcultures that buttressed Catholic identity while permitting interaction with society in general now have to discover and foster in American culture itself the resources they need to express their faith. If these resources are only ambiguously there, American Catholics who have remained somewhat distant from the dominant culture naturally hesitate over their relationship to it.

Minorities as Subcultures

Among the most visible minority groups in the United States today, four are founded on a relationship to faith different from that found in the dominant culture. How these groups relate to both culture and Church might offer insights to American Catholics intent on evangelizing American culture.

HISPANICS

U.S. Hispanics inherit a culture formed in dialogue with the Catholic faith on the Iberian Peninsula and re-formed in Latin America during the past five hundred years. The Hispanic Catholic bishops have described their people's cultural uniqueness as a second mestiza tradition. The original mixture of Spanish and Indian cultures is now a mixture of Hispanic and U.S. values. The cultural values mentioned by the bishops, however, are fairly universal: love of family and community, love for life itself, and respect for each person. These values are integrated through Catholic faith and, especially, through love for the Blessed Virgin Mary. Lists of values evoke cultural loyalties, but their integration presents the distinctive pattern of values and meanings in which the genius of a culture becomes clear.

Hispanics have developed pastoral plans from national Encuentros in 1972, 1977, 1985, and 2000. With sure pastoral insight, the U.S. Hispanic bishops have placed the faith-culture dialogue at the center of the reevangelization of their people. They have pointed out groups among Hispanic Americans in need of pastoral attention: young people, those susceptible to pressure from religious sects, those exploited by unjust conditions of employment and immigration difficulties. The development of vocations to Church leadership is a priority, and the traditional devotions of Hispanic Catholicism must now be complemented by love of Scripture in a country whose believing Protestants have shown us all what it means to reverence the Bible. The emphasis in the pastoral plans is on preserving and deepening the faith of a people traditionally Catholic; there is little on how Hispanic Catholics might be agents for evangelizing U.S. culture.

BLACKS

African American and other black Americans are also, for the most part, baptized Christians. Their original African cultures have been enriched here by Protestant faith. Black Catholics, through the National Office for Black Catholics (NOBC) and the letters of the African American Catholic bishops, are continuing a series of reflections on their experience begun with Negro Catholic Congresses from 1889 to 1894 and meetings of the Federated Colored Catholics from 1914 to 1935. Both the Secretariat for Black Catholics in Washington and the NOBC responded to the 1974 Roman Synod on evangelization by reminding American Catholics that the Church is the object of evangelization as well as the subject evangelizing, since the U.S. Church has not been free of the racism that afflicts the general culture. Where Hispanics talk of the Church, blacks more often talk of the Gospel; the goal of evangelization is a fusion of Gospel truth and black cultural experience.

Like Hispanics, African American and other black Catholics want to see Catholic leaders from their ranks and want responsibility for the Church's mission shared with lay people. Catholic schools in African American neighborhoods are both means of advancement and a way to deepen Catholic identification with black culture. This culture's relation to Protestantism, analogous to Hispanic culture's relation to Catholicism, leads some African American Catholics to ask that styles of worship and preaching incorporate elements from the black Protestant heritage. Finally, no program for evangelizing among African Americans fails to mention the paramount importance of the Church's continuing aid in the struggle for racial justice in the United States.

ASIANS

Americans of Asian background are, with the exception of Filipinos, culturally non-Christian. Their traditional cultures developed in relation to Buddhism, Confucianism, Shintoism, Hinduism, or Islam. Those who are now Catholic in faith are also Buddhist, or Hindu or Confucian in family culture, living in a secularized society rooted in Calvinist Christianity. What insights for evangelizing culture might the complex faith-culture dialogue that is their inner life offer other Catholics? This is still to be discovered, since little has been written about evangelization among Asians in this country. American interfaith dialogue has been most developed with Jewish believers rather than with the Hindus, Buddhists, and Muslims engaged by Catholic bishops in Asia itself. A point of entry for the Church into Asian American experience is, of course, concern for social justice.

NATIVE PEOPLES

Concern for social justice is also a way into the experience of the first Asian peoples to settle here — the North American Indians or native pre-Americans. While few in number and culturally diverse among themselves, the native peoples make unique collective claims on all Americans. Their cultures express a religious relationship to the land from which they have now been largely dispossessed. The current rise of ecological consciousness among the U.S. cultural elite makes American Indian religion fashionable; but among non-Indians there is little evidence of submission to religious demands that developed in a largely untamed natural environment.

Catholics among American native peoples ask for religious leaders from their number. They are also incorporating into Catholic liturgy a few elements from pre-Christian worship; and every document from the annual Tekakwitha Conferences and other pastoral meetings speaks of restoring their collective self-respect with the cooperation of the Church.

What Is to Be Done?

When American Catholics consider the Church in their society, they usually speak of tensions between faith and culture as problems in constitutional law or as clashes of values in a plural-istic society. When U.S. bishops speak of American culture, they sometimes list values that Americans believe are particularly their own: equality, freedom, openness, participation in decision mak-ing, communication. These are values of a popular liberal culture, and defenders of American culture point out that the United States has played a providential role in the history of human liberty. It is unfair simply to reduce American culture to consumerism and hedonism, selfish individualism, and the history of oppression of minority groups. These vices, like American virtues, are also part of larger historical developments. Tabulating collective strengths and weaknesses, virtues and vices, successes and failures can, moreover, distract from the more fundamental question: Does this culture now provide a sound context for human life or does it stifle the human spirit?

In a talk to U.S. religious in San Francisco during his 1987 visit, Pope John Paul II said that an evangelizer of culture brings out evils only to show the power of God's word to heal and uplift, to unify and bind with love. A program for evangelizing American culture, therefore, begins, continues, and ends with love for the people and their culture. The people whom God calls to form Christ's body in a way that respects the best in their heritage are constantly in an evangelizer's prayers. Prayer itself, an activity with no immedi-ately productive goal, evangelizes culture by introducing a rhythm that opens daily life to the transcendent. In a society often driven by short-term goals, the inner discipline needed to live prayerfully creates an alternative sense of time.

Second, the evangelizer of culture will look for the places where significant conversations take place. A culture is a communica-tions network; the Gospel is a message. The evangelizer needs to be present in those places where the messages that form the cul-ture are created and transmitted: taxi cabs, neighborhood taverns, office water coolers, and most of all the electronic media (including television and the Internet) that are omnipresent in our world.

Third, American Catholics need to enlarge their culture's appreciation of human reason. Reason is diminished when it is reduced to calculating means for achieving individual ends. A shriveled intellect cannot insist on truthfulness in public life and fails to recognize its natural ability to seek a transcendent God.

Fourth, because the dominant culture in the United States privileges voluntary relationships to the detriment of others, the evangelizer works to strengthen relations that are given rather than chosen: family, race, linguistic group, the land, and nation itself as our home rather than willed messianic project. Within the context of these relationships, the Church as gift, as ecclesial communion with her source of life in the love of Father, Son, and Spirit, becomes culturally possible. American culture reduces the Church to a voluntary association and treats the nation itself the same way. American cultural myths, by reason of our history, are inevitably voluntaristic. We are a people of choice rather than of blood. One can choose to become American in a way that one cannot become Japanese, Navajo, or Arab. The melting pot myth has enabled the United States to welcome almost anyone and everyone, at least in principle; and its inclusivity can serve the Gospel's universalism, as Pope John Paul II pointed out. It cannot, however, be allowed to destroy the public legitimacy of nonvoluntary relationships and communities. The Catholic evangelizer in the United States will cherish and strengthen the relationships that faith tells us we have no right to "un-choose."

Fifth, evangelizing American culture means purifying our sense of mission. Catholics believe that groups play roles in salvation history; but a collective vocation within God's call to everyone is different from the Puritans' notion of their peculiar covenant with the Lord. Transforming our national purpose in the light of God's plan for all peoples means listening to a source of truth not limited by American experience. Here again, our cultural resources fail us.

We have, in American culture, resources for reexpressing evangelical freedom. Freedom is our major cultural value, and even the Church can talk about what it should mean. We have resources, too, for reexpressing evangelical justice, because justice is another cultural value. Even when we recognize the deficiencies of our theories of justice and our failure to practice it, justice remains a public imperative. The Church can figure in conversations around it and help change institutions and structures. But there are no public resources in our culture for reexpressing evangelical truth, because religious truth is no longer a public virtue. Any truth not immediately verifiable in observation or through the methodologies of the hard sciences becomes private opinion. It enters the public realm under the rubric of personal expression, a value that is the subject of arbitration but not of intellectual research. The public authority, the government, while it must protect freedom and foster justice, cannot teach. But the Church can; and this claim to teach the truth is truly countercultural. It explains why anti-Catholicism is a socially and intellectually respectable prejudice among much of the cultural elite in this country. Since the culture is too narrow for Gospel truth, Catholic evangelizers want to enlarge American culture and broaden its vision.

A Civilization of Love

Pope Paul VI preached a civilization of love, and Pope John Paul II spoke of a new Christian humanism; Pope Benedict XVI encourages every society to be open to transcendence. The popes are not calling for a "Catholic state" of any sort but for the creation of a culture that will be rich enough to provide means for expressing the Catholic faith in culturally distinctive fashion and resourceful enough to support the relationships of universal and local

Catholic ecclesial communion. An evangelized culture will offer no special favors to the Catholic Church, but it will privilege the human person in ways that American culture presently does not and cannot.

Creating a culture that provides a more evangelically authentic environment for daily life in the United States is less a program with clearly defined stages than a movement of gradual growth. Cultural change is slow, but it can be steady if our purpose is clear and our nerves are strong. Evangelizers need a broad vision and strength for the long haul. Evangelizing culture relies on deep insight into the mysteries of our faith and keen vision for understanding the bases of our culture. Evangelizing culture is, finally, a contemplative activity. The dialogue between Catholic faith and American culture takes place in the media, in the schools and the marketplace, and in the public square; but it begins in the heart of every American Catholic who loves both faith and country.

Chapter 3

Sowing the Gospel on American Soil

The Distinctive Contribution of Theology

"WHAT ARE YOU DOING to affect the culture in the United States?"[1] Pope John Paul II asked me this question directly when I was in Rome in the late 1990s for an *ad limina* visit. John Paul often spoke of the Church's mission as including culture-engagement or culture-transformation. "The faith creates culture" was a frequent refrain of his.

There are, of course, many ways that the Church shapes culture, but one of the most significant means to this end is the intelligent and faithful practice of theology. Even in its most technical academic expression, Catholic theology is essentially evangelical in nature and purpose, since its task is to explore the full meaning of the story of God's love for the world in Jesus Christ, crucified and risen from the dead. When theologians are no longer taught by the Church and fired by her evangelical enthusiasm, they may become cultural critics or philosophers of religion, but they cannot carry out the full culture-forming task envisioned by the Church. When theologians speak from within the household of the faith, however, their words can create a culture open to Catholicism. How can authentically Catholic theology help announce the Good News to and within a culture shaped by a complex and uniquely American set of assumptions, values, symbols, practices, and convictions?

The Evangelically Ambiguous Quality of Every Culture

Since we have recognized that every culture is a human artifact and since human beings are both made in the image of God and also fallen, we can assume, on strictly theological grounds, that every culture is evangelically ambiguous — that is to say, both fertile soil and rocky ground for sowing the seed of the Gospel. Accordingly, we may search, with Paul Tillich, for the religious ground of the artistic, political, and institutional life of any society; and we may notice, with Karl Barth and John Milbank, the various spiritual distortions evident in those same cultural expressions. With Origen and the bishops of Vatican II, we may discern the *semina verbi* that are present in non-Christian philosophies and religions; and with Augustine, we may craft an appropriate critique of even a great culture grown decadent. Thus it is in a spirit neither optimistic nor pessimistic, neither overly enthusiastic nor excessively censorious, that we look, with Gospel eyes, at our American culture. Since this is *our* culture, all of us can look at trends and values and past history to understand who we are collectively; but each of us can also look within and seek for identity and self-understanding as individuals. Our culture is a *locus theologicus,* a privileged source for theological reflection.

American Culture as Rocky Ground

What are some of the qualities of our culture that make it hostile, or at least unreceptive, to the proclamation of the Good News? The United States is a nation that has been shaped decisively by Protestantism, with its stress on the power of inner experience. For

Martin Luther and other great reformers, justification is mediated less through an external system of sacraments and ecclesial institutions than through the deeply subjective intuition of faith. When this Lutheran insight passed into the thought-world of Calvinism, it became the inner conviction that one had been predestined to salvation. A particularly powerful insight into the psychological dynamics of this Calvinist feeling of being saved is given by John Henry Newman in his *Apologia pro vita sua*. He recounts there the story of his embrace of evangelical Christianity at the age of fifteen. By an "inward conversion" of great intensity, Newman became aware of two "luminously self-evident beings," himself and his Creator, and of the fact of his final perseverance in grace.[2] At the beginning of the modern age, such subjective certitude had come to replace the objective givenness of participation in Church and sacramental rites as assurance of salvation.

The Emphasis on Experience in American Theology

When, in the seventeenth century, the Reform became more rationalized through the efforts of the Protestant scholastics, the focus on interiority and experience was preserved on the continent in such groups as the Hutterites, the Anabaptists, and the Moravians and in England by the Puritans and the Quakers. Many of the earliest settlers of colonial America were members of these more radical and marginalized Protestant groups. An already subjective Protestantism was expressed in a more markedly inward and experiential form. Think, for instance, of the Quaker emphasis on the inner light and the Puritan — and later Wesleyan — concern for tracking the movement of the divine spirit within one's soul. And in the eighteenth and early nineteenth centuries, during the various "Awakenings" that swept the country, preachers confirmed these tendencies by encouraging their listeners to feel their conversion to Christ in an intensely emotional way and to express it vividly and physically.[3] This is the ground of our contemporary search for what might be called spiritualities without faith.

Experiential Protestantism assumed a new and more intellectual form at the beginning of the nineteenth century in the thought of the founder of theological liberalism, Friedrich Schleiermacher. Trained in a Moravian community, Schleiermacher never lost his fascination with the subjective ground of faith. He simply transposed it, in line with the romanticism of his time, into the "feeling of absolute dependency," claiming that intuition as the self-verifying foundation for Christian dogma.[4] This Schleiermacherian liberalism profoundly shaped the religious thought of both Europe and America, helping to give theological legitimacy here to Unitarianism (Schleiermacher placed the Trinity beyond the range of what could be verified through religious experience) and Emersonian transcendentalism (in his early writings, Schleiermacher spoke of a mystical union with the Universe). Though these more liberal forms of religion strayed far from the classical Christianity of the sixteenth-century reformers, they retained the powerful subjectivism and experientialism of the Reformation.

Paul Tillich, the twentieth-century Protestant theologian standing most clearly in the tradition of Schleiermacher, found a receptive audience among American intellectuals for his correlational version of Christian theology. Tillich understood religion, subjectively enough, as "ultimate concern"; as he saw it, the task of the theologian was to relate the anguished questions of finitude to the answers of the biblical tradition. Through a kind of trickle-down effect, the thought of Tillich has found its way into much of popular narrative theology and into many forms of theological reflection done in pastoral contexts.

And even as our Protestant-formed culture shades today into a post-Christian secularism, the emphasis on subjectivity and experience remains. It can be seen, for instance, in the numberless talk shows, those public confessionals where people discuss their deepest feelings and anxieties and are urged to act them out, sometimes histrionically. And it can be discerned in the myriad forms of New Age spirituality, most of which are grounded in a mysticism of the divinized self.

The Challenge to Revelation and Authority in American Culture

All of this, quite obviously, renders extremely difficult the proclamation of a revealed and doctrinally developed faith. For classical Catholic Christianity, the truths of faith do not arise from common human experience; they come to us through God's gracious self-revelation. More to the point, they cannot be verified, measured, or contained by our subjectivity. In the very first question of the first part of the *Summa theologiae,* St. Thomas Aquinas argues that a revealed *sacra doctrina* is required beyond the philosophical discipline of metaphysics because human beings are oriented to an end beyond what they could in principle grasp through their own powers.[5] Revealed doctrine, and its theological elaboration, are necessary, in other words, because God has not intended that we rest in ourselves, trapped, as it were, in our own experience.

In his critique of Tillich's correlational method, Barth said that the "answers" of Scripture are so surprising and strange that they confound any and all questions that we ask. And in his critique of Karl Rahner's more experiential approach, Hans Urs von Balthasar compares Jesus to a mountain torrent.[6] The torrent cannot be exhausted by the various human channels made to receive its water. What Aquinas, Barth, and von Balthasar suggest is this: experience and subjectivity are most themselves when they are graciously overthrown by the revelation that surpasses them. The exaggerated subjectivism of American culture renders this overthrow problematic.

A related difficulty is that of authority, especially religious authority. When subjective experience is the source, measure, and criterion of truth, any and all authority is seen as arbitrary and invasive. But a doctrinal tradition that is grounded in objective revelation must be preserved and monitored by an authority that transcends subjectivity and is thus capable of real judgment. Newman argued, throughout his career, that the existence of a developing and historically situated dogmatic faith requires an infallible authority in order to discriminate between legitimate evolutions and corruptions.[7] As even a casual survey of American religious culture reveals, acknowledgment of such an authority is problematic.

Another theologically negative dimension of our American culture is what could be called its fundamentally antagonistic social ontology. In addition to John Calvin's influence in America, we have to recognize the presence of Hobbes. As noted earlier, at the heart of the medieval Catholic theological worldview was a metaphysics of *participatio*. God was seen, not so much as a supreme being, but the sheer act of to-be itself (Thomas's *ipsum esse subsistens*), in which and through which all created things exist. This analogical conception of being allowed the medievals to see God in creation and thus to appreciate the essential connectedness of all things to God and, through God, to one another. Because human beings participate in God, they are, willy-nilly, linked to each other in the deepest ground of their existence. This powerful underlying metaphysical account led medieval Christians to appreciate the connectedness of social/political life as natural to human beings and, consequently, to see violence as not only ethically improper but ontologically inconsistent.[8]

This vision began to break down under the influence of Duns Scotus's univocal conception of being (which turned God into a supreme instance of being, set over and against finite realities) and Nominalism (which radically individualized and hence separated God and creatures). Pope Benedict XVI laid great emphasis on this problem in his 2006 address at the University of Regensburg, where he spoke of the relation between social violence and a God totally transcendent to His creation. As we saw in an earlier chapter, the total dissolution of the medieval ontology was realized only in the early modern metaphysical and political thought of Hobbes. Having bracketed the creator God, Hobbes saw, consequently, that the basic form of human existence must be antagonistic and individualistic. If there is no universal ground in the divine being, the war of all against all is the natural state of affairs, and sociality, an artificial contrivance for the preservation of life, is no reflection of ontology. On this Hobbesian reading, the purpose of government is no longer — as it was in classical and Christian thought — civic virtue and social justice, but rather the protection of each individual from the potential threat posed by every other individual. A social ontology of peace gives way to one of violence. "Ought" can find no foundation in "is"; and metaphysics no longer functions as meta-ethics.

This basic Hobbesian view goes through various shadings and permutations in Locke, Thomas Jefferson, and the other American founders, but they share in a common understanding of the essential nature of government. Thus, in the Declaration of Independence, it is the *right* to life, liberty, and happiness that is affirmed; the *form* of that life, the purpose of that liberty, and the proper ground of that happiness are left completely unarticulated. And the role of government is still exclusively protective rather than directive, since ontological antagonism is taken for granted.

When John Paul II spoke against a Western conception of freedom that is detached from justice and truth, it was this peculiarly modern, Hobbesian sense of freedom that he had in mind. When the free choice of the individual is incontestably paramount, the consequences are the materialism, self-absorption, litigiousness, and, above all, violence that so obviously mark our culture. Abortion and domestic abuse, human trafficking, capital punishment, the increasing gap between rich and poor, the appalling violence on our city streets often fueled by drugs, our sometimes arrogant and aggressive nationalism — all flow from an apotheosized freedom rooted, in turn, in an antagonistic, disenchanted metaphysics.

One of the most remarkable and disturbing expressions of this Hobbesian freedom is the *Planned Parenthood v. Casey* decision handed down by the U.S. Supreme Court in 1992, dealing with abortion rights. The majority of the justices determined that "at the heart of liberty is the right to define one's own concept of existence, of meaning, of the universe, and of the mystery of human life."[9] What we see here, with breathtaking clarity, is the complete eclipse of truth by freedom and hence the subjectivizing of any and all moral, metaphysical, or religious claims.

In the *City of God*, Augustine mocked the order of the Roman Empire as a pseudo-justice, based more on fear and oppression than on a dedication to real community. And he clearly showed the relationship between the phony social order of the empire and its inadequate theology: the worship of vain and violent false gods led to a dysfunctional political system. What he proposed to replace it was the *communio* of Christianity, grounded in the love, forgiveness, and compassion of Christian believers, and ultimately in the *communio* of the Trinitarian persons: a good society rooted in right worship. In Pope John Paul II's warnings to the West, we hear an overtone of this Augustinian critique. A freedom that is disengaged from the worship of the Creator God, one that is thus correlated to a false metaphysics, becomes poisonous.

Proclaiming a Christian metaphysics of participation, connection, and compassion is, obviously, difficult in a culture predicated on Hobbesian social and ontological assumptions. In a nation formed by an antagonistic and individualistic sense of freedom, it is awkward to say that our lives do not belong to us, that our liberty is for the sake of the Gospel, and that happiness lies in surrender to the divine will. Ignatius of Loyola is speaking a profoundly Christian language when he says, "Take, Lord, receive all my liberty, my memory, my understanding, my entire will. You gave them to me, now I give them back to you." What Ignatius assumes is a metaphysics of participation and creation: our being is, first and above all, given and then received, and therefore the task is to give it away in love rather than cling to it. "What you have received as a gift, give as a gift." Americans often find this language of self-sacrifice hard to grasp. But not only our values and patterns of thought are evangelically ambiguous — our institutions and social patterns are as well. Political democracy and religious pluralism, both characteristic of America, require extensive theological analysis as carriers of culture, as do the worlds of entertainment and the professions.

American Culture as Receptive Soil

The theological assumption I made at the outset, that every culture is evangelically ambiguous, now compels us to explore the other side of this question: To what degree is American culture *receptive to* the sowing of the Gospel seed? As we saw, John Paul II was a trenchant and honest critic of the modern West, but he was also an admirer of the American experiment, and his theological analyses and meditations on the value of our society can guide us effectively in this section.

Pope John Paul II visited the United States in 1979, 1987, and 1995. On each occasion, he found much to praise in America. During his 1979 pilgrimage, he preached at the Chicago lakefront on the theme of the national motto *e pluribus unum*. Looking out over the throng of about a million people, he reminded them that they had come from a variety of cultural, ethnic, and religious backgrounds. He exulted in the fact that from this diversity they had created something new: "You brought with you a different culture and you contributed your own richness to the whole; you had different skills and you put them to work, complementing each other, to create industry, agriculture, and business; each group carried with it different human values and shared them with others for the enrichment of your nation. *E pluribus unum:* you became a new entity, a new people."[10]

This new people was forged for the purpose of pursuing material wealth, fellowship, and social progress, but, the pope reminded them, "history does not exhaust itself in technological conquest or in cultural achievement only." There is a deeper reality, signaled by the very act of gathering around the table of the Eucharist: "your unity as members of the People of God."[11] What John Paul underscored was the analogy between the secular national *communio* of the United States and the sacred, transnational *communio* of the Church. Like America, the Church gathers people from every corner of the world, benefits from their distinctive contributions, and then draws them into oneness around a common principle: "The Body of Christ is a unity that transcends the diversity of our origin, culture, education, and personality."[12]

John Paul meant to highlight this analogy not only theoretically but practically: the *praxis* of America, as it has painfully but effectively forged unity out of diversity, echoes the *praxis* of the Church as she has brought, throughout the centuries, peoples to Christ. Thus, when America has successfully produced the one from the many, it has participated, however imperfectly, in the divine unifying principle on full display in the Church, namely, Christ's love for the world. This insight was never more dramatically expressed than in the homily the pope delivered at Dodger Stadium during his 1987 pilgrimage. Once more looking out on an audience of striking ethnic diversity, John Paul said, "Christ is Anglo and Hispanic, Christ is Chinese and Black, Christ is Vietnamese and Irish, Christ is Korean and Italian, Christ is Japanese and Filipino... and many other ethnic groups."[13] And this is why the idea and practice of *e pluribus unum* make American culture receptive to the proclamation of Christ's Gospel in universal communion.

When the Puritan settlers arrived in the New World, they expressed the significance of their pilgrimage in explicitly biblical terms. Having passed through the Red Sea waters of the Atlantic Ocean and having left behind the divisiveness and superstition (as they saw it) of Europe, they sought to establish on these shores "a city on a hill," a New Jerusalem where a purified Christian community would gather. This sense of America as a divinely sanctioned place of fresh beginnings worked its way quickly and deeply into the national consciousness. It can be sensed in the rhetoric of the writers and activists of the Revolutionary period, in the western movement of the pioneer generations, in Abraham Lincoln's Gettysburg Address, in the poetry of Walt Whitman, and in the hope against hope of the nineteenth- and twentieth-century immigrants. American culture is shaped significantly by the intuition that we are not the victims of history, inescapably caught in a maelstrom of war, recrimination, and social oppression. Rather, we sense that, here, the rejected are welcomed and even the lowliest, by dint of imagination and courage, can move confidently into an open future.

On October 3, 1979, John Paul II gathered in the rain with three hundred thousand people in Battery Park on the southern tip of Manhattan. There he spoke of this quality of the American soul. "It will always remain one of the glorious achievements of this nation that, when people looked toward America, they received together with freedom also a chance for their own advancement."[14] In the cadences of our own literary tradition, the pope urged us to realize the fullness of this vision: "Break open the hopeless cycles of poverty and ignorance...the hopeless cycles of prejudices that linger on despite enormous progress...the inhuman cycles of war that spring from the violation of man's fundamental rights."[15] What the pope counseled was that the biblical understanding of history as hopeful, open, and providentially guided would find an echo in the American mythology of opportunity and advancement, and hence that prophetic calls to radical social transformation, which might sound strained and naïve elsewhere, would here find a receptive ear.

At the very heart of John Paul's assessment of our culture is a deep and often-expressed appreciation for our ideal of human rights. The Hobbesian conception of rights and freedom, as we saw, has, to some degree, haunted us from the founding of the nation to the present. But it would be an oversight if we ignored the pope's equally passionate endorsement of a properly directed and grounded freedom. In a homily delivered on October 3, 1979, in Philadelphia, John Paul drew attention to the Declaration of Independence, which had been composed and ratified in that city two hundred years earlier. He cited the prologue of the document, which contains "a solemn attestation of the equality of all human beings, endowed by their Creator with certain inalienable rights."[16]

The key word in this sentence is "Creator." In pre-Christian political and social thought, the radical inequality of human beings was taken for granted. In Aristotle's *Politics,* our fundamental differences in intelligence, courage, and physical ability provide the justification for clear social distinctions and hierarchies, including that of master and slave. But with the Judeo-Christian revelation, something radically new was introduced: the idea of a creator God in whose presence all of us, despite our differences, are respected and loved. In light of this biblical idea, it became clear that human social status could never be simply a function of natural abilities or accomplishments. It must rather be rooted in our identity as beloved children of God. Inasmuch as Locke and Jefferson spoke of creation in their articulation of human rights, they showed the influence of this Christian heritage and their departure from a purely Hobbesian construal of the question. In that same Philadelphia sermon, John Paul drew attention to the Genesis account of the creation of human beings in the image and likeness of God. It is this biblical intuition, he implies, that informed the best of the language of "rights" from the founders of the American political culture.

Therefore when the Church speaks—as she must—of the dignity of each individual, created by God and redeemed by Christ, she ought to find a receptive audience in Americans formed by the civil tradition of human rights. When, on Gospel grounds, she defends the weakest and most vulnerable members of a society—the elderly, the unborn, the economically unproductive, the mentally and physically disabled — her words ought to resonate with the deepest convictions of the American soul. In the measure that these "least" among us are legally unprotected, our culture has rejected a creation-centered understanding of rights and chosen a Hobbesian conception. A theological analysis of our rights language would be a powerful contribution to culture and society.

Evangelizing by Way of the Saints

The theological task is not completed with an analysis of our culture's evangelical ambiguity. Theology also reflects on the pattern of holiness evident in those who, formed within the culture, became saints of God. One of the earliest descriptions of the Church is found in the Acts of the Apostles, where the Church is referred to as "the way." This simple and eloquent phrase indicates that Christianity is an entire style and pattern of life involving, certainly, new modes of thinking and seeing, but also new habits of movement and sets of practices, a "way" that addresses the body as much as the mind and will.

In the Gospel according to St. John, when the disciples of the Baptist follow Jesus and seek an audience with him, the Lord says, "What do you seek?" They answer him with a question, "Where do you stay?" And Jesus responds, "Come and see" (John 1:37–39). Then we are told that they stayed with him the rest of that day, emerging from the encounter as convinced disciples. According to John's account, Jesus did not simply illumine their minds or redirect their wills; rather, he invited them into intimacy with him and thereby drew them onto his path, into his way.

The theological project of Hans Urs von Balthasar is one example of theologizing from the pattern of Christian holiness. First, someone is drawn by the splendor of the form of Christ as it is displayed in the Scripture, preaching, and, above all, in the liturgy of the Church. Then, dazzled by the beauty he has seen, that person wants to participate in the dramatic form of Christ's life, playing in the theater opened up by the Incarnation. And finally, having played, the player becomes a preacher and teacher, speaking the truth of Christ, as it were, from within and from experience. The rhythm, as in the Johannine calling of the first disciples, is from fascination to participation and then to communication.

This is why, for von Balthasar, the true theologians are the saints: one cannot speak correctly of divine things until one has participated in them intimately. Does this imply that academic theologians become irrelevant? Of course not, but it does imply that in their work they must consider as a privileged *locus theologicus* the examples of the Christian way that occur in the lives of those who are intimate with God. If von Balthasar is right, Mother Teresa of Calcutta, picking the dying off the streets and treating them with dignity and love, is an icon, not only of enormous evangelical power, but also of great theological depth. Certainly, Pope John Paul II believed that of her.

Among American saints, let us consider Katherine Drexel of Philadelphia. She was born in 1858, the second daughter of Francis Anthony Drexel, a wealthy financier, and his wife, Hannah. Katherine's father and stepmother (her natural mother died just a month after Katherine's birth) instilled in her a keen sense that their riches were simply "on loan" to them and were meant ultimately to be shared with the less fortunate. They lived out this belief by regularly throwing open their elegant home to the homeless and hungry. Traveling widely in the United States while still a young woman,

Katherine saw the gross injustices of her society and became especially sensitive to the plight of American Indians and blacks. When her father and stepmother died, Katherine inherited a vast fortune, and she resolved to use her wealth to help disadvantaged peoples. In 1885, she established a school for American Indians at Santa Fe, New Mexico.

Later, during an audience with Pope Leo XIII, she asked him to recommend a religious congregation that could staff this and other institutions she intended to found. To her surprise, Leo suggested that she herself become a missionary. Taking this as a divine sign, Katherine began her training as a religious with the Sisters of Mercy in Pittsburgh. In 1891, with a few fellow workers, she established the community of the Sisters of the Blessed Sacrament for Indians and Colored People. Requests for assistance came to Katherine from all over the country, and her congregation eventually opened and staffed sixty schools, the most prominent of which was Xavier University in New Orleans, the first such institution for blacks in the United States. In the course of these years of establishments and foundations, Katherine donated her entire fortune to her work. In 1935, Mother Katherine suffered a serious heart attack, but continued to inspire her sisters and devoted herself especially to Eucharistic adoration and prayer.[17]

What do we see in this life? First, we notice that the attitudes and practices that Katherine Drexel inherited from her parents were informed by a deeply Catholic sensitivity to creation and participation: Everything we have received is a gift, and all of us are connected to one another, despite our economic and social differences, by the strongest metaphysical bonds. Thus a fortune, even though fairly earned in the free market economy of America, must be, in its "use," destined for the good of others. This is a truth affirmed by Aquinas and repeated by every papal social teaching document from *Rerum novarum* to *Centesimus annus*. Drexel's parents practiced this truth moderately, and she did so dramatically and heroically. She is, accordingly, a challenge to a "free" economy that can so easily lose its moral moorings, becoming powered by greed and productive of glaring social abuses.

Similarly, in her willingness to give herself to missionary work at the prompting of the pope, Katherine demonstrated the most authentic form of personal freedom. We are free not when we follow the whim of our self-interest but when we surrender to Christ's mission and thus correlate freedom to truth. St. Katherine Drexel's mission, in its scope and nature, was (and is) a powerful challenge to an American culture founded on the principles of equality and respect for human rights but betraying those ideals through its personal and institutional racism. It was precisely as a disciple of Christ that Katherine taught Americans how to be true to themselves as Americans.

We cannot overlook the last years of Mother Drexel's life, a time of increased silence and contemplation of the Eucharist. When the Word of God became flesh, he entered, in a real sense, into all of flesh, since the purpose of the Incarnation was the restoration of fallen creation. The Eucharist, a perpetuation of the Incarnation, is the great sacrament of unity. In it, we see the power that saves, connects, and elevates all things. Thus when Katherine Drexel retired from the active direction of her order and gave herself to contemplation of Christ in the Eucharist, she did not withdraw into inactivity but instead commenced a different form of activity, entering mystically into the truth that grounded and governed the whole work of her community. Most importantly, she did not retreat into private experience (though many Americans might typically read it that way); rather, she entered into a densely objective fact, opened up to her by Christ's revelation and presented to her by the dogmatic teaching of the Church. This period of contemplation permitted her to go radically beyond the limits of her own experience and to explore a reality that would have been otherwise unavailable to her. Mother Drexel's Catholic worship of the Eucharist, in all of its uncompromised objectivity, models the transformation of subjective religious experience into a supra-subjective encounter.

Conclusion

As mentioned earlier, I am uneasy with the term "countercultural," because it sometimes connotes self-hatred. There is truth to the claim that the Catholic believer must sometimes stand boldly apart from his or her culture and speak a word of prophetic critique; but, at its limit, the claim to be counter-cultural strikes me as incoherent. Whether we like it or not, we are shaped — linguistically, intellectually, relationally, bodily — by the culture in which we live. To stand completely outside of our culture is, impossibly, to stand outside of ourselves. More to the point, the language of counterculturalism can give rise to an attitude both mean-spirited and condescending. A culture is transformed only by those who love it, just as individuals are converted only by evangelizers who love them.

What I have suggested is that the best way to evangelize is through the witness and practice of holiness. The saints are experts in loving God and neighbor. The saints will always ratify what is best about a culture, and they will always properly critique what is demonic in it. If we want to know, therefore, how to go about our work of proclaiming the Good News here, we should look to those who, in their souls, in their blood and bones and their practices, embody that Gospel within the context of American culture. Theologians, in reflecting on saints' lives, complete the analysis necessary to understand a culture from within the household of the faith. Even more, theologians sow the Gospel on American soil by their own quest for holiness.

Chapter 4

Making All Things New

Notes on a New Apologetics

I N 1999, A THEOLOGIAN AND PASTOR visited the Archdiocese of St. Louis. John Paul II was at the end of a short trip to that geographically united but culturally and politically divided entity, the American continent.[1] He had just released in Mexico City *Ecclesia in America,* the apostolic exhortation he wrote after the 1997 Synod for America, and he made the purpose of his visit to Mexico and then to St. Louis quite clear. We live in an era of globalization. Technology allows us to move capital and people, consumer goods and ideas, with a new ease. This capacity both unifies and fragments the human family in ways that we do not yet fully understand or even realize.

To prepare for the Great Jubilee, the anniversary of the Incarnation two thousand years ago of the Eternal Son of God, Jesus Christ, who so deeply wished that all might be one, the Holy Father called a series of synods, continent by continent, in order to help the Church rethink her mission at the beginning of the Third Christian Millennium. In calling a Synod for America — north, south, and central as one continent — the pope was asking us to walk together and to be one in faith in a way that is much deeper than the unity created by computers and the Internet, by economic relationships such as NAFTA, by other commercial exchanges, or even by the exporting of films from this country and the creation here of networks such as Telemundo and Televisión with content from Latin America. The pope and the synod encouraged the Church in America to be truly what the Second Vatican Council said she is, namely, a communion, a network or a set of relationships that are created by all the baptized sharing the gifts of Christ. In the sharing of these gifts visibly — the gifts that make visible invisible grace — relationships are created around the Gospel, the sacraments, and apostolic governance that have the power to convert those who live in that communion, that network, sharing those gifts. They sanctify the Church's own members but also transform culture and social structures and all institutions that exist, finally, in order to serve the good of human persons at every stage of their earthly journey on the way to the heavenly homeland.

The communion of the Church is to be at the service of the solidarity among the peoples of this continent and of others. As we see in the stories of Christ's encounters in the New Testament with the woman at the well, with Nicodemus, with Levi the tax collector, and with Saul, an encounter with Jesus has three results. First, there is a personal conversion, a shift in one's self-consciousness so that one's ego is displaced and Christ becomes the center of one's life. Second, this conversion takes place within ecclesial communion. One cannot meet Christ, in the way that he wants everyone to meet him, outside of his body, the Church. To fully understand him, not just as a cultural hero, historical figure, or a myth of our own construction, the encounter must be within the network of ecclesial communion. Third, that personal encounter, which results in a strengthening of ecclesial communion, creates a leaven for solidarity among peoples.

Encounter, conversion, communion, solidarity are the dynamics of what the pope called a new evangelization — "new" because we are in a new moment. We live in the beginning of a new millennium and in a new situation. For the first time, we are in a self-consciously global order.

The Call for a New Evangelization

Karl Rahner used to speak about the years of the Second Vatican Council as the first time that the Church came together not only as a universal Church — for the Church was universal already at Pentecost — but as a world Church in the phenomenological sense, or as we might say a generation after Rahner, as a global Church.

Pope John Paul II, in the era of globalization, called the continents together in individual synods, continent by continent, to reconsider the Church's mission, because in this new situation there is also something new in the history of the Church. Individuals sometimes turn away from an encounter with Christ, but that has always been the case. Now, however, whole groups and cultures and countries once Christian have turned away. The Good News is neither good for them, nor is it news. "We've heard it before," they seem to say. We live in cultural apostasy.

The pope first started talking about a new evangelization in Haiti, in 1983, nine years before the quincentenary of the European discovery of the Americas. He called for an evangelizing effort new in ardor, new in method, but obviously not new in content, for it is rooted in the original kerygma: *Jesus Christ is Lord.* It needs a new vocabulary, however, for what those words mean and how we explain them to those who do not know Jesus Christ need to be rethought. The pope did not give us the methods or the words, because he expected us to work these out ourselves. Pope John Paul made that clear during my own first *ad limina* visit as a bishop from Washington state with the bishops of the Pacific northwest in 1993. We asked him, "What do you mean by this new evangelization that you have been speaking about for ten years?" He responded, "It's up to the bishops of each place to determine what shape it takes for you." Together we have to think about a new evangelization in the light of the continent and its needs, from within the cultural context that is ours. Our city is not just St. Louis or Mexico City, Chicago or Miami; our "city" is a continent and, finally, a globe. The context of evangelizing has changed.

Historical Turning Points

All earthly cities, as St. Augustine has pointed out, are an amalgam of the City of God and the City of Man, because of the respective choices made at different times for or against the God who orders our loves, saves us as persons, and unites us in Christ's body and in human societies. Errors and sins are always present in some way in this field of wheat and tares. But in some eras, the sources of disunity and its nature are more critical than at others, because history has turning points. Our present day is one such turning point.

In the early Church, coming to understand what it means to say *Jesus is Lord* and to understand how Christ is truly *Son of God* and *Son of Man,* resolving the controversies about Christ's natures as both God and man, deeply threatened unity around the Lord. The Church weathered the storm of the Christological controversies, working through the theology of Christ and of the Trinity in ecumenical councils. The Church's witness to Christ in the death of martyrs had converted her persecutors and other enemies in the Roman Empire. But less than a hundred years after the end of persecution, St. Augustine analyzed the impending fall of this Roman Empire, eroded from within by the love of self and pleasure and beset from outside by peoples whom he and other Romans called barbarians.

In the aftermath of the fall of the Western Empire, civilized life in her territories was disrupted. Always missionary in her heart, the Church responded to the new situation with new tools, new translations of Scripture, new ways of evangelizing, so effectively converting these barbarian tribes that, within a few hundred years after the fall of Rome, an even greater Europe was again Christian. The *oikumene,* the known civilization of the time, was entirely — globally, if you will — Christian. After a long period in which the Church was the leading cultural and, sometimes, political actor, the Great Schism and the Protestant Reformation visibly divided the Church and the civilization she had formed. Once again, the response was to draw closer to the Lord, to purify our hearts, and to evangelize Europe and the New World.

Part of evangelizing after the Protestant Reformation included a clearly apologetic moment. Apologetics — rationally responding to questions about the Catholic faith — goes back to the Acts of the Apostles and the letters of St. Peter and St. Paul, where we are told and shown how to give reasons for the hope that is in us. An apology for the faith has to be made to various people in different ages. In an age that was reeling from the division of the Church after the Reformation, the "enemies of the faith" were the classical Protestants: Lutherans and Calvinists and Zwinglians.

The method of apology, the way of doing apologetics, was to separate ourselves, first in our mind and to some extent in our heart, and certainly in our behavior and actions, from those who would lead us astray. It was a defensive kind of apologetics, and it set the tone for the Church for four hundred years after the post-Reformation Council of Trent (1545–63). Even as we knew people, especially in a country such as ours, who did not share our faith, we continued to learn about how to argue against positions that, if we had checked, they might not have been holding any longer themselves. In the midst of this wave of evangelizing and the apologetics of the counter-Reformation that went with it, another crisis, one with which we are still grappling, emerged, far more destructive of the faith in many ways than was the division of the Church. The acids of what has come to be called modernity, of the Enlightenment's radical theological and philosophical skepticism, began dissolving the formerly Christian culture in both Catholic and Protestant lands so quickly that by the early 1800s, in the wake of the French Revolution, the Church was again besieged by secularist ideologies. When the Church throughout the 1800s spoke about liberalism, what she meant was the French Revolution.

At a time when recognition of human rights under liberal theories and regimes was advancing politically, the abuses of those rights paradoxically also spread. The Industrial Revolution, which called for an elaboration of the social teaching of the Church in the modern era under Leo XIII, was followed by the global slaughter of tens of millions in two World Wars. It was partly in reaction to these terrible divisions that Pope John XXIII called the Second Vatican Council; he hoped to use it to tell humanity that we are one race, one people, one family of God. Since then, divisions within the Church and within culture itself have become more pronounced and, at times, the rhetoric more strident. We are still trying to understand what the preeminent modern value of freedom means, and how it corresponds to the truth that sets us free, the truth given us by divine revelation. We are still trying to grapple with how we are to situate ourselves vis-à-vis the earth and the physical world that we are increasingly able to master and to exploit. At perhaps the final frontier of the modern project, the revolution in biology, we pursue a kind of absolute freedom to dominate the God-fashioned gift of the human body itself.

A New Moment

This is a new moment with a new situation calling for a new evangelization that has to include a new apologetics. Rightly, the catechetical renewal after the Council stressed that the most important goal in evangelizing is simply to set forth the faith on its own terms, not to argue against adversaries. What was sometimes forgotten in the euphoria of the 1960s, however, was that convinced adversaries to the faith are still with us — perhaps not classical Protestants any longer, but others whom we will discuss below.

During the Synod for America, I suggested that an integral part of the new evangelization must be a new apologetics — a loving and nondefensive but nonetheless clear response to the arguments against the Catholic faith. These include arguments raised on the one hand by those who misrepresent God's Word by reading the Bible as a code, and on the other hand claims by others that all religions, but especially Catholicism, are an illusion that destroys personal happiness and critical scientific intelligence. Today, as two thousand years ago, Catholics must be able to give a clear account of the hope that is in them (1 Pet. 3:15). A clear account of our own faith does not preclude a strengthening of ecumenical relations and excludes directly attacking any other faith community.

Apologetics is important first of all within the Church herself. We need to give reasons for the faith not only to enlighten those who do not share it but also to strengthen those within the household of the faith. This is one of the reasons why so many renewal movements begin with small groups in which Catholics begin to express the faith that is in their hearts in an atmosphere where they know that what they say will be understood because the faith is mutually held. In rehearsing the expression of faith among believers, members of these groups will find the courage to express the faith also to those who do not share it.

Apologetics within Christianity

Apologetics in this first instance is always an exchange within the Church — sometimes a very theologically sophisticated exchange — which gives well-considered reasons for our belief in the light of revelation and of critical intelligence. This is the task of each age in order to give deeper understanding of what we profess in the Creeds and in the doctrines of the Church. This conversation is essential for ecclesial communion. Its highest expression is an ecumenical council. The early controversies about the divinity and humanity of Jesus Christ constituted an especially critical period within the Church and in the development of her doctrines. Hanging in the balance were the exact meaning and the gravity of Christ's words and acts and our memory of them in the Church, the nature of the God in whose image all human beings have been created, and the unity of the Church herself. Behind the results of each of these early councils are reasoned arguments about how to interpret divine words and actions, about what meanings these interpretive methods will yield, about how the contents of revelation can be understood using available philosophical concepts, and about the cultural errors exposed by divine revelation.

Behind these arguments are the great theologians of the early councils: Athanasius, the Cappadocian Fathers (Basil of Caesarea, Gregory of Nazianzus, Gregory of Nyssa), John Chrysostom, Cyril of Alexandria, Maximus the Confessor, Andrew of Crete. Each of these great preachers, many of them also great bishops, was a theologian and apologist. Many of them endured great hardship for their tenacity. Bishop Athanasius survived his sixteen years in exile, while John Chrysostom did not survive his exile. They were preceded and followed by other great apologists who defended the faith not only internally from errors within the community but from both paganism and any heretical aberration that set itself up against the Church. Their names and titles are familiar: Clement of Rome, Ignatius of Antioch, Justin Martyr, Irenaeus of Lyons, Tertullian, Clement of Alexandria, Origen, Cyprian, Eusebius, Augustine — and then into that "middle age" that was inaugurated with Abelard, Aquinas, and the scholastics. Aquinas is not only the master of the *Summa theologiae*, he is also the writer of an earlier multivolume tome, the *Summa contra gentiles*, a work to help evangelists answer the objections of Muslims.

When the Reformation divided the Church's visible unity, a new era of intra-Christian apologists, many of them Dominicans, Franciscans, and Jesuits, sought to reform, defend, and propagate the Catholic faith. When Enlightenment thinkers challenged Christianity as a social and cultural whole, Catholic thinkers as varied as Frédéric de La Mennais and Joseph De Maistre, François-René de Chateaubriand and Jean-Baptiste Henri Lacordaire, countered with an apologetical, historical, and political theology. From these turning points in the history of the Church and the history of the human race, from these periods of crisis, the effective evangelization that was a response brought us to where we are today. We possess a new recognition that we cannot simply present the faith on its own terms, essential though that is, because the terms are not understood by people outside the Church and are often misunderstood within. We have to present the faith in context, a global context today, which affects not just non-Catholics but ourselves as well. We live in the world as well as in the Church, and the space between them is porous. It must be so, for the function of the Church is to love the world and proclaim within the world that Jesus Christ is the leaven, the center of communion, creating solidarity among peoples.

In "apologizing" for the faith, one runs the risk of being misunderstood or even hated. The new apologetics has to respond, to give reasons for the hope that is in us in terms that others will understand. We also have to do so in a nondefensive way, because we are taught by *Evangelium nuntiandi* and *Redemptoris missio* that dialogue is now a part of evangelizing. Dialoguing and evangelizing follow different dynamics and internal logics, but they cannot be separated. To evangelize in a dialogical way means that we accept into our lives the other precisely as other. We cannot reject persons even as we refute their arguments. This is a new imperative for a new apologetics, one that the Second Vatican Council imposes in sending us out to unite a divided world as apologists for the Catholic faith.

Who are the people the new apologists must pay particular attention to? There are two groups: secularists on the one side and fundamentalists on the other. What does American "secularism" look like? While Pope Benedict XVI praises a culture that still permits religious language in public, Pope John Paul II often pointed out that the fault line of our culture — of Western culture, and specifically of our culture in the United States — is that we have been willing to sacrifice objective truth in order to save subjective freedom, understood particularly as freedom of choice by an autonomous self. He was insistent that this fault line will eventually erode our civilization from within, just as the willingness on the part of Marxist societies to sacrifice personal freedom for the sake of justice (understood as a brutal equality) eroded those societies from within.

Secularized Society

In our case, then, in secularized and postmodern society, where there is no longer any single focus, where even science itself, while understood as true, is no longer *the truth,* where there are many points of perspective, we are no longer in the modern world where there was a single source of truth in science falsely set in opposition to the faith. Now any and every truth claim puts personal freedom in jeopardy. In this postmodern world, the relationship between truth and freedom has to be the object of particular attention by Catholic apologists who are intent upon evangelizing. We are, of course, free; but we are often isolated in our freedom by our interpretation of freedom as autonomy.

At no time was this clearer to me than in the contrast between the 1999 visits of John Paul II to Mexico and to the United States. In Mexico City, the papal visit was a public celebration. The streets between the airport and the papal nunciature, as the papal cortege moved into Mexico City itself, were lined on both sides by youngsters. The people were held back by a living chain of thousands upon tens of thousands of very young people, teenagers, and men and women in their early twenties. They were a living boundary to mark off both sides of the twelve-mile route. These same young people entered into the hotels where the bishops stayed. They controlled our security; they vouched for us as we came in and out; they checked on us as friends, and they took care of us. "What can I do for you?" *"¿Qué le puedo hacer?"* They told us their names, they spoke of their families and faith, of why they were serving us. There were undoubtedly police officers among us and them, but the security officers were not highly visible. It was the young people in relationship to one another, in relationship to the Holy Father, in relationship to the bishops, and all of us in relationship to Christ who made it possible for that visit to be what it was.

In St. Louis, that same kind of unity around Christ, the Holy Father, and the bishops was visible, especially among the young people and at the main Mass. In those situations where the Church was able to establish the same climate that was characteristic of Mexico City, the same response of faith was made visible. But in the streets of St. Louis, the security of the Holy Father had to be handed over to the Secret Service. Understandably enough, they wanted to deliver a live pope at the end of his visit. The way they assured that was not to connect him but to isolate him from the crowds. It seems the best way to protect in our society is to eliminate systematically as much contact as possible between an individual who needs to be protected, such as a president or a pope, and other people. The pope was secure, but it was very difficult, except when the Church intervened, to have human contact with the Holy Father. In Mexico the protection was through relationships; in St. Louis, the protection was through isolation. During the visit of Pope Benedict to

Washington, D.C. and New York City in April 2008, the security was far more sophisticated and everyone was respected. But the massive security measures discouraged any spontaneous gesture that departed from the carefully choreographed events we now accept as necessary. We are used to isolation, both of the famous and of ourselves.

Individualism can be construed positively. It has often been positive in our history, and a sense of the dignity and generosity of the individual is part of our gift as Americans to the whole world. It leads to respect for personal rights and can foster a fervent sense of responsibility for loving oneself and others. It can encourage a healthy optimism about the possibility of accomplishing something: not for us a kind of a fatalistic culture that looks to a *caudillo* or a *Führer* in order to save people. It promotes a reluctance to see oneself as a passive object of a historical process, one who needs to turn to the state or, finally, to violent revolution for relief.

The individualism that has marked U.S. culture since the beginning has, in many ways, therefore, been positive. But like every cultural reality, there is an underside to individualism. No culture perfectly expresses the Gospel, and therefore every cultural phenomenon is evangelically ambiguous. In the tale of Mexico City and St. Louis, two notions of what it means to be human were in evidence. The one formed more closely in dialogue with Catholicism has its own problems — Mexico is not the promised land; its people live with poverty and various forms of oppression and violence. But the understanding of the human being that is formed more in relation to Protestantism also has its strengths and weaknesses. In one culture, the human person is freed, fulfilled, and protected by relationships to God and to the truths that God has revealed. In the other culture, relationships are often seen as constraining or even threatening individual freedom. Marriage itself is often no longer a total and mutual donation of self; it has to be hedged by a prenuptial agreement. Almost every relationship is commercialized in some way, and individuals rely more on laws and bureaucratic processes than on other people for protection.

We live with a crisis of relationships, and also with a crisis of intelligence. Pope John Paul II addressed this latter crisis in *Fides et ratio,* explaining that the twin crises of atheism and moral relativism stem from a lack of confidence in human reason's ability to arrive at the truth. It is not that we dismiss faith because we are so sure we have the truth; it is rather that we dismiss faith as a source of truth because nothing can give us the full truth. There is no absolute truth. In this view, even science, a construct that enables us to work in a pragmatic way to manipulate nature to our own purposes, is not true in a necessary way. The human intellect has lost confidence in its ability to know unchangeable truth. In the face of triumphant human reason at the end of the nineteenth century, the First Vatican Council taught that faith is not irrational. Ironically, at the end of the twentieth century, the Church is saying that faith must rescue reason from its own self-inflicted wound of skepticism.

Doubt that human reason can understand the truth of things as they are is the result of a rationalism that separates human thought from any relationship to the data of God's self-revelation. In such a cultural milieu, the new apologetics must therefore be grounded in a philosophy that grants the sciences their rightful autonomy but not a hegemony; it must make use of a philosophy that is open to contemporary concepts, especially those that promote an appreciation for human subjectivity and for the centrality of human freedom in our experience. In an effective apologetics, reason finds itself strengthened in its dialogue with faith, and vice versa.

Fundamentalism

On the other side of the apologetical conversation in our era are the fundamentalists, both non-Christian and Christian, whose faith is not critical, who have not been subjected to the acid of modernity and emerged with a refashioned faith in a postmodern culture. Theirs is a faith devoid of self-criticism, a faith that simply asserts itself and refuses to judge any other position except in the light of faith itself. There is no mediating discourse possible, no natural law theory or philosophical reflection to connect the truths of faith to society in ways that are acceptable to those who do not believe in revelation. The Catholic Church is in a unique position in the dialogue between faith and culture in a new millennium. The Church's roots are premodern, but she has gone through modernity in a way that enables her to carry on a certain number of conversations that fundamentalists are less able to enter into.

As I discuss elsewhere in this book, the most important conversation in the next hundred years is that between the two faiths that are growing most quickly in this postmodern era — Islam and Christianity. If we can come together without the defensiveness of the past and the bloodshed of a thousand years when Islam was a constant threat to Christendom and Christians fought to reconquer once Christian lands, we might be able to envision together a world that will be a better home for the whole human race. We can agree with Islam about the perils of modernity. We can agree particularly with their critique of the moral relativism into which Western society has fallen.

My own birthplace, Chicago, is also home now to many thousands of Muslims, most recently arrived and often living a faith that has not yet come to terms with modernity. I watch from my windows overlooking Lincoln Park and sometimes see a Muslim woman in *chador* with her children in tow, completely covered up, even in summer; and running by her are joggers in their underwear. I wonder what must be going on in her heart. What about her children? How will they be Muslim in this kind of society? Muslim parents worry about this. When I speak with them, it's very easy to talk about the moral issues that preoccupy Catholic parents as well.

If we enter into a more religious conversation, they might mention verses from the Koran that speak about Jesus and his mother, Mary, but in ways that are not totally acceptable to Catholics. Then the conversation might issue into a dialogue about how to live together, and that conversation is important not only to Catholicism and Islam, but to the world as a whole. What we might be able to show Muslims is how a premodern faith, such as theirs and ours, can go through modernity into postmodernity and still survive; what they might be able to show us is a way to be part of a postmodern society and not allow one's faith to be corrupted or smothered. If together we can face postmodern culture, even though we are very differ-ent in our understanding of what God asks of his people, then we might heed the call of Pope Benedict XVI to build a global culture safe for both critical reason and traditional religion.

Within Christianity itself, of course, there are fundamentalist movements that also are a reaction, in part, to modernity. The rationalism that was applied to the Bible in the "new criticism," the historical criticism of the last century, caused some Protestants to assert five fundamentals of the faith that are to be accepted without criticism. Catholics accept these fundamental truths, but we also are able to recast them, even in the Creed, in more self-consciously critical ways. The second component of modernity that was rejected by fundamentalists, because it seemed to attack the truth of God's creating the world as the Bible describes it, was Charles Darwin's understanding of the evolution of animal species through natural selection by random variation. Histori-cal criticism and evolutionary theory were at the heart of modern self-understanding. They are now somewhat relativized, although Darwinian evolutionary theory is being put forward as a philos-ophy in its own right. These developments left a certain number of Christian groups removed from liberal Protestantism and dis-trustful of critical intelligence. If this is where reason has taken us, some say, if it gives us biblical criticism and Darwinian evolution, then we can't trust reason itself. This reaction isolates a faith community from the culture and from other religious communities. In American fundamentalist communities, it is the personal experience of one's emotional attachment to the Lord and to his truths that is finally normative. While fundamentalist belief is not irrational, the evidence for it is private, religious experience interpreted without the philosophical and ecclesiological foundations Catholics would see as necessary to be faithful to the data of revelation itself. This kind of fideism or fundamentalism can easily lapse into an uncritical emotivism.

A new apologetics on our part, therefore, must not only be philosophically rigorous in order to talk with secularists; it must also be biblically enriched, with an attendant focus on history, languages, and interpretative methods. The faith that enables fundamentalist Christians to walk with the Lord and to love him must be respected because in its fundamentals it is ours.

Four Characteristics

What characteristics, to conclude, are necessary for a new apologetics? First, the new apologetics must have a deep understanding of the Catholic faith on its own terms. This is where we must begin, but we cannot end there. An apologist understands not only what is taught, but why it is taught, along with the historical context of our beliefs.

Second, the new apologist must fully understand the positions of the others whom he or she invites into dialogue. In our context this means being as scientifically and philosophically sophisticated as secularists and as biblically knowledgeable as Christian fundamentalists. In the spirit of Vatican II, this also presupposes an openness to these positions as other than our own, not only in order to better critique them but also in order to recognize the potential positive implications of what the others are asserting, even for ourselves.

Third, the new apologist must create responses to these challenges through positive articulations and explanations of the faith — a faith that employs terms and concepts understood by one's interlocutors without diminishing the substance of the faith. We have a right to use our proper vocabulary, but we also need to translate it or use it in such a way that it is not needlessly puzzling to others.

Finally, and most importantly, the new apologetics must be a personal and nondefensive loving response to arguments against the Catholic faith even by those who in fact hate the Catholic Church. The new apologetics must be a clear response to the arguments against the Catholic faith raised by those who, on the one hand, believe that all religions are stifling illusions and, on the other hand, those who misrepresent the Bible. But our response must also be permeated by humility and respect, two dispositions that we have occasionally lacked, as John Paul II said in his confession to God of sins done in the name of truth during the last two thousand years. We must love enemies of the faith, of course; and we must also love Holy Scripture more than do fundamentalist Christians, and love the world more than do secularists.

The Church will fulfill her mission when she ministers with her Lord's combination of respect for persons and for truth. This is a combination much in evidence in Jesus' encounter with those whom we read about in the New Testament — the Samaritan woman and others. As Catholics, our encounter with others reaches out to everyone, for the Church is universal, and especially must we meet those who are most broken, even those who are our enemies. Since no evangelist is himself totally in possession of the Gospel of Jesus Christ, the call to encounter Christ, our friend, our Lord, is always made with humility. Further, our modern appreciation for the subjective dimension of human acts and human freedom dictates that the call or the explanation of who Christ is has to presuppose the good will of those in the conversation, even if in practice we quickly discover this not to be the case. Finally, while the Church is Catholic, she is also apostolic. The Church every-where reaches out with the faith that comes to us from the apostles, a particular faith, a set of truths that make their claim upon us. We proclaim them without compromise, for this is the truth that is received, the data given us by historical revelation. We proclaim them with a joy that should attract.

Integrating the apostolic and the catholic aspects of our mission, uniting the objective and the subjective aspects of the human person, synthesizing Gospel truth with universal charity: these are the tasks that face a Church challenged and graced by her Lord to make all things new through a new evangelization in our time.

Chapter 5

Ancient Traditions in Contemporary Culture

Catholics and Jews in Dialogue Today

T HE NEW APOLOGETICS is new in part because it brings dialogue into its method. It both demands and creates an attitude of openness to the other. Chicago is a place that offers examples of fruitful dialogue among people of diverse faiths. The Parliament of the World's Religions first met in Chicago in 1893 and now has its permanent home in the city. Chicago has also been a center of ecumenical and interreligious collaboration on social justice issues, racism, and economic fairness, as well as a locus of more formal theological dialogue. For the past decade, Catholics and Jews in Chicago have honored the address given by Joseph Cardinal Bernardin at the Hebrew University in Jerusalem in 1995, by hosting an annual lecture presented alternately by Catholic and Jewish scholars. Christian-Jewish dialogue in the Archdiocese of Chicago is deeply rooted in friendship and in mutual respect.

This history leads to reflection on two major themes: (1) the Second Vatican Council's statement on the Church and the Jewish People in the conciliar text *Nostra aetate*, and (2) the relationship between religion and society in a global context. Both of these are issues that are central to the faith and lives of Jews and Christians alike, but the second is only rarely reflected on together.

Nostra aetate

To the first issue, *Nostra aetate*'s fourth chapter inaugurated a profound transformation in the Catholic Church's understanding of her relationship to Judaism and the Jewish people, both at the time of her origins as a Church as well as today. Subsequent statements from the Holy See in 1974 and 1985 further developed the implications of the Council document. We continue to explore the theological dimensions of this new understanding.

Pope John Paul II gave strong impetus to such theological reconsideration in his many addresses on the relationship between Christians and Jews. His talks on this relationship fill two published volumes. The late pope's elaboration of how Catholics are bound to Judaism in their own self-identity is among the most important legacies he has left the world. Benedict XVI wants to assure the continuation of John Paul II's legacy, something that the cardinals, discussing among themselves before the conclave that elected him, wanted to see continued. The meetings Pope Benedict has had with world Jewish leaders, his visits to synagogues in Cologne and New York City and to Israel itself have worked to strengthen that relationship.

Prior to his election as pope, Joseph Cardinal Ratzinger had written some articles offering new insights into the paths followed by Judaism and Christianity on the road to redemption. Pope Benedict XVI has continued to promote this theological exploration, both through his own writings as well as through the work of the Holy See's Commission for Religious Relations with the Jewish People.

The three basic assertions of *Nostra aetate* are: first, that the Jews remain in covenant with God after the coming of Jesus Christ; second, that Jews were not collectively responsible for the death of Jesus, whether in his day or later; and third, that as Jews, Jesus and his first disciples lived and were formed by the Jewish faith. This formation occurred during the period before both Christianity and Judaism took on further definition after the fall of Jerusalem and the expulsion of the disciples of Jesus from the synagogues toward the end of the first century. These three points remain the basic building blocks for further theological reflection, and Benedict XVI has in his past writings reflected especially on the third point.

Nostra aetate was necessary because, over the centuries, anti-Semitism and anti-Judaism had become sinful realities within the Church and in many societies that were (at least nominally) Christian. Pope John Paul II, in his personal writings, such as *Crossing the Threshold of Hope*, and in the poignant prayer he inserted into the Western Wall in Jerusalem, made it clear that anti-Semitism cannot be tolerated within the Church. In the fundamental agreement signed by the Holy See and the state of Israel, both parties commit themselves to work against anti-Semitism in whatever forms it might reappear. Regrettably, that commitment remains necessary today, a fact reaffirmed in the joint communiqué from the 2004 meeting of the international Vatican–Jewish Committee in Buenos Aires.

Religion and Contemporary Global Society

Religion and contemporary global society is a theme derivative from the dialogue between faith and culture. My personal interest in this topic has been shaped by the years I spent living outside the United States as part of the government of my own international missionary congregation, the Oblates of Mary Immaculate. Returning to the United States, I became concerned less about protecting Catholicism as a mainstream religion than about preserving Catholicism as a religion true to Christ and universal by its very nature. Catholicism is always and inevitably "other" in any society, but it is "other" in particular ways in American society. One can belong to and contribute to the identity of a society by being authentically "other," by being integrated without being co-opted.

Suspicion about Religious Faith

In a talk given in Chicago in 2004 on "Catholicism in American Public Life," I hoped to say something substantive and nonetheless avoid controversy. I was invited to speak before the 2004 presidential election, with the expectation that I would, in fact, say something controversial. The contribution to the public conversation that the media make is to offer an ongoing commentary on events, featuring from time to time voices that otherwise might not be heard, so that people live in the illusion of freedom to criticize the status quo, even as they are manipulated into preserving it. In my talk, I noted that "public life is, of course, much broader than political life. Catholicism," and, one could add, Judaism and Islam, "is a complete way of life, a life of faith which is a total response to God who loves us and reveals himself to us, a way of life with proper behaviors and convictions and ideas, based upon...[biblical] faith."[1] In America today, such faith is increasingly suspect for at least two reasons:

> One reason stems from the suspicion that faith will limit personal freedom. Since freedom is our most precious value, both in public life and private life, any deterrent, any obstacle to human freedom, anything that is a threat to personal freedom, is automatically suspect. Ever since American freedom was expanded after World War II to include sexual freedoms of all sorts, religion, and particularly Catholicism, has come to be regarded as a threat.[2]

A second reason that faith is suspect stems from the conviction that religion is a cause of social violence. This is especially true after September 11, 2001. This conviction ignores the historical fact that more people have been killed for the cause of national independence or to defend an already established state — or even for values such as freedom or democracy — than were ever killed in the name of Moses or Christ or Mohammed. But once religion becomes suspect, it has to be controlled and society moves toward a secularized ethos:

> When the public realm is constructed without reference to a way of life based on faith, when public life doesn't admit that faith is compatible with its own nature as public, we have the beginning of a secularized ethos. Philosophically, of course, a secularized society rests on the conviction that spirit does not have power. Matter has power. We harness the power of matter for our own purposes all the time, especially through science and with technological advances. But spirit, which believers say is the most powerful reality of all, does not have power in a secularized worldview. At best, [therefore,] religion is poetry that can console, but it doesn't give the truth about anything, and it doesn't have any access to a power that is not material, because matter is all that there is.[3]

Therefore, the truth claims that any religion might make are automatically discounted as irrational or superstitious and further cause for suspicion. Believers can react in different ways to this kind of ethos, which is more or less strong in different parts of the country and different parts of the world. Very often we begin by trying to clarify who God is, hoping that God's power, providence, and presence will be neither a threat to personal freedom nor a cause of social violence on the part of those who worship God. We try to present a God who is not a caricature, someone out to get us, and with that argument we hope that opposition to religion will be attenuated. Sometimes that maneuver works; very often, it does not. Yet as we noted earlier, in the Catholic perspective, God has out of infinite generosity created the finite realm *ex nihilo*. Because of his unique relation giving existence from within yet standing outside of the entire created order, he is not one being among others; because he acts from generosity, he is not a violent or manipulative god; because he creates all things, all creatures are related to each other in ontological intimacy.

What this should mean is that our way of conceiving social relationships must be in accord with the most fundamental relationship between God and the order that he has created. Religious people and religious institutions have often failed to be true to this God we believe in, and nonbelievers sometimes base their antireligious convictions on our sinful behaviors as well as our ill-understood beliefs.

Still, even when all the explaining is done, some people do have a principled opposition to religion itself, or at least organized religion, if not to God, however they conceive God. Where we see this religious conflict with secularism most starkly is in the behavior of the institutions of the state, which carry the public order. Now that secularism has assumed something akin to the role of an established religion, or at least a public ethos, we see the state intervening to protect its citizens *from* religion rather than to promote the free exercise *of* religion. The jurisprudence of the Supreme Court of this country began about fifty years ago to make the switch from protecting the free exercise of religion to protecting people from religious interference in their nonpractice of religion. This creates a quandary for the Catholic American, and, I suppose, for many other people of faith as well:

> The definition of life itself, of the nature of marriage, and of what is religious and what not are now in the hands of the government, especially through the courts. The United States no longer has, therefore, the type of limited governmental institutions that preserved individual freedom in our past. A state increasingly bureaucratized and courts that meddle in areas

that [should be] outside of government's limited jurisdiction in a free society have effectively broken the social contract.[4]

A Cautious Assessment

The Church's gaze was focused beyond the United States to the entire world during the Second Vatican Council. At that moment in the 1960s, there was an optimism about modernity that seemed quite appropriate. Blessed Pope John XXIII, however, was less optimistic about modern society than he was about the Church. He saw the Church in a position of internal strength, united doctrinally (which is why Vatican II was a pastoral council rather than a doctrinal council) and ready to engage pastorally, boldly, in a dialogue with a world weakened in his lifetime by divisions of class and race, by conflicts and wars based upon nationalisms and totalitarianism, but a world filled nonetheless with God's love and goodness, which were the source of his confidence in the future.

The last forty years have seen a weakening of the Catholic Church's internal unity, because ecclesial renewal has been too often confused with self-secularization. Secularism itself, the ethos of the world on its own, divorced from divine providence, has become more assertive as it has gained control of many of the reins of state power. None of this means that the dialogue between faith and culture in this country or elsewhere is now a stalled conversation between a sectarian faith and a hostile culture, a dialogue of the deaf. We have not yet come to that pass; there are too many good people around, whether secularists or religious people, to bring us yet to pitched battles. But the conversation continues more cautiously, aware of inherent contradictions that were able to be overlooked in the enthusiasm of the 1960s and 1970s.

If society is becoming increasingly suspicious of institutionalized religion, perhaps a cooperative and friendly dialogue between biblical faith and American culture remains strong. The psychological

counterpart of cultures co-opting faith ideologically is the assimilation of individual believers to cultural mores not rooted in faith.
When both Catholics and Jews immigrated to the United States,
we came to a culture shaped by Protestantism. It can be argued
that we secularized American culture for religious reasons before
the irreligious secularizers began their work. Catholics worked to
secularize the public ethos of the country because we did not want
to become Protestant in order to become American, and Jews secularized it because they did not want to be Christians in order to
be Americans. We both succeeded, and now we have to ask, "What
has happened as a result?"

A century ago, both Jews and Catholics were assimilating into
what was basically a biblical culture, with many points of contact
among all of us who look to Scripture as the written witness to
God's self-revelation. While never formally exploring the question
from within the contemporary faith–culture framework of discussion, the instinct of early Catholic Americanizers, such as James
Cardinal Gibbons of Baltimore and Archbishop John Ireland of
St. Paul, was to believe that the biblical faith we had in common
with Protestants would allow for successful assimilation of Catholics into American society without loss of their Catholic faith. In
1930, with the cutoff of European immigration to this country
after World War I, George Cardinal Mundelein, one of my prede-
cessors as archbishop of Chicago, was a leader among the second
generation of Americanizers in the Catholic hierarchy, and he held
similar convictions. It was up to us to create Catholicism with an
American ethos, and this project was considered possible because
the culture was benign and, in fact, biblical in its roots.

In 1990, with these same convictions, I suggested that Catholics
might look to Protestants for help in the religious dialogue with
modernity, since Protestantism was born at the beginning of the
modern age and, having been more at home in this kind of culture,
could give us some clues.[5] Two decades later, and from the vantage

point now of a diocesan bishop trying to hold people together in the Catholic Church, I would be far more cautious. The very elements within American Protestant culture that would have allowed this linkage have also been eroded by the secularizing trend that affects all of us, including Protestants themselves. What remains of the original Protestant ethos in contemporary American culture has been deformed into a secularized echo of Calvinism, particularly in the cultural emphasis on the notion of individuals determined by situations beyond their personal control, with the result that many perceive themselves to be victims. The present societal ethos tends to regard people as victims not of Calvin's sovereign God but of inadequate parenting, societal prejudices, and institutional injustice. As a result, the biblical message of freedom rooted in truth is treated at best as just one more personal option and at worst as a reactionary opposition to progressive cultural trends that are seen as liberating individuals from societal and institutional oppressions and dogmatisms of all sorts. The communitarian ethos of both Jews and Catholics, and even of Protestants, receives cultural short shrift. Society becomes a collection of individuals. Religious claims are at best private, and at worst morally oppressive.

What might be an adequate response to society's impression or even conviction that religion is almost always oppressive? If it is not enough to clarify what we believe, then we should do something genuinely new, using religion to create a new culture: That was the great project of John Paul II's papacy, and I want to conclude with a few considerations about that possibility here.

Creating a New Culture

Speaking about religion and society during one of his visits to Canada, Pope John Paul II said that secularized culture is really a "new culture," in the sense that it is a collection of values distinct from the biblical culture it replaces. It is up to believers to work with this fact and to create from it a different kind of new culture, one that perhaps would not be explicitly Christian or Jewish or Muslim but would nonetheless be open to religious influences in a way that the pope believed secularized culture, closed to transcendence, is not.[6] The pope also identified some concerns about where this "new culture" would move on ethical issues, and he questioned whether it had the capacity to be a foundation for understanding and for fostering our common human identity. Over twenty years later, it is clear that these words spoken in Canada were prophetic for our country, too. Biblical faith's "otherness" within American culture today is etched most clearly in ethical questions and in diverse understandings of the anthropology of the human person.

John Paul II was a philosophical anthropologist, sharply aware of the identity of the human person as shaped by cultures and by various ideologies. The papal biographer George Weigel explained:

> Beginning with his late teenage years under Nazi occupation, [Karol Wojtyla] gradually came to the conviction that the crisis of the modern world was first of all a crisis of ideas, a crisis of the very idea of the human person. History was driven by culture, and the ideas that formed culture. Ideas had consequences. And, if the idea of the human person that dominated a culture was flawed, one of two things would happen. Either the culture would give birth to destructive aspirations, or it would be incapable of realizing its fondest hopes, even if it expressed them in the most humanistic terms.[7]

Although he was a trained philosopher, John Paul's critique of modern culture was not born solely of philosophical speculation but from his personal experience, above all as a priest and bishop. His experience of the Nazi occupation of Poland, then of the atheistic communist regime imposed upon his people and, still later, his contact with secularism in the West caused him to think beyond America's standard church–state framework for discussing social questions and beyond the faith–science tensions that are the modern framework for defending intellectual freedom.

In Switzerland in 1984, John Paul II, discussing "the purpose and the limits of scientific method," said that the challenge now is "to work toward a new synthesis of knowledge. Such a synthesis would be 'wisdom', [and] it cannot be created without a philosophy, a metaphysics. It can be accomplished, [furthermore], only if intellectuals can work in freedom, guided by truth."[8] The pope clearly defends freedom, but always as a precondition for seeking for and finally arriving at truth. It is beneath human dignity to live in falsehood, and it is dangerous for human destiny to live in religious falsehood. All peoples and disciplines should be welcome in a public discussion about the truths and falsehoods that underlie public policies and the truths and falsehoods of religion itself. Unfortunately, in the present day, almost any religious truth claim just brings public dialogue to a halt.

The Role of Interreligious Dialogue

How then can we be instruments in creating a new culture, here, in this place? I firmly believe that interreligious dialogue is intrinsic to the creation of such a healthy culture, secular in some ways but open to transcendence. We have to foster this dialogue with the culture not just as individual religions and faiths but as religions and faiths who have created our own dialogue as a model for enlarging the public conversation, a model of how public dialogue can take place. It appears to me that, in the coming displacements and revaluing of national sovereignty, the often-discussed dialogue between church and state will actually become less pressing than interreligious dialogue, particularly as major faiths become again the main carriers of culture. A renewed commitment to interreligious dialogue is therefore needed. There are several conditions for such a renewed engagement.

First of all, to be a partner in interreligious dialogue, one must be a believer. The methodology of comparative religions or of any discipline that would bracket one's personal convictions serves only to distort interreligious dialogue. We cannot talk about religion as if it were "out there" and we were somewhere else. All of us go into these conversations precisely as believers. A commitment to faith brings us into this conversation, and we cannot bracket faith for the sake of a quiet dialogue. Participants' faith must guide and govern their lives and their speech, even in dialogue. Only in this way will they be authentic representatives of their own religious communities to the dialogue partners, to the "other" with whom one is now intrinsically related by reason of mutual willingness to engage in dialogue.

The second measure of a genuine interreligious dialogue is a commitment to what is held or practiced in common. I am not referring to finding the lowest common denominator between two traditions. Rather, I am calling for a personal religious commitment to what is at least analogously common between two traditions. The conciliar document *Nostra aetate* says it this way:

> The Catholic Church rejects nothing that is true and holy in these religions. She looks with sincere respect upon those ways of conduct and of life, those rules and teachings which, although differing in many particulars from what she holds and sets forth, nevertheless often reflect a ray of that Truth which enlightens all.... She therefore has this exhortation for her sons and daughters: prudently and lovingly, through dialogue and collaboration with the followers of other religions, and in witness to Christian faith and life, acknowledge, preserve, and promote the spiritual and moral goods found among these men and women, as well as the values in their society and culture.[9]

This is not a mere description of what we have in common — indeed, it is not a description at all. It is more a methodological point, a protocol for respecting what we do not have in common. As a Catholic, I must both respect the truth in Judaism and preserve and promote the spiritual and moral goods of Jewish faith and the values of Jewish culture and society, even though they are not mine in the same way that they belong to members of the Jewish faith.

Obviously, such a rule is demanding. It is personally demanding in the sense that it is a religious obligation for me. I must exercise that respect as a Catholic. But it is also quite demanding on my relationship with Jews. For our relationship to be guided by this rule or measure, another rule is required to enable both of us to respect the "other" honestly and authentically and at the same time remain true to ourselves. The third rule of interreligious dialogue, therefore, is a commitment to the truth and to the search for it together. Partners must "attempt to agree on criteria for judging what each would accept as true, even when it is to be found in a different belief system" and when that truth is not yet shared.[10] Without question, this third rule is the most demanding on the dialogue, and it is not always clear what it entails. But as we speak together, we recognize that it is there. And if we speak and it is not there, we recognize that as well. It is the condition for the possibility of the last rule for pursuing interreligious dialogue.

The rule of commitment to what is in common is essential, because it enables this commitment to flower into action — particularly common action. The fourth and last rule of interreligious dialogue is to be genuine in searching for common action that does not betray particular beliefs. We are not in dialogue with disembodied ideas; we talk with persons. As we discover our respective engagements and personally commit ourselves to their promotion, we do so making common cause with others equally committed. The commitments that need to govern our dialogue therefore include: a commitment to our respective faiths; a commitment to respect for what joins us in dialogue; a commitment to the search for truth and its criteria; and a commitment to shared action to create a culture not closed in on itself.

Finally, in asking how a religion can be itself with full particular authenticity and at the same time contribute to interreligious dialogue and to the creation and enrichment of a new culture, I must ask myself about both my own religion and my own culture. My experience of Catholicism is characterized by the fact that I am a Catholic in America and Catholic as an American. That situation is probably more complex than the experience of being Catholic in other cultural settings, if for no other reason than the competitiveness between the Catholic faith and American universalist pretensions. If Catholics fail to engage American civil religion, we could become members of a sect, abandoning the requirement for visibility that a biblical religion places upon us. Secularism will have triumphed by default. But then freedom itself will be weakened, and we will have betrayed the living God. Other religions in this country, with different relations to its culture, must also engage the question of American civil religion; it would be better, where possible, to do so together. I believe that together we might engage our culture on many points, but there are two themes that even secularists recognize as culturally significant.

First of all, there is the relationship between freedom and desire. We can examine that relationship together to see where personal desires prevent individuals from exercising genuine freedom. Even if one can fulfill all his or her desires for things or for experiences or for power, one is not necessarily free. There are many without faith who would agree with this assertion. Freedom to pursue one's own desires and dreams does not automatically create happiness. Can we speak to this fact and ask: "What therefore is missing in this cultural project? What truly fulfills a desire for freedom itself?"

Second, there is the relationship between individual and community. As premodern faiths in a postmodern culture, both Catholics and Jews bring to our culture what is often perceived to be lacking: a law deeper than the political for discerning right from wrong, and a communitarian ethos that speaks to contemporary loneliness, isolation, and alienation. Our response to this lack of community does not issue from the culture itself or its terms of discourse, because our faiths precede this culture's creation. We need to envision *as religious people* an alternative to the society now being secularized rather than accept a society where every religion is privatized. Believers engaging in interreligious dialogue could help shape a multireligious society as the framework for a truly free society. I use the term "multireligious" rather than "pluralistic," because a multireligious society would prevent each religion from being co-opted by the ideology of pluralism. Religious authenticity itself can, in dialogue with other religions, contribute its own richness to the formation of a new culture, a different kind of society.

We can go forward together without a blueprint because our commitment to the rules for effective Jewish-Christian dialogue is strengthened by a shared sense of the living God working in human history. This sense is shared as well by Muslims, with whom the rules for effective dialogue are not yet as strongly defined. The confidence remains, however, because while the process is ours, the goal is God's.

Chapter 6

A Necessary Conversation

Catholics and Muslims in Dialogue

C ATHOLICS AND JEWS have been sharing the same countries and talking on various levels for centuries, with the Jewish communities often being in the minority.[1] Catholics and Muslims have also been sharing many of the same countries and talking on various levels for centuries, with Catholics and other Christians often being in the minority. Unfortunately, animosities seem to have intensified in the last hundred years. This is a matter of concern not just for Christians and Muslims but for the world.

In the next millennium, as the modern nation state is relativized and national sovereignty is displaced into social arrangements still to be invented, it will be increasingly evident that the major faiths remain carriers of culture.... Interreligious dialogue is more basic to the future of faith, therefore, than is church–state dialogue, important though that remains. And among the dialogues, that between Christians and Muslims promises to be the most significant for the future of the human race. Islam did not undergo the Renaissance and the Enlightenment and therefore enters the postmodern world as a fully universal faith without having undergone the experience of modernity that shaped European culture and the Christian faith. The conversation between Christianity and Islam is not yet far advanced, but its outcome will largely determine what the globe will look like a century from now.[2]

I delivered these words in an address at the Library of Congress in June 1999. To a degree no one could have foreseen or imagined, that proposal has become timely, even urgent. The disaster of September 11, 2001, sent tremors throughout the world, and its implications have alerted reflective Catholics and Muslims to the need to come together in a world that is deeply troubled and in the throes of radical change. The dialogue between the Catholic Church and Muslims is at once more pressing and more clearly fraught with complexity. What lines of communication are open?

Islam in Dialogue with Catholicism?

Since the Second Vatican Council, the Catholic Church has believed that the dialogue with Islam is not only possible but necessary, despite the experience of much previous history. At the beginning of the history of Islam, St. John of Damascus (A.D. 675–750) had proposed that, while the faith of Islam might be unacceptable, it had brought many people to give up idolatry and to worship the One God; his advice was for Christians to engage with Muslims in firm but prudent dialogue.[3] The advice was not taken, for the most part, and the relationship over many centuries became one of polemic and conflict. But history taught its own lessons, and the Second Vatican Council decree *Lumen gentium* agreed that

the plan of salvation also includes those who acknowledge the Creator. In the first place these are the Muslims who, professing to hold the faith of Abraham, along with us adore the one and merciful God who on the last day will judge all mankind. (16)

This statement was repeated and expanded in the conciliar decree *Nostra aetate,* the Declaration on the Relationship of the Church to Non-Christian Religions. Moreover, as Pope John Paul II noted in his book *Crossing the Threshold of Hope,* the Church has to be prepared to enter into dialogue because "the religiosity of Muslims demands respect,"[4] including their submission to God, their worship of him, their fidelity to prayer, their goodness to the poor.

At the same time, there are other considerations. The pope points out that although Muslims adore the One God, in Muslim teaching Islam denies the fullness of God's self-revelation in Christ: "It is impossible not to note the movement away from what God said about himself, first in the Old Testament and then finally in the New Testament through his Son."[5] Islam denies the fullness of God's self-revelation in Christ, though the Qur'an is very protective of Jesus' uniqueness in the history of salvation.

Yet how well founded is a Catholic hope for dialogue with Muslims? One has to face the fact that it is not easy; there are daunting obstacles. In the first place we must ask: Who is the dialogue partner? It might be observed that in the Council documents, in most papal writings, and in official Catholic statements, there is talk of dialogue "with Muslims" rather than "with Islam," and with good reason. There is no one Islam. As Cardinal Ratzinger observed some years ago, "There is no single authority for all Muslims, and, for this reason, dialogue with Islam is always dialogue with certain groups."[6] The Catholic Church comes to the dialogue as a universal Church, but it is not possible to find any one person or institution that can speak for Islam as a whole or can finally enunciate Islamic orthodoxy.[7]

Relevant Historical Aspects of Islamic Faith

The Qur'an is central to the faith and life of Muslims as a religious record that, in greater or lesser degree, gives shape to each Muslim society. It is believed to be literally the word of God come down into the heart of Mohammed. It is a revelation given once and for all. Christians believe the Word of God was made flesh definitively in Jesus Christ; for Muslims the Qur'an is the utterance of God's word, though not as hypostasis, as a human being. The Qur'an is God's word made text. Hence some Muslim scholars rule out the possibility of a development of doctrine from God's eternal speech in the Qur'an; when the classical Islamic exegesis has allowed some notion of doctrinal development within the Qur'anic corpus, it has been restricted to the form of exegesis rather than development as such.

Over the centuries Islamic law, which specifies the response of the believer to what was revealed to Mohammed, has been interpreted by lawyers, teachers, and commentators to form a body of commentary on Qur'anic law standing alongside the Qur'an. Though not regarded as inspired in the same way as the Qur'an itself, it carries tremendous weight, bearing the authority of centuries of established consensus and practice. This is the Sharia, the principles of Islamic law, which, more than legal norms, constitute "the open way of the Command" (Q 45:18). The Sharia is the path or way of God into which are incorporated the legal rules revealed in the Qur'an (which, as such, are not subject to change) as well as all the traditions and opinions that clarify these fundamentals.[8] This process of interpretation went on until the eleventh century A.D., when the Sharia took on its sacral character and was canonized and closed to further development.[9] This canon has been the primary lens through which Muslims have pursued authoritative interpretation of the Qur'an. There have, however, continued to be differing tendencies in interpreting and applying it in various regions.

There are elements in the Sharia doctrines that, as they are usually stated and often invoked, appear to end the hope for dialogue. The strict application of jihad would seem to require that if Islam is in control of a country, it must bring the whole of that society under the rule of Islamic law, even by force. This demand is usually presented as integral to fidelity to the Sharia. Where Islam reigns, unbelievers are to be subjugated, while Jews and Christians are to be under the rules of "dhimmitude" and therefore treated as citizens with diminished rights, who are circumscribed severely in their public religious practice.[10] The contemporary outcome of a literal application of these doctrines is vividly and painfully evident in the horrible situation of Christians in the Sudan at the present time. Yet the jihad and the dhimmi, however interpreted, are part of the classical Islamic stance and are generally held to protect the spirit of Islam.

This classical position is currently modified in differing directions by what is called the Muslim revival. At its root, this is a movement of return to Muslim origins; but it can result in quite different outcomes. Fear of Western imperialism, often understood as Christian aggression, finds expression in a literal interpretation of the Qur'an and Islamic law. The revival then becomes a movement to restore the all-embracing law of God found in Islam, even by violent means, and it holds that political institutions separate from Islamic religion are illegitimate. This current of revivalism is rooted in much of Islamic history; it is strong at present and allows little space for dialogue, either in theory or practice.[11]

Yet the revival includes other significant developments that give a more hopeful picture. Over the past century, as part and parcel of contemporary Muslim thinking, movements of reform and intellectual renewal have emerged in Islam. They are not identical in their beginnings or expression, but generally they also invoke the precedent of early Islam in order to question and even abolish current practices that render Islam exclusive and keep it apart from contemporary culture.[12]

Within Islam, one finds a certain space that includes distinct differences between the mainstream and the fringes, between orthopraxy and deviation. Even the major division within Islam, between

Sunnis and Shia, arose over a historical conflict about the political leadership of the community, not over any question of doctrine.[13]

Walid Saif, the Jordanian participant in the Muslim–Christian dialogue organized by the World Council of Churches, comments:

> Theoretical and conceptual revisions are often triggered by practical encouragement and realistic constraints in the field of action.... The challenges posed by concrete realities, and even by secularism itself, are partly, at least, responsible for many Muslims and Islamists to revisit, debate and revise old ideas which, for long, have been considered indisputable religious facts, while, in reality, they are part of the socio-cultural traditions, or the product of interpretive efforts situated in time and space.[14]

If Dr. Saif is correct, the intra-Islamic debate significantly conditions the possibilities for the Christian dialogue with Islamic religion. The Sharia binds the Muslim as a believer, as a human being, and as the citizen of a theocracy. It is in the interplay of these three that the debate has to take place. The debate shapes how the *Umma*, the Muslim community both worldwide and local, is understood and lived. Because the *Umma* in classical Muslim understanding is an inextricable mix of society, state, and religion, the shape of the Muslim community is also affected by cultural and political factors as well as doctrinal considerations. At any given point in history, one or the other of these factors may become more or less influential.

Considerations from Recent History

What is that history in recent times? The twentieth century saw scholars and commentators, both in Islamic countries in the Middle East and in the West, trying to come to terms philosophically with what was happening as the former achievements of Islam paled in light of the new world of technology. The almost frightening economic power of the West brought with it a changing concept of what it means to be human, along with the conviction that religious and political authority are completely separate. This is a world in which Christianity also has to struggle to survive, as well as one that holds formidable threats for Islam.

In the 1930s strong voices began to emerge in some Islamic lands and among numbers of Muslim scholars in the West in favor of some kind of intentional connection with modernity and the dominant world and philosophy of the West. These were thinkers, scholars, and students of social institutions who had in mind the Muslim cultures that had flourished during the Christian Middle Ages. In these medieval cultures, they found a model of the Sharia presented and lived in a way that favored manufacture, commerce, and the beginnings of science, contributing even to Christian philosophy and resulting in a society that, in modern terms, was relatively free.[15] In the name of Islam, as it had been at certain times and in some places, scholars in the early twentieth century could begin to argue against a theocracy based on a literal and restrictive interpretation of the Qur'an and the Islamic Law. Their vision was of a modern, pluralist society for Muslim countries, so that Islam could take its place and play a strong part in a world that had little room for a closed society.

This "Islamic Liberalism" has become a part, even an influential part, of current Muslim thought; but it has had to struggle and has undergone reverses in the face of the dominant trends in Islamic revivalism. It continues "to argue that Islam, properly understood, is compatible with — or even a precursor to — Western liberalism."[16] There is also secularism, in the modern sense of the privatization of religion, among some Islamic thinkers, but what I am describing here is rather the approach that comes from a concern to renew the impact on today's world of the Sharia as public law. It would claim to return to the sources, that is to the Qur'an and the practice of the Prophet, not to take shelter there, [not] to drown current cares there, but to draw from thence elements for the renovation and revitalization of Islamic philosophy.[17]

It is liberalism with an "Islamic essence,"[18] confident of "the need for Islamic contributions to modern problems"[19] and ready "to argue that the West is suffering from a spiritual crisis that Islam may help to cure."[20] Islamic "liberalism" has to face the same challenges faced by Catholic liberalism, although the two movements relate differently to modernity. The broad challenge is to prove their fidelity to their respective sources of divine revelation.

The Islamic world has now drawn together with a renewed sense of solidarity. In the face of the obvious crisis of the Western moral order, "the Islamic soul [has] reawakened."[21] The revival is therefore wider than fundamentalism. It is, rather, a consciousness of Islam as a vigorous religion that also in the West might become the religious force of the future. Muslims see Christianity as debilitated by secularism and, in an increasing number of places, as being pushed to the fringes of society. This is both a challenge to Muslims and a temptation. The temptation is simply to think that zeal and intensity in preaching and living the Sharia could convince and win over the West. With its clarity and simplicity of teaching, Islam does have a real attraction similar to that of some forms of Christianity, and not least for young people who want something better than they find in the complex, corrupt, and seemingly faithless societies of the West. The real challenge to Muslims, however, is to read the situation in the light of their own origins and history, along with the experience of the West, and to realize that if they try to stand alone or to assume a mode of conquest in the emerging global society, they risk losing all and being swallowed up by the disintegrative powers of Western secularism. Islam stands at a point of decision that will have enormous implications for Islam itself, for Christianity, and for the well-being of a global society.

Of course, any Catholic–Muslim dialogue that seeks to engage Muslims on a fairly extensive front will be complex. The *Umma*'s total organization is different from that of the Catholic Church, which recognizes an essential distinction between the organization of the faith community and the organization of the civil society. The Catholic approach inevitably seems to Muslims like an abandonment of the claims of an all-sovereign God on the whole of life. Yet even Islam distinguishes between the *Umma*, the total Islamic society, and the *jamaá*, a congregation at prayer. Christianity's stance is certainly God-centered in maintaining a separation between Church and world. "Only when Israel's faith emerges from the chosen people" and, in Christ, "becomes the faith of all people, does it become detached from politics and prove to be an element that stands above political divisions and differences."[22] This conviction does not leave the state bereft of religion or outside the realm of God but allows God, through the instrumentality of the community of believers, to stand over against the state and judge it. The Church has a role — not of force but of prophetic criticism[23] — to speak God's word of truth, accepting the weakness of her position in order to allow this politically separated word to be her strength.

Reasons for Hope

What hope, then, can there be that the two religions can maintain a dialogue? I am proposing, in the first place, that the history of Muslim civilization seems to show the Sharia being implemented in concrete situations in a way that does not preclude genuine coexistence with other faiths and even permits a certain mutual exchange of ideas and intellectual discovery that might almost be called a cross-fertilization.

By bringing even the nonnegotiable dimensions of the Catholic and Muslim faiths into dialogue, we might have reasonable hope of creating a mutual and sympathetic knowledge, a measure of real understanding that would allow Catholics and Muslims to uphold the necessary place of religion in a global civilization. This is something that takes on a new urgency as the aggressive unbelief of some Western molders of public opinion use the events of September 11, 2001, to try to secure the rejection of all religion because it foments violence, in the hope of effectively excluding religion from public life. Catholics and Muslims can have a common concern to uphold religious freedom in societies where, if some have their way, religious freedom will be severely restricted.

This is not simply wishful thinking or a hypothetical proposal. Already Catholics, other Christians, and Muslims are cooperating at a world level on practical moral issues that derive directly from essential Christian and Muslim teaching. They are cooperating in a way that has profound implications for a world moral order. This cooperation began in 1994 with a response to disturbing developments at the UN International Conference on Population and Development in Cairo. That conference set out with the object of bringing about "a radical shift in the world's population policies."[24] Driven by a strong international secularist and feminist agenda, the conference strove to achieve the acceptance by all nations of women's right "to control their reproductive lives," a code phrase to cover not only access to artificial birth control but also to abortion on demand as a human right. Pope John Paul II at once identified in the project a vision of sexuality and morals that favored the individual over the family, promoting "models of behavior that are the fruit of a hedonistic and permissive culture."[25]

Other Christians, too, along with Muslims, were uneasy about the conference. Mustafa Mahmoud of Egypt described the project as "a well-designed explosive to blow apart [Muslim] religious identity."[26] At the conference itself, inspired by the stand taken by the pope, a pro-family group emerged. At the level of governments, it included the Holy See, Latin American countries, and some nations from the Middle East and Africa. They were joined by non-governmental agencies representing some Catholics, Evangelical Christians, Mormons, and Muslims. The common denominator among these rather disparate groups was clear internal identity along with firm doctrinal and moral stands that at times have been a source of division among them but that now enabled them to devise a common strategy for the protection of human life.

Among the governments taking a stand were representatives of Islamic countries that stand a bit apart — Libya, Iran, Egypt, Sudan, Iraq — some of which actively persecute Christians living within their borders. They were perceived by the delegation of the Holy See as allies on this issue rather than as friends in general. This distinction is important, because the Holy See was not ready to compromise its stand on freedom of religious practice. The Taliban in power then in Afghanistan was not represented at the Cairo conference.

Several of the Muslims present were able to work with Catholics and other Christians in considerable amity. Austin Ruse, who coordinated the Catholic human life concern in United Nations circles, said that the pope was the rallying point for this quite varied coalition, which operated again at the later Beijing meeting on women's issues and in preparations for the 2002 meeting on children's rights. A number of these participants also came to the defense of the Holy See when its status in the United Nations came under attack. They came to consider the Holy See as the conscience of the UN. This role has served to clarify the issues for some of the Muslim delegates and has encouraged them in speaking out to good effect and taking the lead on the floor of the meeting.

The outcome of all this is what has been described as the most important Muslim–Christian dialogue in the world. It is still in the process of development, since the problems raised by the work of the UN are tenacious and do not admit of easy solution. Yet already there is clear evidence that Catholics, other Christians, and

Muslims are able to work together in a way that, beyond practical cooperation, touches on important moral principles and expresses a sense of mission arising without compromises from strongly held Catholic, Evangelical, and Muslim identities. This cooperation is significant as a contribution to a nascent global moral culture. It provides a voice for Catholics in countries whose governments work out of a morality opposed to the Catholic faith.

The world-shaking events of the past several years have inevitably posed or sharpened certain questions that challenge the proposal I made at the Library of Congress, reawakening fears of theocracy, holy war, and religious intolerance. These developments have to be given full weight where the Catholic Church engages in dialogue with Muslims. I believe they do not, however, nullify the arguments I have brought forward to show that an interreligious dialogue between the Catholic Church and Muslims is possible and even necessary for the well-being of a coming world civilization. Nor is my proposal gainsaid or weakened by Muslim reaction to Pope Benedict XVI's address at Regensburg University in 2006. The speech became the occasion to relaunch dialogue between Catholics and Muslims on a surer and more organized footing. Muslim–Catholic dialogue is inevitably a dialogue with limits and one that will continue to face difficulties. This is already, I believe, the experience of the Holy See through its Pontifical Council for Interreligious Dialogue. The pioneering work of the Council is of first importance, and it now needs to be extended to take a higher profile in the Church and at the level of world events. In the kind of world that is emerging, dialogue has to take place for the sake of what Islam believes itself called to be as well as for the sake of what the Christian faith believes itself to be. It is indispensable for assuring the abiding sense of human dignity needed to undergird a public moral order in the developing global civilization.

The Meaning of Dialogue

There is, of course, no single Muslim position on dialogue, nor does one easily find a developed *ex professo* statement of what it might mean. Yet it is possible to delineate a Muslim dialogical stance, drawing conclusions from the Qur'an that seem justified in terms of Islamic history and of the existence of a reformist movement in Islam and making use of the diversity of interpretations of Islamic law.

For Muslims dialogue means "one must speak the truth, be sincere, and assume that the other person is sincere and also telling the truth."[27] It includes awareness that "interreligious collaboration does not imply giving up our own religious identity but is rather a journey of discovery."[28] The Qur'an says,

> Nearest among [people] in love to the [Muslim] believers you will find those who say "We are Christians," because among them you will find people who have renounced the world, and they are not arrogant. (5:83)[29]

Those Muslims who engage in dialogue claim to find in the Qur'an texts concerning diversity and God's purpose that indicate that a plurality of religions is envisaged in God's design. Dialogue becomes a way for Christians and Muslims

> to live out their faith in relation to each other, sharing as partners common concerns and aspirations and striving together in response to the problems and challenges of our time.... It seeks to discover and appreciate common values of Christianity and Islam.... Dialogue is motivated by a religious vocation and is founded on religious values.[30]

For Catholics dialogue means that without renouncing their own convictions they will meet with Muslims, accepting them as they are and being accepted in turn, in order to understand the truth together as far as possible. Dialogue is not convergence toward a lowest common denominator, nor is it a relativizing pluralism.[31] It includes the desire to know the other as the other truly is and wishes to describe himself. In the dialogue with Islam, Catholics have not always avoided, in an attempt to find shared beliefs and common ground, the danger of "catholicizing" Muslim concepts and terminology and reading into them a Catholic sense that they cannot possess. Essentially dialogue is a service to truth. The parties explain their respective faiths and communities, thereby hoping to grow in mutual understanding and in obedience to revealed truth. Dialogue also entails the rejection of all coercion. Catholic participants will acknowledge and respect the positions of the dialogue partners even while disagreeing with them, and they will refrain from anything that might do violence to the partners' understanding of revelation. This will be especially so in matters of worship; neither Catholics nor Muslims can agree to pray together, though each can be present while the other prays.[32]

There can be no dialogue without mutual respect. Catholics come to dialogue convinced that

> Christians must remember that God has also manifested himself in some way to the followers of the other religious traditions. Consequently it is with receptive minds that they approach the convictions and values of others.[33]

Such a position can be formulated clearly by the Church because Henri de Lubac, two generations ago, so effectively drew attention to the writings of the Fathers and to the principles of St. Thomas Aquinas, which uphold both the necessity of the Church and the possibility of salvation beyond its visible confines, distinguishing always between the possibility of salvation and its actual realization.[34]

A sound, if not always easy, basis for such respect is the firmness with which both Christians and Muslims hold to the truth of God's revelation, mediated through Christ in the Church or through the Qur'an in Islam. On the Catholic side, the declaration *Dominus Jesus,* published in 2000 by the Congregation for the Doctrine of the Faith, asserts that the Catholic Church, the path to salvation willed by God and biblical revelation, is unique.[35] This belief has to be laid on the table in any dialogue in which the Catholic Church takes part. At the same time, the Church expects to hear from her Muslim partners the corresponding Muslim position. The ability to talk about such crucial theological issues, looking at commonality of understanding and approach while equally respecting and seeking to understand the strong divergences, is what grounds dialogue truthfully and gives reality and substance to hard-won cooperation on issues of justice and peace in working toward a public moral order.[36]

Dialogue is neither a win-lose confrontation nor a round of mutual capitulations. Muslims will continue to assert the absolute claims of the Qur'anic revelation. Catholics cannot for the sake of dialogue eliminate the absolute sense and power of Jesus' claim.[37] It is certitude about that real uniqueness that impels Catholics to keep seeking genuine dialogue. Yet the practice and living of dialogue requires Catholics to have a deep sense that the truth they uphold is not their achievement but is the gift of the Lord, who revealed that truth in giving himself to death upon the cross. To enter dialogue is to embrace the humility of the Crucified Jesus while demonstrating the wonder of crucified love.

The experience of the past several decades shows that where there is mutual respect and a shared love of the truth along with a spirit of dialogue, possibilities will open up for practical cooperation on behalf of human well-being. "In dialogue," said Pope John Paul II,

we who believe in the goodness of God have a special duty to address the problems of our people and search together for solutions which can make modern society more just, more human, more respectful of the rights, dignity and human freedom of each individual.[38]

As a number of different statements make clear, the pope would not allow us to retreat from the fact that this is a specifically religious contribution to society.[39] "We should witness to the spiritual values of which the world has need. The first is our faith in God."[40]

Christians and Muslims can work together bearing witness before modern civilization to the divine presence and the loving providence that guide our steps. Together we can proclaim that he who has made us has called us to live in harmony and justice.[41]

The pope opened up a new prospect for interreligious relations, proposing that "the concrete basis for a sincere, profound and constant dialogue between believing Catholics and believing Muslims might be cooperation in solidarity."[42]

Dialogue in Solidarity

Can the notion and virtue of solidarity be for both Catholics and Muslims an immediate goal in dialogue, possibly an organizing concept for promoting Catholic–Muslim cooperation in shaping public morality in a global society? In his encyclical *Sollicitudo rei socialis,* Pope John Paul II proposed solidarity as a category for a Christian approach to economic, cultural, political, and religious dimensions in the contemporary world, as a virtue committing the Christian to the common good, as a means of seeing the other as a neighbor. This solidarity arises from awareness of God as Creator and of the other as made in God's image. In Catholic understanding, solidarity is rooted in the life of the Trinity, in which the communion of the Church is a participation. In this sense "solidarity is the fruit of communion,"[43] and solidarity becomes a Christian virtue.

The source of Islamic solidarity is the acknowledgment and worship of the one God. The oneness of God is the basic doctrine on which Islam rests. The Qur'an, which offers "guidance for mankind" (2:85), is itself the charter for Muslim solidarity. Those things that make for solidarity, such as orderly creativity, sustenance, guidance, justice, and mercy, fully interpenetrate in the Qur'anic concept of God as complex unity. This all-powerful God, through his merciful creativity, measures out everything, bestowing upon everything the range of its potentialities, its laws of behavior, its character. The solidarity of the universe and of human beings is in obedience to God. The Muslim community is to be "the best community produced for mankind, who command good and forbid evil and believe in God" (Q 3:10).

The Qur'an enjoins Muslims to establish a political order on earth for the sake of creating an egalitarian and just moral social order among all peoples. The Muslim community is to be God's instrument, "calling to goodness and prohibiting evil."[44] In this solidarity in carrying out God's plan for the world, Muslims are "brothers" (Q 49:10). They are together as impregnable "as a building faced with lead." To the unity of God corresponds the fellowship of believers.

The word used to designate the Islamic community, *Umma,* signifies the collectivity of believers and necessarily includes the idea of political and social order. It carries a sense of uniformity that does not reflect the oneness in difference, the plurality in unity, that is the nature of God in trinity and that ontologically shapes the Church as communion. This asymmetry in our understanding of God makes it difficult to find commonality of a theological nature between the Catholic Church and the *Umma.*[45]

Yet, even if in different ways, Catholics and Muslims do come to a knowledge of the only God as the one who is unique, a God who wills to establish personal relations between himself and human beings to whom he presents himself. We give a similar if not identical response in faith to God. Along with an absolute insistence on the transcendence of God, Islam has a real concern for the interconnectedness of the human and the divine, not excluding the immanence of God in another (Q 24:35) and in human experience (Q 50:16). God is "nearer to you than your jugular vein" (Q 50:16). God has interacted with humanity to draw people together as Muslims who live by his revealed law, which reflects the will of the Creator (Q 22:40–41).

Can the Catholic response of faith in God's plan and the reception of the gifts of social solidarity and ecclesial communion, alongside the Muslim response of faith in the one God, expressed in the *Umma* and the Muslim concepts of a civil society based on God's law, be the context for interreligious dialogue and the basis of a solidarity that Muslims and Catholics can together foster in a global society?

Dialogue in Faith

The achievement of such solidarity will depend, in part, on the possibility of Muslims and Catholics mutually recognizing and respecting the faith response of the other. Faith is mentioned in the Qur'an fifty-five times. It is asserted that the faith of the Muslim is of higher quality than that of the Christian or the Jew. Islam is described as the faith of Abraham, which is a response to and an effect of revelation. The believer surrenders to God's Word and Law, and faith enters the heart. The Asharite theologians describe it as affirmation with the tongue, confirmation in the heart, and practical living in submission to God. The latter is done by the famous five pillars: (1) confession of faith in the one God, whose prophet is Mohammed, (2) worship of God, (3) almsgiving, (4) fasting, and (5) pilgrimage, which keeps one on the straight path (Sharia). Confession of faith initiates one into the *Umma*, the community of faith; pilgrimage is an expression of that community itself. Faith entails *islam* (submission to God as his servant) and *iman* (inward assent and cooperation). Protected by God and helped by his strength, the believer must manifest his faith in zeal for the things of God and for the extension of God's lordship. This is done by a serene and complete obedience to God's will.

In Fr. Henri de Lubac's description of what faith means for the Catholic, one sees a similarity of experience that might give some ground for a sense of solidarity. Faith, says de Lubac,

> is the fundamental religious act, the one which establishes true religion, which effectively establishes man in his true relationship with God.... Only the Being who is at once personal and transcendent, who is the Absolute and the absolutely Personal, the source and home of all spirits, is worthy to receive the homage of our faith. So we do not just believe in "someone" but in God alone.... God is unique in all respects; he cannot be included in any genus[46]

Faith in the Christian sense, however,

> has a unique and exclusive character. It is not a global notion which could adapt itself to various modalities — Christian faith, Muslim faith, the paganism of the ancient Greeks or Buddhism.... It is the word which designates a unique fact: the reply given by man to God who has come to him in Christ.[47]

Faith teaches and enables the Christian "to begin loving as God loves."[48] Faith moves the believer from truth to trust, from understanding to courage.

As it works out for a Catholic and a Muslim, similarities in the experience of faith are in a constant dialectic with the dissimilarities, and this dialectic does not rule out dialogue but, in fact, makes it more necessary. De Lubac identified the reason for dialogue when he said that Christian faith "introduces events, history, joined to the

Absolute of personal being and of love."[49] In dialogue, Catholics and Muslims, in fidelity, will reach the point where they have to put hard questions to each other. Both have a concern to uphold a God-given identity. In history, this has at times led both Catholics and Muslims to coercion and the infringement of human rights. While making strong claims for herself, however, the Catholic Church has been able to look again at the question of religious liberty and, with ecumenical partners, has been able to address the question of proselytism as distinguished from evangelization. There is a clear conceptual distinction between imposing and proposing. Muslims have yet to make this distinction in the same way, to my knowledge. Further, Catholic understanding of the teachings of Jesus distinguishes always between church and world, between church and state; it recognizes the autonomy of the secular in its own sphere. In Islam, so overwhelming is the claim of God on the human being that religion welds together all elements and levels of human life and activity. This belief becomes in the social order a sometimes aggressive proselytism expressed in the war of religion (jihad), not just as an event but as a permanent dimension of the *Umma*. Real peace would then be impossible outside the realm of Islamic law.

In its more theologically and spiritually developed forms, however, Muslim thought sees the essential meaning of jihad as the personal struggle to submit one's will and all of one's life to God. This internal submission has external consequences in public practice, of course, but it does not of itself demand a Muslim theocratic social and political order. Were this understanding to become determinative in Muslim life generally, then there could be constructive interaction with the Gospel teaching on peace and nonviolence and with Catholic social teaching on human rights.

Here, too, questions such as the dhimmi, or second-class status demanded by the Qur'an for Christians and Jewish believers, will have to be examined. As practiced, this amounts in a number of Islamic countries to repression, denial of religious liberty, and open persecution. If Islam is to be true to itself and if it is to be, with Christianity, a force for moral probity in our rapidly globalizing society, Muslims will have to be prepared to criticize the behavior of other Muslims in some countries where Christians and those of other faiths are actively persecuted; they will have to be prepared to question Muslim communities that allow their mosques to be used as places where terrorists can gather and from whence they can spread ideologies disguised as faith. Similarly, Catholics have to acknowledge and act upon the obligations that Catholic moral and social teaching place on us to uphold fully the religious freedom and civil rights of Muslims in the United States and to reject anything that could marginalize them or discriminate against them. The test of Catholic–Muslim dialogue lies in our being able to take up such questions in order to build a solidarity based on mutual respect and trust and to give a witness to our respective faiths in a secularized society. The dialogue on the notion of faith begins in a shared belief that human existence is fundamentally a response to God, that no human being is autonomous. The meaning of human life is defined essentially not by progress in freedom but by intensity of holiness. Can Muslims and Catholics grow holy together?

A Shared Future through Dialogue

The Qur'an envisages that civilizations will rise and fall. As Muslims and other people fail to live by God's law, there will be breakdown in society. Then a fresh start with an altogether "new generation" of people becomes necessary. The discontinuity of a civilization can be the occasion for shedding the evil in human conduct and society, while the good can be taken up or revived as a legacy for a new civilization. While "the foam on the top of a torrent disappears, that which is beneficial to mankind, the alluvium, settles down upon the earth" (Q 13:17). Will it be possible for

Catholic–Muslim dialogue to lay foundations for universal solidarity by consciously setting out to reclaim something of that alliance with Muslim civilization that contributed to the beginnings of the Christian Middle Ages,[50] a reclamation that enables us together to shape a morality for a postmodern global society?

As the West seemed to be shifting on its moral foundations, Muslims responded to the invitations of Pope John Paul II and took part in the gatherings for peace at Assisi in 1986 and 2002. The Qur'an teaches that war is the work of Satan (2:208ff.) and counsels: "O all you who believe, enter into peace." This admonition is addressed to Muslim believers, and the impact of this call has caused Muslims to agree with John Paul II that

> this dialogue will be especially important in establishing a sure basis for peace and warding off the dread spectre of those wars of religion which have so often bloodied human history. The name of the one God must become increasingly what it is: a name of peace and a summons to peace.[51]

In this message for the beginning of the millennium, the pope asked that the dialogue of the Catholic Church with other religions continue to be strengthened.

> In the climate of increased cultural and religious pluralism, which is expected to mark the society of the new millennium, it is obvious that this dialogue will be especially important in establishing a sure basis of peace and warding off the dread spectre of those wars of religion which have so often bloodied human history. The name of the one God must become increasingly what it is, a name of peace and a summons to peace.[52]

The ideal of Islam is obedience; the truth and gift of the Christian Gospel is love. Obedience and love are both needed to ground a public moral order for a global culture. The God who is truly transcendent and immanent in both Christianity and Islam is to be known and experienced in the communion that is his being and his gift. Human communion is grounded in the self-giving love of God and reflected in the self-gift of those who would belong to him.[53]

Christian love is powerful in the witness given by the deaths of seven Trappist monks in Algeria in 1996. Their prior, Father Christian de Cherge, left a testament that speaks to every effort of dialogue between Catholics and Muslims. He wrote that in his time in Algeria, he had found the Gospel he had learned at his mother's knee in the reverence of believing Muslims.... In his coming death, he said,

> ...this is what I shall be able to do, if God wills: immerse my gaze in that of the Father to contemplate with him his children of Islam as he sees them, all shining with the glory of Christ, fruit of his Passion, filled with the gift of his Spirit whose secret joy will always be to establish communion and to refashion the likeness in playing with the differences.[54]

Pope John Paul II thanked God

> for the witness of love given by these religious. Their fidelity and constancy give honor to the church and surely will be seeds of reconciliation and peace for the Algerian people with whom they were in solidarity.[55]

The price and condition of dialogue and of true, faith-filled solidarity is self-giving love. This love is the condition for the possibility of dialogue. Wherever and whenever it is found, this love gives hope for our efforts now to shape a future global society open to faith in God and intent upon peace for all his creatures.

Chapter 7

The Universal Church and the Dynamic of Globalization

A T THE BEGINNING of the third Christian millennium, inter-faith dialogues find their place in discussions about a new world order. In the early 1990s, with the collapse of Communism in Eastern Europe, the Cold War ended. This meant both the end of the bipolar political arrangement of the world and, as it has turned out, the end of an economic order that divided the world into capitalist and socialist economies. The triumph of Anglo-American capitalism was short-lived, however, because its crisis has left the world without a sure model for economic globalization. Searching only for economic profit without external social or political regulation led to the collapse of financial institutions and the discrediting of the theories that gave them legitimacy. The new economic order already exceeds the grasp of any nation's exclusive influence.

What has replaced the post–World War II world order, which perdured for more than four decades, is what has come to be called globalization. While it is still emerging as a new world order, its contours and directions are becoming clearer. Given the effects of this world order on human persons, it is incumbent upon the Church — which has been entrusted by Christ to care for all — to engage this global culture as she does all cultures: both to affirm what is good and noble about it, and to confront its shortcomings and evils with the light and power of the Gospel.

What Is Globalization?

Globalization is a phenomenon so vast that it is impossible to define or grasp it comprehensively. But let me begin with an image that may help set the stage for understanding globalization, both at the technical and the spiritual levels.

July of 2009 marks the fortieth anniversary of one of the most remarkable events of the twentieth century: the occasion when in the course of the Apollo 11 mission an earthdweller first set foot on another celestial body, the moon. One of the most powerful images to emerge from the adventures of travel in space was that of our own planet earth seen from outer space. This is an image now familiar to all of us. From the perspective of the earlier *Apollo 8* spacecraft in December 1968, the earth appeared like a sapphire orb, illumined against the blackness of space. As one gazes at this gem, one cannot see lines of political division or other boundaries and barriers that mark and sometimes divide the human community. Instead, the image from space is one of a profound unity.

Globalization in its most positive sense is an aspiration here on a divided earth toward the harmony and unity seen from space. Globalization holds up the hope and the promise of a truly united human family, bound together in deep communion. It is from such an image and such a hope that we should take our cues about dealing with a process that has the potential to link all humanity together in ways only inchoately discerned. That image of earth from the *Apollo 8* spacecraft offers the basis for a spirituality that can guide us to meet the missionary challenges globalization presents, a spirituality more adequate to the vision given us by a truly Catholic faith.

What, then, is globalization? Put most simply, globalization is about a simultaneous expansion and compression of time and space. On the one hand, globalization has connected people and places around the world in a way not earlier known to humanity. On the other, those very connections have created a density of relationships that can become overwhelming and even oppressive to the human community. The computer provides an image of both expansion and compression: the Internet and the World Wide Web represent the expanded interconnectedness of the world; the computer chip, with its compression of information into a very tiny place, gives us an image of what the world has become.

The twin forces of expansion and compression create a lively dynamic and reveal the deep contradictions within globalization. But first we need to understand how globalization operates in our world today. It involves four major dimensions of our lives: technological, economic, political, and cultural.

The Technological Dimension

Globalization, we might say, began in 1492, but the kind of globalization we now know became possible because of the rapid advances in communications technology. The rise of the personal computer in the 1980s and the advent of the interconnections of the World Wide Web and the Internet in the 1990s have created a communications network that can move large amounts of information extremely rapidly. It has dramatically expanded the scope and cut the time of communication. This possibility of connecting so many people and institutions, and making their interactions fast and relatively effortless, lies at the foundation of globalization as we are experiencing it.

In addition, the ease of long-distance transportation has led to quick growth in both the migration of peoples to improve their political and economic lot and the rapid movement of capital and consumer goods. Such migration and movement are, of course, not new. But they are now emerging on a scale not known in earlier ages.

The Economic Dimension

Globalization has made itself particularly felt in the economic dimension of human life. The rapid transfer of information and

capital allows for business transactions at a greater pace and intensity. The economic order emerging is a form of worldwide market
capitalism. It was assumed it would resemble in many ways the liberal capitalism of the end of the nineteenth century, but a form
of capitalism less and less under cultural or governmental control
and regulation has become suspect in the present economic crisis.
Nevertheless, economic globalization continues to link more and
more national economies. It also represents one of the profound
paradoxes of globalization. Despite its ability to improve life for
all, it has—at least to this point—widened the gap between a few
immeasurably wealthy groups and individuals and an ever greater
number of people imprisoned in economic hardship or even misery. The 2007 report of the United Nations Development Program
(UNDP) indicates that the gap between rich and poor is growing
ever wider rather than narrowing. Likewise, despite its ability to
link together everyone in this new economic arrangement, it has
mostly linked those most privileged, whether from rich or poor
countries.

The Political Dimension

The combined political effect of communications and transportation technology, of the powerful economic forces of global capitalism, and of the pervasive cultural images circulated in daily life
is a weakened nation-state. Communications leap over national
boundaries. A global market economy limits government control,
reducing the importance and the power of the nation-state. Additionally, economic agreements between nations have created blocs
that undercut national sovereignty: the European Union, NAFTA,
and Mercosur are all familiar arrangements. Finally, the collapse
of the bipolar Cold War world order has been accompanied by an
increase in small-scale wars, most often fought now within nation-
states rather than between them. These wars are creating large

numbers of displaced persons and refugees on a scale not seen since the end of World War II.

As the political order shifts, the nation-state will not disappear, but its powers and roles are changing. We are also witnessing the rising importance of transnational, nonstate organizations such as the Non-Governmental Organizations (NGOs) in the political order. Especially important, for good and ill, are those accredited at the United Nations.

The Cultural Dimension

In this interconnected web of relationships fostered by communications technology, a kind of global culture has emerged. This culture is marked especially by signs of consumption: food, clothing, and entertainment. Many of these signs of consumption emerged, at least initially, from North America: McDonald's hamburgers, Coca-Cola, T-shirts bearing product advertisements, athletic shoes, rock music, videos, and movies. These products come from public companies owned by investors throughout the hemisphere and around the world. Although these cultural signs are received and interpreted in different ways in different cultures, they do provide a common cultural language, especially among the youth of the world. Along with a wider choice of cultural goods and lifestyles, a kind of universal skepticism about the human intellect's ability to grasp truth has arisen, perhaps because many people come to regard truth as one more consumer choice. The postmodern mind deconstructs traditional truths and resists intellectual synthesis.

Paradoxically, postmodern diversity seems to lead to homogenization of culture. The homogenizing powers of the economic forms of globalization give the impression that there is no alternative to neoliberal capitalism. Can the business economy described by Pope John Paul II in *Centesimus annus* — one based on private property, a free market, and personal economic initiative, but designed so that the economy serves the person rather than the person serving the economy — emerge from our present global economic order? The homogenizing powers of cultural globalization seem to be breaking down forms of art, music, and even language in local cultures. Although Spanish continues to be the language most spoken in the Catholic Church today, English has emerged as the language of globalization.

These homogenizing forces are keenly felt. Because of their sheer size, these forces appear to many people as beyond their control. At the same time, there continue to be signs that these cultural forces of homogenization may not become as all-embracing as they now appear to be. The United Nations Development Program has called for greater regulation of economic globalization, which indicates an awareness of the problem, but gives no solution. Studies are also showing that, while global cultural signs may pervade a culture, they have not eradicated local cultural expressions and sometimes cause a reaction that intensifies a local culture. Observers increasingly recognize that, to understand globalization, we must look not only at its homogenizing aspects, but at the global intersections with the local. Very few people beyond a small managerial and cultural elite live exclusively at the level of the global. Most people feel its impact as it interacts with their local setting.

One of the most common postures in the face of globalization is *resistance* by reasserting local identity. This has been one of the common causes for the increased number of wars in the world today. It has led in some instances to religious identity being invoked as a means to establish a clearer local identity and a source of difference from one's neighbors, often with violent consequences. It has also contributed to the revival of language and local customs in other places. In both instances, the local is experienced more intensely because of the incursion of the global.

This interaction of the global and the local has combined with the migration of peoples, both voluntary and forced, to produce cultural interactions unprecedented in intensity and scale. Many of the countries in the Americas, for example, have long been multicultural. What is new is the intensity of the interaction between cultures. The United States and Canada are now the second and third most multicultural countries in the world (after Australia). The United States now contains also the fifth largest Spanish-speaking population in the world.

The jostling of cultures with one another has led to cultural fragmentation and the emergence of new cultural forms. Cultures have always borrowed from one another, but what we are seeing today is a cultural fragmentation, especially in urban settings.

Because of a combined experience of powerlessness in the face of globalization, resistance to its encroachments, and the fear of fragmentation of basic cultural values, groups around the world are responding with what is sometimes called fundamentalism. Fundamentalism is a self-consciously noncritical reassertion of identity and autonomy by selecting certain antimodern, antiglobal dimensions of local (especially religious) identity, and making them both the pillars upon which identity is built and the boundary against further global encroachment. If globalization is leading to an unacceptable homogenization, some seem to say, the postmodern world may find protection for the local in premodern phenomena. Human freedom might thereby be finally disconnected from modernity, and a genuinely new postmodern order could be born in the dialogue between premodern culture, such as some Islamic societies, and the postmodern culture of secularized Christianity.

Globalization: An Evaluation

How shall we evaluate globalization? There has been a tendency, especially in religious circles, to focus on the negative dimensions. Much of that evaluation is on the mark. But to focus exclusively on the negative dimensions of globalization ignores two important

considerations. First, there are some positive dimensions of globalization, and they must be properly acknowledged. Second, one
cannot simply condemn globalization outright, since all cultural
phenomena are evangelically ambiguous, and there is no alternative
in view. Globalization can neither be ignored nor easily escaped. If
the Church wishes to engage the world — as it was made so clear
she should at the Second Vatican Council — we must not simply
evade or even condemn such a powerful force in the contemporary world. To that end, I wish to look at both the positive and the
negative consequences of globalization.

Positive Dimensions: Globalization as Opportunity

Here I would like to note two positive dimensions of globalization.
Together they represent the *opportunity* that globalization offers.
The first dimension is the possibility of a more interconnected
world. With the communications and transportation technology
we now have, we have the chance to become a genuinely connected
human family. For a Church that calls herself catholic, this is of
great spiritual importance. That vision of a united earth from the
Apollo 8 spacecraft is the possibility now being held out to us. The
implications of this possibility have been expressed over and over
by Pope John Paul II in his call for greater human solidarity.

This brings us to a second and related positive side to globalization: the increased opportunity for human development through
access to information and the shrinking of distance. Communications technology in this newly global era has enabled more effective
protection of human rights. The movement against the deploy-
ment of land mines, for example, was conducted entirely over the
Internet. The televised display of famine and war-induced suffering
has mobilized public opinion and forced governments to react to
these human tragedies. Globalization in medicine is bringing about
campaigns to totally eradicate certain diseases. In other words, the

access to information and the shrinking of distance can improve the quality of human life in significant ways.

Negative Dimensions: Globalization as Ideology

Three main areas have attracted the attention of globalization's critics.

First, there are the values that have often driven economic and cultural globalization: namely, the search for economic profit as the highest human goal and the definition of the human being as a producer and a consumer. If profit alone — and especially short-term profit — is seen as the organizing value of an economic system, then human beings and societies suffer spiritual want.

To value human beings primarily in the light of how much they consume is an affront to a basic principle of theological anthropology, namely, that we are created in the image and likeness of God. To define people on the basis of how much they can buy and consume destroys our sense of the person, who discovers his genuine self through generosity and self-giving. These negative phenomena are, of course, not tied uniquely to globalization — they have existed in every economic order since the fall of Adam and Eve — but their scope today makes them particularly powerful.

The second negative dimension of globalization is the ever-widening gap between the rich and the poor. The global economy promises those who submit to its ways a better way of life. But the experience of many is exclusion or exploitation rather than inclusion and participation in this growing wealth. In response, more and more voices are calling for greater regulation of the global economy in order to distribute its wealth more equitably. The problem, of course, is that there is no single political authority for a global economy, nor do most people really want a world government. Still, economic dynamics cannot be severed from politics and culture. Look at the differences, for example, between the post-Marxist Polish and Hungarian economies and that of Russia. The first two had the cultural context to make the economic shift more humanely where Russia apparently did not, at least until their oil revenues came to the rescue.

The third negative dimension has to do with the fracturing of cultures and ways of life, which the homogenizing forces of globalization bring in their wake. Part of human dignity is the right to culture, to an authentic but distinctive way of being human. This is a point John Paul II tirelessly reiterated in his travels around the world. To deprive peoples of their language and way of life, to force them into other patterns of living, is to rob them of a basic dimension of their humanity. Further, the fundamentalist response to cultural globalization is often accompanied by human rights abuses and conflict.

The Church's Missionary Challenges in an Age of Globalization

What, then, do the possibilities and the challenges of globalization mean for the Church's mission today?

John Paul II first spoke of globalization in his Message for the 1998 World Day of Peace.[1] In that message, he recognized how the world was changing. In view of political and especially economic changes, he posed a series of questions about inclusion and justice. In order to create a more equitable society and bring peace in the world, he laid down two guidelines: (1) have a greater sense of responsibility for the common good, and (2) never lose sight of the human person as the center of any social project. "The challenge, in short," he said, "is to ensure a globalization *in solidarity,* a globalization *without marginalization.*"[2] In light of these words of the Holy Father, I propose to identify two tasks that might define the Church's mission in an age of globalization, and three resources the Church brings to these tasks.

Two Tasks

1. THE PROCLAMATION AND DEFENSE OF THE DIGNITY OF THE HUMAN PERSON

At the very foundation of a globalization that is just and equitable is the dignity of the human person, a theme that Pope John Paul II returned to again and again, from his first encyclical, *Redemptor hominis*, to his last breath. Without this focal point, any project for society is bound to go astray and enslave rather than liberate. We must make the truth about the human person the center of our missionary proclamation in a globalized world. The redemption we have received in Jesus Christ is testimony to how God perceives and loves each human being. Pope Benedict XVI made a similar point when noting that "only charity can encourage us to place the human person once more at the center of life in society and at the center of a globalized world governed by justice."[3]

2. CREATING A CULTURE OF LIFE

Since our response to human dignity is deeply affected by the values of our culture, the second and related major task facing a Church is the conversion of culture. In the words of the postsynodal apostolic exhortation *Ecclesia in America,* the cultures that globalization touches must be guided by a moral vision that "rests on the threefold cornerstone of human dignity, solidarity, and subsidiarity" (no. 55). As the apostolic exhortation explains, this transformation involves both the inculcation of these positive values in every culture and in interactions between nations, and also the attendant reduction of the negative effects of globalization on the poor and weak. The global conversion of culture also involves supporting those international organizations that strive to create and sustain a culture of life.

Let me give an example of a proper response to one issue that is of special importance to the countries of the Americas: massive external debt. Dealing with this central issue in our peoples' lives requires two strategies. On the one hand, we must mitigate the negative effects of the debt, especially interest payments that drain away resources from an already impoverished country and especially hurt the poor. This requires concerted efforts by lender countries and institutions to reduce debt or, in some cases, even to completely cancel it. While some efforts have been made by the world financial institutions and the major industrialized countries to acknowledge this issue, all have so far been inadequate. But we must also foster an internal culture within each debtor nation that will assure that loans and investments received are used for the common good and for genuine human promotion. Thus, cultural elements that encourage cronyism, corruption, and fraud must be eliminated within the country itself. As Christians, we are called upon to work at both of these tasks.[4]

Three Resources

I. THE CHURCH'S CATHOLICITY IN AN AGE OF GLOBALIZATION

One of the great resources the Catholic Church brings to the mission of evangelization in an age of globalization is its very catholicity. I understand catholicity here in both of its theological dimensions: its extension throughout the entire world and the fullness of truth that it brings to the human family.

Extended throughout the entire world, the Catholic Church is a transnational institution that brings special resources to a globalized world. In an age when transnational institutions (such as NGOs) can render a special service to mankind which no single nation can, the Church has networks of communication to build solidarity among nations and throughout the human community. The challenge before us now as a Church is to use the network we already have even more effectively. Missionary institutes and organizations have a special role to play in this. Communion among local churches is meant to be the leaven for solidarity among peoples.

The message of faith that the Church preaches provides a moral and spiritual vision for a just and equitable society in an age of globalization. The truths she has received from Christ embolden the Church to proclaim: the dignity and centrality of the human person for any social project; solidarity among all members of the human family; the presence of both good and evil in every culture, and the reconciling mission of Jesus Christ to bring all things on earth together in an offering to God (see Eph. 1:10; Col. 1:20).

Let me sketch how I see the working out of these truths. A Church that is truly catholic proposes the message of salvation to all people without exception or distinction; all are called to the banquet table of the kingdom of God. The effectiveness of this proposal is grounded in our own continual conversion, a continual "change of mentality" (*metanoia*), a constant turning away from a radically autonomous and isolated self, a change brought about by the encounter with Christ in his body, the Church. In this constant conversion, ecclesial communion, our relation to one another in Christ, is deepened. The inculturation of the faith — the conversion of a society and culture brought about by preaching who Christ is in a language understandable to the people — begins with identifying *semina verbi* present in every culture and then moves to identify the demonic elements also present in any culture. This discernment becomes visible in the lives of the evangelizers themselves, who are witnesses to the power of God's grace. Catholic evangelizers must be in profound conversation both with Christ and with the people he places on their path.

2. THE CALL FOR A NEW EVANGELIZATION

The New Evangelization, first called for by Pope John Paul II during a visit to Haiti, takes into account how the world has changed and asks how the saving message of Jesus Christ can be heard by those who, having once accepted the Gospel, now have deliberately put it aside. This conscious rejection of the faith is present not only in the "new Areopagoi" of the mass media and of science, of which the pope spoke in the encyclical *Redemptoris missio* (#37c), but also in the changed outlooks of many men and women today, entire groups of whom live in a world where the old compass points no longer guide them. Keeping the principles of the New Evangelization in mind will make our mission more effective in a globalized world: it is biblical; comprehensive in attending to all peoples; dialogic in its respect for freedom of conscience; culturally adapted even as it transforms societies; innovative in its use of the new media of communications. It is also the responsibility of all members of the Church.

The New Evangelization presupposes both ecumenical and interfaith dialogue. Since Christ and his Church are one, ecclesial disunity is a scandal that weakens the preaching of the Gospel. Globalized economies, societies, and cultures will respond only to a genuinely unified Church. As the faith communities become again the primary shapers and leavens of culture in the next millennium, interfaith dialogue becomes ever more imperative. Especially crucial is the dialogue between Catholicism and Islam, both of which are growing. The relationship between Catholics and Muslims will define globalization more profoundly than any economic or political arrangements.

3. THE CELEBRATION OF THE GREAT JUBILEE

A third resource for the mission in a context of globalization was the celebration of the Great Jubilee and its aftermath. The Jubilee carried with it messages that are central to mission. First of all, it expressed the gratuitous character of the love of God, who offered his own Son for the salvation of our world. In a world where every relationship threatens to become commercialized, where acts of generosity and gratuity are seen as diminishing possible profits, the message of how God acts gratuitously to save the world brings us into a genuine new world.

Second, Jubilee means in the Bible the cancellation of debt and a new beginning. If authentic globalization is about inclusion and participation, then such inclusion and participation must be made possible by giving the poor a fresh start. The Church brings her resources to bear upon imagining a new beginning where justice and then peace will have a better chance because both are grounded in love.

Conclusion

To carry out this missionary activity, we must have a missionary spirituality that will sustain, guide, and nourish us. I return here to the image of earth seen from space: our world is, after all, quite small in the total scheme of the cosmos. It is fragile. Its divisions and barriers are of human making, and believers should strive to see where the world has come from and where it is going.

The world in all of its dimensions has come from God. It is God's creation and bears the imprint of his own image. It has therefore a dignity, a goodness, and a beauty that cannot be denied, no matter how much sinfulness has disfigured the world's countenance. The world is on a journey beyond its brokenness and divisions to a new harmony and communion with God, a journey that the Letters of Paul to the Ephesians and Colossians call reconciliation. In the midst of the fracturing that the world experiences more acutely because of globalization, the message of reconciliation of all things in Christ is a truth our world must hear, whether or not it is understood or accepted.

Several decades before talk about globalization became common, Pope John XXIII called the Second Vatican Council to revitalize the mission of the Church in the world. He called the Council so that the Church, as a global and universal assembly, could be more visibly the sacrament of the unity of the human race, after national, cultural, and economic divisions had led the world into war and bloodshed in the first half of the twentieth century. The call to mission that is truly Catholic is the true call of the Council. For various reasons, the Council has not yet been effectively received as a call for the Church to change the world. Much energy has been expended in changing the Church according to various patterns; not enough energy has been given to changing ourselves with the help of the Church so that we can change the world.

This change begins with Jesus Christ and ends in him. He is the kingdom of God in his person. The greatest challenge to the mission of the Church in a new global order remains what has been the greatest challenge for the last two thousand years: how to overcome the obstacles to discipleship and accept with glad hearts the freedom that Jesus Christ, savior of the world, wants to give the whole world.

Chapter 8

One Lord and One Church for One World

Redemptoris missio

TWO THOUSAND YEARS after the world first heard the name of its redeemer, we received an encyclical letter, *Redemptoris missio,* that told us that the mission entrusted to the Church by this redeemer "is still only beginning." The mission is beginning anew in a globalized society whose severe crises give renewed force to the Lord's command to teach and make disciples of all peoples.

"The Redeemer of man, Jesus Christ, is the center of the universe and of history,"[1] are the opening words of another letter, *Redemptor hominis,* the encyclical with which Pope John Paul II began to call the Church's attention to the approach of the third millennium at the beginning of his service as bishop of Rome. From that beginning in 1978, the Holy Father saw the potential for this great anniversary of God's mercy to reawaken faith in Christ. At that time, the pope proclaimed a season of expectation, a "new Advent"; and he continued to hold out the mystery of the redemptive Incarnation before the Church and the world from the beginning of his pontificate until his death.

Pope John Paul II urged us to expect a great outpouring of grace on the occasion of the Great Jubilee and to anticipate a "new springtime" of Christianity.[2] His confidence in the power of the Good News to address the concerns of every human person, every generation, and every culture remained always unshaken. His conviction that missionary evangelization is "the primary service which the Church can render to every individual and to humanity"[3] appeared to increase, in fact, in proportion to the difficulties proposed against it.

Pope John Paul II's witness to Christ the Redeemer grew more intense over the course of his pontificate. In his first encyclical, he laid out his commitment to the course set by the Second Vatican Council. He recapitulated the Christological teaching of *Gaudium et spes* and examined its implications for human dignity and human rights. In a particular way, *Redemptor hominis* challenged the Catholic people to witness to the truth of Christ by taking up their mission to transform the social order. In his later years, the pope's focus on Christ the Redeemer appeared to be motivated by a growing concern that the waning commitment to the mission *ad gentes* reflected a crisis of faith in the central mysteries of our religion:[4] the Incarnation, the Redemption, and the Holy Trinity. This motive became explicit in *Redemptoris missio.* I would like to review, first, how *Redemptor hominis* and the earlier apostolic exhortation of Pope Paul VI *Evangelii nuntiandi* prepared the way for *Redemptoris missio;* second, the Christological and the Trinitarian foundations of mission in this encyclical's argument; and, third, the challenges *Redemptoris missio* continues to put to the Church today in a new pontificate.

Preparations in *Redemptor hominis* and *Evangelii nuntiandi*

Redemptor hominis

"The Redeemer of man, Jesus Christ, is the center of the universe and of history." Drawing on the Sacred Scriptures and on the

Christology expressed in *Gaudium et spes,* article 22, John Paul in *Redemptor hominis* asserted that the revelation of God in the Word made flesh is not of special interest only to Christians. On the contrary, it expresses the final truth about God, a truth all have a right to know. And it expresses the final truth about the dignity and destiny of humanity, a truth all people yearn to discover. Jesus Christ provides an answer to the fundamental human questions.[5] In fact, the mystery and vocation of the human person can be discovered only in Christ, for he is the "new Adam," the new "head" or source of the human race who, "in the very revelation of the mystery of the Father and of His love fully reveals man to himself and brings to light his most high calling."[6]

The pope never tired of repeating the Christocentric teaching of *Gaudium et spes:* that the Son of God has, by his Incarnation, united himself in a certain fashion with every human being; that he has, by his paschal mystery, restored to humankind the divine likeness lost by the first Adam; that in him, humankind has been raised to an incomparable dignity.[7] That Christ the Redeemer has fully revealed what it means to be human he calls the "human dimension of the mystery of the Redemption." The "divine dimension" of this mystery is the revelation of the Father's eternal love. It is the Father who sends Christ to reconcile humanity to himself through his cross. On the cross, Christ reveals that God is "love." Apart from an encounter with love, human life is incomprehensible. The Good News is that God's forgiving love — a love stronger than death, always ready to forgive, coming in search of the lost — is also mercy. And the revelation of divine love and mercy in human history, he affirmed, "has taken a form and a name: that of Jesus Christ."[8]

But knowing the truth about God and about the human vocation imposes a grave obligation on believers. We are obliged to bear witness to Christ everywhere because he belongs to everyone. "Jesus Christ is the chief way for the Church," and every single human being, because each is united with Christ, is also "the way for the Church."[9] Throughout this encyclical, when the Holy Father spoke of mission he had in view all that threatens human dignity and robs human life of meaning in the concrete historical situation of the modern world.

Preparation in Evangelii nuntiandi *(1975)*

Redemptor hominis was written only a few years after the Synod on Evangelization (1974) and the subsequent apostolic exhortation of Pope Paul VI *Evangelii nuntiandi* (1975), but it speaks less about evangelization in the technical sense and more about the broad theological vision and pastoral program emerging from John Paul II's sustained reflection on the accomplishments of the Council. It is possible and instructive, however, to compare the perspective of *Evangelii nuntiandi* with that of *Redemptoris missio*. Each was written to mark an anniversary (the tenth and the twenty-fifth, respectively) of the closing of the Council.[10] Each invites an examination of conscience, offers an assessment, and proposes a new challenge to interior renewal and a fresh commitment to mission. They emerge from different contexts, however, and manifest two quite different concerns. *Evangelii nuntiandi* broadens the concept of mission to include all of the Church's evangelizing activity; in particular, it establishes the profound link between the verbal proclamation of the Good News and the work of human promotion and liberation. *Redemptoris missio,* on the other hand, reaffirms the permanent validity of mission in the specific sense of mission to "the nations"; it addresses the question of motivation for mission and takes up more explicitly the question of the internal obstacles to mission.

Four themes addressed in *Evangelii nuntiandi* are taken up and developed in *Redemptoris missio:* (1) the link between the proclamation of salvation in Christ and the work of human promotion and liberation; (2) the primacy of direct (verbal) proclamation of

Christ with the intention of conversion; (3) the problem of a new reluctance to assume this primary task; and (4) the fundamental motivation for mission.

Pope Paul VI, gathering the fruits of the third Synod of Bishops in *Evangelii nuntiandi,* invited the whole Church to meditate on the question the Synod considered: "after the Council and thanks to the Council, ... does the Church find herself better equipped to proclaim the Gospel and to put it into people's hearts with conviction, freedom of spirit and effectiveness?"[11] The Church must remain faithful to the message of Christ, on the one hand, and to the people of our time who need to hear it, on the other.[12]

For *Evangelii nuntiandi,* evangelization names a complex and dynamic activity that cannot be equated simply with the first proclamation of the Gospel, with preaching, catechesis, and administering baptism and the other sacraments, but extends beyond all these to include the transformation of humanity from within. "The Church evangelizes," Paul VI stated, "when she seeks to convert, solely through the divine power of the message she proclaims, both the personal and collective consciences of people, the activities in which they engage, and the lives and concrete milieux which are theirs."[13] According to this broad definition, evangelization is directed not only to the conversion of individuals but also to the conversion of cultures. It aims to plant the Church in order to inaugurate the kingdom of God, a social order transformed by the values of the Gospel, a civilization of love. It describes the salvation offered by Jesus Christ as "liberation from everything that oppresses man but ... above all liberation from sin and the Evil One, in the joy of knowing God and being known by him, of seeing him, and of being given over to him."[14] The salvation the Church announces certainly cannot be reduced to material well-being, but concern for human promotion is not "foreign" to evangelization. Indeed, there are profound links — anthropological, theological, and evangelical — between evangelization and human liberation.[15] This "broad" definition of evangelization serves in a particular way to address the urgent question of the Church's witness to the Gospel in traditionally Catholic countries and cultures. It is introduced in order to respond to the challenges posed by the theory and praxis of liberation theology and to various challenges to the concept of mission posed in contemporary debate.[16]

Paul VI explained that "the Church links human liberation and salvation in Jesus Christ, but she never identifies them."[17] Evangelization is incomplete without the witness of life (for example, the work of human promotion), but it does not exist at all without the explicit proclamation of who Christ is.[18] The content of the Good News is that "Jesus is Lord," and that in "Jesus Christ, the Son of God made man, who died and rose from the dead, salvation is offered to everyone as a gift of God's grace and mercy."[19]

Pope Paul VI expressed concern about a certain reluctance to announce the Gospel that has emerged among Catholics in the years since the Council.[20] What is especially disturbing is the attempt to justify such reservations by citing the Council's teachings. These "excuses," according to the pope, are entirely without foundation. What are these excuses? One is that direct evangelization constitutes a violation of religious liberty. In response to this objection, the pope agreed that it is wrong to "impose" the Gospel on anyone, but it is not wrong to "propose" the truth of the Gospel and of salvation in Jesus Christ to the consciences of those who do not know it. On the contrary, to make this presentation is to respect their liberty by offering them the possibility of accepting the Good News which, by God's mercy, we have received. A second objection to announcing Christ as Lord states that conversion to Christ and membership in the Church are unnecessary, since "uprightness of heart" suffices for personal salvation. In response to this objection, Paul VI agreed that God can bring the unevangelized to salvation by means known to him alone, but he did not concede that this excuses Christians from bearing witness to the revelation of God and his way of salvation in Jesus Christ. If God sent his Son, he argued, "it was precisely in order to reveal to us, by his word and by his life, the ordinary paths of salvation."[21] We have been commanded to bear witness to this revelation and must consider whether we place our own salvation in jeopardy by failing to preach it to others. The proclamation of the Gospel, Pope Paul VI wrote, "is a question of people's salvation."[22]

This reference to "people's *salvation*" points to the question of motivation for mission. Clearly, the objection regarding the possibility of being saved by "uprightness of heart" arises from the Council's new optimism about the salvation of nonbelievers. This teaching, found in *Gaudium et spes,* article 22, appeared to some to eliminate one traditional reason for mission: the "salvation of souls." The problem of coordinating the new optimism with the missionary mandate is recognized in *Ad gentes,* article 7: "So, although in ways known to himself God can lead those who, though no fault of their own, are ignorant of the Gospel to that faith without which it is impossible to please him (Heb. 11:6), the Church, nevertheless, still has the obligation and also the sacred right to evangelize." Pope Paul VI highlighted two motives for mission: the confession of the truth and the love of neighbor.[23] *Evangelii nuntiandi* exhorts all evangelizers to proclaim the Good News with joy, as a service of love for others, in a spirit of grateful obedience to God.

Development of These Four Themes in Redemptoris missio

In *Redemptoris missio,* Pope John Paul II repeated the message of his first encyclical, *Redemptor hominis:* the Church's vocation is to proclaim Christ as the universal Mediator and only Savior of humankind. In the years since the Council closed, the number of those who have not heard the Gospel and joined the Church has almost doubled.

Pope John Paul II candidly acknowledged the present experience of crisis in mission and asks whether it may not reveal a crisis in faith.[24] Today, on account of the many changes that have taken place in the modern world and on account of new theological theories that attempt to account for the salvation of those who have not heard the Gospel, some members of the faithful raise the following questions with all seriousness:

> Is missionary work among non-Christians still relevant? Has it not been replaced by interreligious dialogue? Is not human development an adequate goal of the Church's mission? Does not respect for conscience and for freedom exclude all efforts at conversion? Is it not possible to attain salvation in any religion? Why then should there be missionary activity?[25]

These questions, which echo and add to the "excuses" mentioned in Paul VI's *Evangelii nuntiandi*, are generated by a new self-criticism on the part of missionaries and missiologists, by the "destabilizing" effects of interreligious dialogue, and by a new optimism regarding the value of non-Christian religions as the means of salvation for their adherents. More dramatically, they reflect the "paradigm shift" that characterizes a postmodern attempt to come to terms with religious pluralism by denying that any religion has the right to make universal claims about its own belief, its image of God, and its normative character.[26] Before examining the unique contribution of *Redemptoris missio* in responding to these questions, let us note how it reinforces and develops the four themes set out in *Evangelii nuntiandi*.

First, *Redemptoris missio* reasserts the profound link that exists between the explicit proclamation of the Gospel and the work of human promotion by employing the expression "integral salvation" (or liberation). Jesus came to deliver us from all that enslaves us.

Second, like *Evangelii nuntiandi*, *Redemptoris missio* insists that proclamation of the Good News is the "permanent priority of mission,"[27] toward which all other forms of missionary activity are directed. Faith is the response to preaching, and the content of Christian preaching is the mystery of God's love and mercy made visible in Jesus Christ, crucified, died, and risen from the dead. The proclamation of God's Word, inspired by faith, "has *Christian* conversion as its aim: a complete and sincere adherence to Christ and his Gospel through faith."[28] Conversion leads to repentance, baptism, and entry into Christ's body, the Church.

Third, Pope John Paul II gave this theme a sharp definition by making the mission *ad gentes* the direct focus of his encyclical. "The mission *ad gentes*," he wrote, "has this objective: to found Christian communities and develop churches to their full maturity."[29] Whereas *Evangelii nuntiandi* adopted the concept "evangelization" in order to encompass the totality of the Church's activity, *Redemptoris missio* gives renewed attention to "missionary activity proper," that is, the specific mission directed to non-Christian peoples whose lives are not yet touched by the presence of the Church and whose culture has not felt the influence of the Gospel.[30] This new emphasis is not exclusive, for the Holy Father clearly identified the needs of other situations addressed by the Church's missionary activity, namely, the pastoral care of established Christian communities and the "new evangelization" of formerly Christian countries and sectors where a living sense of the faith has been lost.[31] In addition, he acknowledged the positive aspects of the newer expressions of missiology that prefer to speak of all the Church's activities as part of her "mission."[32] The emphasis on the mission *ad gentes*, however, is vitally necessary, for today some question the value of this kind of missionary activity and the Church's right to engage in it. They ask whether the goal of conversion is appropriate and whether it is necessary. The pope replied by pointing out the vast areas of the world, especially in Asia, Africa, and Oceania, that had not been evangelized for the first time. He reaffirmed the value of the geographic conception of mission that has come under criticism since the Council and argued that the situation of the majority of the human race which, in fact, has not yet been reached by the Gospel, requires special attention and missionary zeal.[33]

The problem of the new reluctance to undertake the mission *ad gentes,* mentioned first in *Evangelii nuntiandi,* is openly addressed in *Redemptoris missio.* The two "excuses" mentioned by Pope Paul VI were that respect for religious freedom forbids direct proclamation and that it is, in any case, unnecessary since "uprightness" of heart suffices for salvation. In response to the first, Pope John Paul II repeated the argument that the Church "proposes" and does not "impose" the Gospel to persons who are free to accept or reject it. The Church's mission, in fact, promotes human freedom.[34] The Church rejects the view that the call to conversion addressed to non-Christians is "proselytism," for every single person has the right to hear the truth of the Gospel. It is not enough, as some would suggest, to limit one's missionary service to promoting human development and helping people preserve their own religious traditions. Confident proclamation of salvation in Christ flows from conviction that he truly holds the answer to the deepest human longings. In response to the second "excuse," the pope reaffirmed that salvation in Christ is concretely offered to every person, and that it is accessible by virtue of the grace won by the sacrifice of Christ and communicated by the Holy Spirit, which relates a person mysteriously to the Church. The person in whose heart grace is secretly at work must cooperate freely with this grace in order to attain salvation. This assurance that grace is offered to all does not dispense Christians from the missionary mandate, for the grace has a name that all should come to know and love. The faith we have received lays upon us an obligation and stirs up a desire to bear witness to God and to Jesus Christ, without whom no one is saved. The pope charged that lack of interest in the missionary task results in large part from indifferentism and religious relativism ("one religion is as good as another"). Lack of missionary fervor may, in fact, reveal a deeper problem, a crisis of faith in Jesus Christ.[35]

Fourth and finally, *Redemptoris missio* confirms the teaching of *Evangelii nuntiandi* that love is "the soul of all missionary activity" and "the driving force of mission."[36] It also endorses the idea that mission is motivated by the desire to confess the truth revealed by Jesus Christ.

Both encyclicals presuppose the missionary mandate given to believers by the Lord himself. But the question continues to be urged today, and so the Holy Father probed still more profoundly, "Why mission?"[37] Why, indeed? Christianity's contemporary confrontation with the great religions of the world has not only generated a need for new theories to account for the activity of the Holy Spirit outside the "boundaries" of the Church; it has also generated serious doubts about the validity of Christianity's own truth claims. Taken together, the new self-criticism that acknowledges errors and flaws in past mission theory and practice and the new experience of interreligious dialogue lead some to conclude that direct proclamation with the intention to convert is ethically irresponsible. They regard mission *ad gentes* as morally unacceptable in principle on the grounds that it presumes Christians are allowed to judge other belief systems as deficient. Religious truth claims, it is alleged, inevitably lead to intolerance, violence, and religious "imperialism." Again, some who survey the evidence of religious pluralism conclude that the mission *ad gentes* is not only ethically dubious but also epistemologically indefensible. It is preposterous, they think, to imagine that Christians have the resources to persuade non-Christians of the truth that they profess. But if they cannot expect to do this, they are not justified in holding that the majority of the human race lacks the truth about God and about humankind. On these grounds, too, they demand that Christians surrender their "truth claims" and concede that Christianity is only one of many equally authentic religious traditions.[38]

As the controversy surrounding the declaration *Dominus Iesus,* which made extensive use of *Redemptoris missio,* bears witness, these doubts are widespread; they trouble simple believers and theologians alike. They confront believers with a most daunting challenge, for it appears to those who stand outside the faith that Catholic Christians are impossibly arrogant and intolerant! At the same time, for those within the Church, the truths we profess represent a most precious treasure we desire to share with all men and women. To deny them would be to betray the gift we, apart from any merits of our own, have received from God's mercy. It is this "new" situation that prompted Pope John Paul II to proclaim: "*Mission is an issue of faith,* an accurate indicator of our faith in Christ and his love for us."[39]

Why mission? Our faith compels us to affirm the truth of what we believe. Concern for "evangelization," considered as identical with the totality of the Church's activity, does not require us to face directly the issue of Christianity's truth claims; concern for mission *ad gentes* does. It puts us face-to-face not only with alternative belief systems but also with a theory of religious pluralism that demands the surrender of those truth claims. This leads us to consider the special contribution of *Redemptoris missio,* its specific attention to the Christological and Trinitarian foundations of mission.

The Christological and Trinitarian Foundations of Mission in *Redemptoris missio*

"The Redeemer of man, Jesus Christ, is the center of the universe and of history."[40] We have observed that Pope John Paul II began his first encyclical with the confession of this key truth claim. Two decades later, he told us to focus on the *universal* salvific significance of Jesus Christ. He prepared the world to commemorate the date on which "God entered the history of humanity and, as a man, became an actor in that history."[41] He also sounded a clarion call to faith in the face of new challenges and the crisis of mission accompanying a crisis of faith. In *Redemptor hominis,* the Holy Father asked what path the Church should take. He answered that the only direction for heart, intellect, and will was toward Christ. Faith in Christ the Redeemer and in the salvation he alone offers to humanity emerges again as the reference point and anchor for the teaching of *Redemptoris missio.* "The Church's universal mission is born of faith in Jesus Christ," he wrote.[42]

The Christology of this encyclical on mission is found in its first three chapters, "Jesus Christ, the Only Savior," "The Kingdom of God," and "The Holy Spirit: The Principal Agent of Mission." Here the pope offered a very concise response, based in the New Testament, to the theories that give rise to doubts about Christianity's truth claims and the validity of its mission *ad gentes.* Three Christological points are identified in the first chapter: (1) salvation comes only from Jesus Christ, the one Mediator for the whole world and the full revelation of God; (2) Jesus Christ is the Word made flesh and there is only one "economy of salvation," that given in him; and (3) the new life offered in Christ is the gift of God's love. Let us consider each of these in turn as it relates to the question "Why mission?"

First, salvation comes only from Jesus Christ, the one Mediator for the whole world and the full revelation of God. Christians affirm this as true not only for themselves, but for everyone, for "there is no other name under heaven given among men by which we must be saved" (Acts 4:12). This belief excludes belief in other "gods." New Testament Christology is *theo*centric and monotheistic: Christ, the "one Lord," participates in the uniqueness of the "one God" (1 Cor. 8:4–6). He, the only-begotten Son sent by God, makes God known in the fullest possible way. "This definitive self-revelation of God is "the fundamental reason why the Church is missionary by her very nature."[43] Her vocation is to bear witness to the truth that Jesus Christ is the one, universal Mediator established by God (1 Tim. 2:5–6) and that no one can come to God except through him and in the power of the Holy Spirit. This conviction does not exclude "participated forms of mediation of different kinds and degrees" but these "acquire meaning and value only from Christ's own mediation."[44] According to the Declaration *Dominus Iesus,* this text does not exclude further theological investigation of whether and how "the historical figures and positive elements" of other religions "may fall within the divine plan of salvation." It does, however, exclude the theory that revelation in Jesus Christ is "limited, incomplete, or imperfect," or that it needs to be complemented by revelation found in other religions.[45]

Second, Jesus Christ is the Word made flesh and there is only one "economy of salvation," the one given in him. In the face of contemporary theological proposals adduced in favor of religious pluralism, *Redemptoris missio* asserts the unity of Christ against two errors, one that would separate the Word of God from Jesus Christ, and another that would separate Jesus of Nazareth (or the "Jesus of history") from the Christ (or the "Christ of faith"). The first error attempts to drive a wedge between the Word of God and Jesus Christ. But the Church teaches that Jesus is the Word — "who was in the beginning with God" (John 1:2) — made flesh, a single, indivisible person. According to *Dominus Iesus,* this affirmation excludes two alternative theories. In the first place, it excludes the theory that proposes that Jesus is "one of many faces which the Logos has assumed" in human history to offer salvation. In the second place, it excludes the theory that "there is an economy of the eternal Word that is valid outside the Church and is unrelated to her, in addition to the economy of the incarnate Word."[46] According to this theory, the Word has a saving influence that is independent of the historical event of the Incarnation and the cross. But the Church teaches that "one and the same" subject, the person of the Word, exists and operates in two natures. It is he, Jesus Christ, who has redeemed us by his death and resurrection.

There is only one "economy of salvation" for the whole world, the one mediated by the Incarnate Word.

The second error attempts to drive a wedge between Jesus of Nazareth and the Christ, as if the "Jesus of history" were someone other than the "Christ of faith." Christology must hold together two truths: the individual, concrete reality of Jesus as a historical figure, and his universal, cosmic, and absolute significance. Contemporary Scripture scholarship focuses attention on what historians can know of Jesus apart from his resurrection, and tends to reserve the title, "the Christ," for the transcendent reality of the Risen Lord. This new usage, which appears to name the two natures of Christ but does not, represents a paradigm shift that is often the source of considerable confusion.[47] Like the first error, this error also threatens belief in the concrete particularity and permanence of the Incarnation. In the case at hand, it tends to support the erroneous idea that "the Christ" transcends humanity in some "inclusive" divine way. In practice, it is often put in the service of a new "adoptionism" that portrays Jesus as a human person in whom God's spirit dwelt and who became "the Christ" at his resurrection. Such a Christology is content to remain agnostic about the personal preexistence of the Word and says nothing of the Incarnation.

The Church, in the language of dogma, confesses one Christ who is identical with Jesus of Nazareth and is personally the Word of God incarnate. Just as we say that Jesus Christ is the Word (or Son) of God incarnate, not "someone else," we also say that Christ the Risen Lord is the crucified Jesus of Nazareth, not "someone else."[48] The dogmatic tradition holds fast to the unity of Christ by referring every name by which he is known to the one "Person." The Church is able to confess the unity of Christ by calling Mary the Mother of God. Christian faith speaks of Christ as one in whom the "fullness of God" dwelt, God's "beloved Son" who is utterly unique and the bringer of universal salvation. It affirms that Jesus Christ not only belongs to human history but also transcends it as its center and its goal. Belief in a single economy of salvation implies belief that God's gifts of salvation, the "spiritual treasures" given to every people, are never given independently of Christ. We affirm that Christ has united himself with *every human being* by his Incarnation, and that his Holy Spirit offers *everyone* the possibility of sharing in the paschal mystery. We reject the view that Christ is Mediator of salvation only for some, or that he reveals only some aspects of the truth about God and the truth about the human person. It is not possible to remove the "scandal" of the Christian claim that we are saved in "no other name" and remain a believer.

A third Christological point in this chapter is that the new life offered to the world in Christ is the gift of God's love. The salvation he brings is a "participation in the very life of God: Father, Son, and Holy Spirit."[49] *Redemptoris missio,* as already noted, uses the expression "integral salvation" in speaking of Jesus' mission. This entails, negatively, liberation from everything that oppresses and, positively, the prospect of divine filiation. "See what love the Father has given us, that we should be called children of God: and that is what we are" (1 John 3:1). In this sense, the Christian concept of salvation is utterly distinctive. Without the revelation of the Father's love and intimate participation in it, the human person does not yet know his full dignity and value in the divine plan.[50] The faith conviction that God has communicated *himself* to us in this radically new way in Christ is what drives the Church's mission.

The second and third chapters of this encyclical contain two additional points relevant to our question: (1) the God whose kingdom we proclaim is the God revealed by Jesus Christ, and (2) the mission of the Holy Spirit reveals that he is the Spirit of Christ the Redeemer. These two clarifications are offered, again, in response to theories that advance the possibility that there is more than one divine economy of salvation. These theories err by discounting the role of Christ as Mediator and Redeemer. They have the net effect of dividing the work of salvation among the Persons of the Trinity.

In chapter 2, the pope observes that some kingdom-centered theologies proclaim God but remain silent about Christ, and that they celebrate creation but remain silent about salvation.[51] The kingdom that Jesus preached, however, was the kingdom of the God he revealed, that is, the kingdom of a Father full of compassion and mercy. Jesus invited all to repent and believe and so enter this kingdom to enjoy "liberation from evil in all its forms" and communion with one another and with God. This kingdom was already "at hand" in Jesus' very person, and the Father's love for the world was fully manifest in the gift of Jesus' life on the cross. Because the resurrection marked the definitive inauguration of this kingdom, the apostolic preaching joined the proclamation of the Christ-event to the proclamation of the kingdom. Any theology of mission that attempts to find common ground with non-Christians in a "theocentrically" based understanding of the kingdom but remains silent about Christ is deficient on two counts. It fails to acknowledge that Christ is the revelation of God's kingdom in person, and it promotes a false theocentrism, for it promotes the kingdom of the "one divine reality by whatever name it is called,"[52] not that of the God revealed by Jesus as "Abba." Christian theocentrism cannot fail to speak of Christ, for it is Trinitarian. Likewise, any kingdom-centered theology that emphasizes the mystery of creation but remains silent about Christ's redemptive work and the Church that mediates it to us is deficient, for it fails to include what is specific to the Gospel and to the identity of Christ as Lord and Redeemer.

Reflecting on the mission of the Holy Spirit in chapter 3, the Holy Father noted that some contemporary theories attempt to account for the salvation of non-Christians by proposing a separate economy of the Holy Spirit.[53] The Church teaches, of course, that the Spirit "fills the earth" and is at work sowing the "seeds of the Word" in human hearts, cultures, and religions in order to prepare the way for the Gospel message.

The activity and influence of the Holy Spirit, however, is never divorced from that of Christ. The same Spirit who was active in Jesus' life is active in the Church. The "seeds" he sows are "seeds of the *Word.*" The offer of salvation he makes is that of sharing in Christ's paschal mystery. The Spirit, therefore, is "not an alternative to Christ," the pope explained, "nor does he fill a sort of void that is sometimes suggested as existing between Christ and the Logos. Whatever the Spirit brings about... serves as a preparation for the Gospel and can only be understood in reference to Christ, the Word who took flesh by the power of the Spirit."[54] According to *Dominus Iesus,* it is contrary to Catholic faith to propose "an economy of the Holy Spirit with a more universal breadth than that of the Incarnate Word, crucified and risen."[55] The mission of the Spirit is always linked to that of the Son; it is not independent of or parallel to his mission. The Church teaches, in fact, that there is only one economy of salvation, a Trinitarian economy.

Insofar as faulty theories of salvation appear to discourage the mission *ad gentes,* the crisis of mission is revealed to be a crisis of faith. This crisis calls forth a defense and clarification of the Church's faith in Christ and his work of Redemption. This inevitably entails a defense of belief in the Blessed Trinity.[56] Both *Redemptor hominis* and *Redemptoris missio* are clearly Christocentric in emphasis, but they presuppose that the Trinitarian missions are the source of the Church's missionary nature, as *Ad gentes* taught.[57]

In past generations, Catholic theology of mission was rooted primarily in Christ's "mandate" to "go forth and make disciples of all nations" (Matt. 28:19–20). Today, missiologists prefer to seek the source of Christ's mandate and of the Church's mission in the mystery of the inner-Trinitarian relations and in the divine missions of the Son and the Holy Spirit *ad extra.* The Church's mission, in this perspective, is a participation in the *missio Dei.*

The gift of salvation is, in fact, "participation in the very life of God: Father, Son, and Holy Spirit."[58] It "consists in believing and accepting the mystery of the Father and of his love, made manifest and freely given in Jesus through the Spirit."[59] The one economy of salvation for the whole world is an economy of divine self-communication in love, a love also described as mercy.[60] In his self-emptying love and vulnerability — in the womb, in the manger, in the company of sinners, on the cross — God's Son made man reveals the face of the Father as love and mercy. He longs to share with every person the glory and the love he has from the Father, and so he send his disciples into the world that everyone may know and believe (John 17:21–23).[61] The Holy Spirit, Lord and Giver of Life, is sent forth into the whole world to offer "the human race 'the light and strength to respond to its highest calling.'"[62]

Challenges to the Church in Fulfilling Her Mission

A text is always written and read in a context. The textual context of *Redemptoris missio* was created by the documents on the Church (*Lumen gentium*) and the Church in the World (*Gaudium et spes*) from the Second Vatican Council, by Pope Paul VI's encyclical *Evangelii nuntiandi,* and by Pope John Paul's constant proclamation of the mystery of redemption in and by Christ. The ecclesial context revealed in *Redemptoris missio* is marked by a crisis of faith that makes it difficult for Catholics to love so deeply that they desire to proclaim Christ to the world. God's motive in sending his Son to save us was love of the world (John 3:16). The Son's motive was his love for his Father and for those the Father had given to his care (John 17). The Church's motive for mission is love for her Lord and all those he died to save. If we do not love, we will not act. But it is faith that tells us who God is in Christ and whom God loves. It is faith that tells us how to love. A crisis of faith weakens the charity that is the soul of the Church, and a Church so weakened cannot act, cannot be missionary. A Church filled with the love born of faith is eager to share Christ's gifts with the world. She will discover new forms of missionary cooperation and will hold her missionaries, especially those who have given their lives to the service of the mission *ad gentes,* in great honor and esteem. The best way to continue to reflect on *Redemptoris missio* is to examine ourselves as Christ's body in the world and take the steps necessary to stir up the love that marks an evangelizing Church, a missionary body.

The world in which the Church evangelizes has continued in recent years to develop within a pattern called globalization. This is the social context in which *Redemptoris missio* must now be read and implemented. Because of technological advances in communication, growth in the movement of peoples and ideas, and increase in the transfer of capital and goods, our very experience of space and time is altered. But growth in contacts between individuals and among peoples is not the same as a deepening of relationships, and evangelizing means bringing people into relationship with another through their relationship to Jesus Christ. How make use of global communications to transform contacts into relationships? If contacts made possible in an era of globalization give birth to genuine dialogue among cultures, new paths for evangelization, new ways of mission, open up in the new global Areopagus.

We speak often, especially since the Council, about the Church in the world. For the world to become truly global in the solidarity born of Gospel love and social justice, we should speak as well about the world in the Church. The Church, if she is faithful to her Lord, will not only proclaim who he is but will act to become herself the womb, the matrix, in which a new world can gestate and be born. Listening and welcoming, the Church is the locus of interfaith encounter, of interreligious dialogue, of the intercultural collaboration among religions and people of good will. In this context of universal mutual respect, created by the Church, she offers the gifts that transform the world and bring salvation in this life and the next. In her own inner life, the Church, like her Risen Lord, transcends and encompasses human history.

Why mission? The primary service the Church can render to the world is to direct the gaze of all toward Christ the Redeemer, "the center of the universe and of history," in whom God's love and mercy are fully revealed. Christians take up this service out of love for God and for their neighbor, but also in order to imitate God's own self-giving love by sharing with others the riches of their radically new life. Our obligation comes "not only from the Lord's mandate but also from the profound demands of God's life within us."[63] Just as within the life of God, the dynamism of self-emptying love from the "fountain-fullness" of the Father overflows in the missions of the Son and of the Spirit, so "the love of Christ urges us" (2 Cor. 5:14) to share the Good News of God's love with the world. Why does the Church bear a mission to the world? Because we are a graced people, and the grace bears a name above all other names (Phil. 2:9–11): Jesus Christ, Redeemer of the world.

Part Two

THE CHURCH'S LIFE
Hierarchical Communion

Chapter 9

The Crisis of
Liberal Catholicism

An Internal Dialogue

O N JANUARY 17, 1998, I celebrated a Saturday evening Mass at Old St. Patrick's Church in Chicago during a National Center for the Laity meeting.[1] I had not prepared a homily because I understood someone else was to preach and I was only to give a few remarks at the end of Mass. More important, I had been told the day before by the apostolic nuncio that Pope John Paul II would announce on Sunday that twenty bishops, myself included, were to become cardinals, clergy of the Holy Roman Church. As I sometimes do at turning points or crises in my life, I turned to Cardinal Newman for counsel when I learned that I was to be named a cardinal. Fresh in my mind as I celebrated Mass at Old St. Pat's were the words of Newman's speech when he accepted the official notification of his being named cardinal. He explained on that occasion that all his life he had contested liberalism in religion, *liberalism* in that context meaning religious relativism. Reading his speech led me to reflect on the context of religion today. When I came to say a few words after I read the Gospel, I thought that, in the absence of a prepared homily, I might try to provoke a discussion among all these rather liberal folks in front of me. I believe I did so.

Here are the remarks I wrote down as best I could remember them later that night:

We are at a turning point in the life of the Church in this country. Liberal Catholicism is an exhausted project. Essentially a critique, even a necessary critique at one point in our history, it is now parasitical on a substance that no longer exists. It has shown itself unable to pass on the faith in its integrity and inadequate, therefore, in fostering the joyful self-surrender called for in Christian marriage, in consecrated life, in ordained priesthood. It no longer gives life.

The answer, however, is not to be found in a type of conservative Catholicism obsessed with particular practices and so sectarian in its outlook that it cannot serve as a sign of unity of all peoples in Christ.

The answer is simply Catholicism, in all its fullness and depth, a faith able to distinguish itself from any culture and yet able to engage and transform them all, a faith joyful in all the gifts Christ wants to give us and open to the whole world he died to save. The Catholic faith shapes a Church with a lot of room for differences in pastoral approach, for discussion and debate, for initiatives as various as the peoples whom God loves. But, more profoundly, the faith shapes a Church which knows her Lord and knows her own identity, a Church able to distinguish between what fits into the tradition that unites her to Christ and what is a false start or a distorting thesis, a Church united here and now because she is always one with the Church throughout the ages and with the saints in heaven.

I regret now giving offense to some people because of my use of the adjective "parasitical" to describe a set of ideas and a movement that defines itself and takes life from an idea of Church no longer adequate to the Church's self-consciousness since the Second

Vatican Council. But I regret as well the later, deliberate misrepresentation of what, I still believe, was clearly expressed. To criticize an idea or a movement is not to condemn or despise those who believe in it. I have a number of friends, mostly from my time in graduate school, who regard the Catholic Church as a hypocritical system. Their judgment on the Church doesn't mean they believe me to be a hypocrite, and I take no personal offense at their misunderstanding of a Church I love as my mother and spouse. I understand what they are saying, even though I think they are profoundly wrong. I am saddened by their convictions and pray for their conversion, but they remain friends. Conflating ideas with the persons who espouse or even cherish them makes critical conversation impossible, in the Church or anywhere else. If everyone felt insulted when cherished convictions are criticized, we would have to close most public discussions about anything of ultimate or even of purely personal importance.

These remarks at a turning point in my own life combined with a second, perhaps providential, circumstance: *Commonweal* editor Margaret O'Brien Steinfels was present at that Mass. That evening during supper and in a later *Commonweal* editorial, she asked me to "please explain" my remarks, especially the part about "simply Catholicism." I do so here, not to offer a last word, since my remarks were offered as a thesis and not as an indictment, but perhaps to help advance a conversation important to all Catholics and especially to those without a vested interest in personal conflict, those disturbed by the divisions that too often paralyze the mission of the Church in our time.

Liberal and Conservative

To clarify terms, let me examine several factors that enter into the definition of "liberal" and "conservative" and that need to be made explicit to advance the discussion. First, there is the political context, from which the terms take their primary meaning. Political liberals and political conservatives both define themselves in relation to government and its exercise of power. Conservatives, though suspicious of state power, usually associate themselves with the constituted authorities, giving them the benefit of the doubt so that the order that saves us from anarchy and social violence can be maintained. Liberals contribute to the common good by beginning most often with a suspicion of abuse of authority and a critique of the exercise of power. They are a "loyal opposition" — loyal to the goals of good government but not to the established rulers when the rulers themselves impede the achievement of those goals.

In the economic context, so closely connected with the political but not identified with it unless one is a Marxist, liberals are more concerned with the distribution of wealth and look to government to see that the political equality of all citizens is mirrored, at least roughly, in their economic equality. They tend toward suspicion of vast accumulations of wealth comparable to their suspicion of government, because both are instances of power. Wealth's "social mortgage" easily becomes a social penalty. Conservatives, on the other hand, tend to be more concerned with the conditions of the creation of wealth and understand that the right to economic initiative cannot be separated from other individual rights and freedoms. In a business economy, they argue, all are enriched eventually, even if there are serious inequalities for a time. The effects of governmental deregulation of the economy can be softened, in the meantime, by personal (as opposed to state-sponsored) generosity toward the poor.

The political and economic contexts shade easily into the psychological. In the psychological context, "liberal" and "conservative" describe attitudes or mind-sets toward societal change. Conservatives are closed to changes that threaten good order, and liberals are more open to the risk of proposed change. Grossly caricatured, therefore, conservatives tend toward being "closed-minded" and liberals toward being "open-minded."

In epistemological theory, the point of reference is neither political government, economic order, nor mental attitude toward societal change. Rather, respective stances toward the foundations of knowledge also differentiate liberals and conservatives. This was the context of Cardinal Newman's Biglietto speech, as it was the context for his *Essay on the Development of Christian Doctrine* (1845) and his *Essay in Aid of a Grammar of Assent* (1870). Conservative certitude and the legitimate quest for certitude about the foundations either of faith or of an intellectual discipline can be pushed into fundamentalism; liberal criticism of the same foundations can degenerate into skepticism or the relativism that Newman constantly contested.

Finally, there is the context of American religion, the historical context in which we Americans profess the Catholic faith. In this country, as noted in an earlier chapter, liberal religion treats God as an ideal; it falls to human beings, therefore, to bring about change. Religious language is seen as poetic and does not so much offer accurate truth claims about God as express an experience. Regardless of how elevated the liturgy, the sacraments, too, reflect human rather than the divine truths; in this agnosticism about God's nature, the focus of religion becomes social justice.

For conservatives, however, God's agency and presence are real, religious language about God is not metaphorical but literal, and any social agenda tends to recede in the face of the expectation that it will be God who inaugurates genuine change in history.

Neither of these historical and current models of American religion is able to capture the Catholic sense of the Church as mediator of God's life and teacher of God's truth, the Church as a hierarchical communion, an organic body that comes into being as the gifts of Christ are shared, a body to which one is joined in order to be changed, to be converted, so that, with the help of God's grace, one can accept Christ's mission to preach the Gospel to all peoples and transform the world. Before turning toward "simply Catholicism," however, I wish to stay with the historical context in exploring what I understand by the phrase "liberal Catholicism."

First, I will provide a brief sketch of the "necessary" liberal Catholic project, which began in the mid-1800s and culminated with the still inadequately received Second Vatican Council. Second, I will discuss why I believe it is not unfair to call contemporary liberal Catholicism an exhausted project. Third, I will briefly critique "a type of conservative Catholicism" that makes the same error as liberalism in its excessive preoccupation with the Church's visible government. Lastly, I will attempt to draw the basic outlines for the always original voice that is "simply Catholicism."

A Necessary Project

By the early 1800s, the Church was besieged by a movement that she had, at least in part, helped to create: the Enlightenment or modernity (here, I will use these terms interchangeably). While difficult to define, modernity has at least the following two premises at its core. First, all men and women possess a dignity or value that dictates, using Immanuel Kant's formulation, that they never be treated as a mere means but always as an end. All human beings ought to be *free* from unfulfilling conditions simply imposed upon them by other human beings. While the specific conditions conducive to personal fulfillment are still a subject of great debate, particularly in a "postmetaphysical" era wary of any essential or even general conception of human fulfillment, these conditions are generally referred to as "rights." These rights exist in two forms: "negative" rights (i.e., "freedom from"); and "positive" rights, which are conditions that must be received from others and thus imply further duties that deeply condition freedom. Given its emphasis on every person's freedom from being used by others, this first strand of modernity has come to be known as "liberalism." It is political and economic, psychological, epistemological, and religious, as outlined above, yet each context blends into the next. In Marxist psychology and cultural criticism, for example, acceptance of a revealed religion creates a form of personal as well as social alienation that impedes the creation of a just economic order.

The second core premise of modernity is the imposing of scientific method as the point of contact between human beings and the world and society into which they are born. Science is the means to social liberation as well as the unique means to liberation from the strictures of the material world. It is a method of knowing that tightly circumscribes what can be considered truly "known" and thus simply "true." As much as it was about rights, the Enlightenment was about science as *the* means to human fulfillment. In general, the founders of modernity believed that through observation of sensed objects and induction, the laws of the material and human worlds could be discovered and that their discovery would make possible the perfecting of life in this world. Since medieval remainders such as religious claims and dubious conceptual "universals" neither promoted human fulfillment nor accorded with the epistemological rules of the scientific method, they were to be consigned to the status of interesting examples of now-superseded consciousness made irrelevant by human progress.

The Enlightenment and its two strands — liberalism and science — did not, of course, emerge spontaneously. Their precursors are well known and are located in that thousand-year period we call the Middle Ages. Enlightenment thinkers radicalized or appropriated, and then combined, what had been bequeathed to them: humanism, philosophical nominalism,[2] the Copernican revolution, and the implications of the Reformation. From humanism came the Enlightenment celebration of the universal dignity and rights of the individual and a commitment to moral perfection in this world. From nominalism, they adopted skepticism about traditional ethics and theology. From the Copernican revolution came a supreme confidence in science as the primary means through which the improvement of life in this world would occur. From the Reformation and its consequent religious pluralism developed the secularization of politics and culture.

Of these sources, humanism has Christian roots, as has the conviction that a well-ordered universe contains an intrinsic intelligibility. The Reformation is an obviously Christian movement. The gradual recognition of the dignity of all men and women and of their capacity for responsible freedom is difficult to understand unless one traces them, at least in part, to the gradual working out of the social implications of the Incarnation. The Enlightenment, therefore, was not devoid of *semina verbi*. The challenge for the Church lay in distinguishing the erroneous aspects of modernity from those that were compatible with, and even developments of, the Christian faith. The challenge was compounded when major Enlightenment figures regarded the Church's doctrines and her hierarchy as the primary enemies of modern enlightenment, thus signaling their unwillingness to assist the Church in her growth and making it easier for those in the Church to ignore the Enlightenment's possible contributions to a new Christian humanism.

In some ways, the relationship between the heirs of the Enlightenment and Christian believers remains stuck in that partly unnecessary opposition. The Church's first historical encounter with the Enlightenment project — which it would thereafter simply refer to as "liberalism" — was the French Revolution. The memory of thousands of priests and nuns exiled, imprisoned, tortured, and executed, of state control of religion and the suppression of the Church, of a dictator who was a Lenin before his time, determined the Church's officially negative attitude toward liberalism for a century. Formal denunciations of liberalism, in whole or part, appeared in Pius IX's *Syllabus of Errors* (1864) and in Leo XIII's *Immortale Dei* (1885), *Libertas praestantissimum* (1888), *Longinque oceani* (1895), and *Testem benevolentiae* (1899).

But in the midst of the controversy, a group now known as the "liberal Catholics" began to distinguish and assess the various aspects of modernity — cultural, political, and economic. Their names are familiar: Frédéric de La Mennais, Charles de Montalembert, Jean-Baptiste Henri Lacordaire, Frédéric Ozanam, John Dalberg-Acton, John Henry Cardinal Newman, and Johann Joseph Ignaz von Döllinger. While profoundly different in their analyses and their conclusions, common to each one's thinking was a rejection of certain *cultural* aspects of modernity, particularly materialism, secularism, moral relativism, and individualism. Also common to each was the conviction that only a unified, energetic, convincing, and engaged Church could solve these developing cultural problems. In their search for means to promote such a Church in the midst of pluralism and increased state power, they began to use the Church's own history in order to question the Church's nineteenth-century thinking on the *political* and *economic* aspects of liberalism. While state-protected religious freedom had been associated with indifferentism, they pointed out that religious establishment also held the potential for state interference and even suppression, not to mention the potential for Church corruption. They argued that freedom of religion would make the Church more effective, and the American experience, for all its difficulties, supported this conclusion. The clash between faith and culture could best be addressed by embracing liberal political and economic institutions rather than by rejecting them out of hand.

The Church's careful assessment of economic and political liberalism continued throughout the better part of the twentieth century, adding new rationales and nuances that are now part of Catholic social teaching. Rights language was appropriated not only to protect private property and the free market but also to protect against their misuse by early capitalists. Because of their dignity, all persons possessed the right to family wages and safe working conditions. As the ultimate guarantor of human rights, the state had the duty to exercise a concern for the poor and family life and intervene in the economy when necessary. A representative, well-constituted democratic state would be more likely to intervene appropriately. But the state was not to be the only solution to social problems. Nonstate institutions such as unions and social service agencies were equally or more capable of solving social problems; a limited state was apt to be less corrupt and more efficient; and the relational and self-constituting nature of the person meant that voluntary, mediating institutions were critical for the formation of persons and culture. Most important, the family was identified as the foundation of any culture and the building block of any society, and the state had the obligation to protect and foster family life. From this logic, the principle of subsidiarity was crafted and endorsed. The Church's engagement with the modern world it had both resisted and helped create eventually resulted in the endorsement of a free society found in *Dignitatis humanae* (1965), *Gaudium et spes* (1965), and *Centesimus annus* (1991).

An Exhausted Project

Do these societal developments and the liberal economic and political institutions born of them provide models for the Church's internal life? Yes and no. As the teaching of the Second Vatican Council — particularly that of *Lumen gentium* — makes clear, the Church is not merely a society. In the early modern era, Robert Cardinal Bellarmine, arguing against a Protestant conception of the Church as simply invisible with adventitious visible expression, created an ecclesiology of the visible Church defined as a society. The Church could be understood by looking at the kingdom of France or the Republic of Venice. This reactive model is flawed to the extent that it loses the relationships between the visible and invisible gifts that constitute the Church. These relationships are the stuff of ecclesial communion; they are created among and for us when the gifts of Christ are shared. These gifts, beyond invisible grace itself, are the visible government of pastors in succession to the Twelve, the Gospel as developed in the creeds and Catholic doctrine, and the seven sacraments, which sanctify men and women through the action of the Risen Christ. Through these gifts, Christ is always present as the way (our shepherd or pastor), the truth (our teacher), and the life (our sanctifier).

Because her relationship to her Lord is one of dependence, and because her relationship to her apostolic foundation is normative, the Church's teaching and constitution cannot simply be apprehended and analyzed at will, using societal categories from any age. Yet neither is the Church's history unrelated to the designs of providence. Given historical circumstances, concepts such as personal rights, political sovereignty, and democratic equality can contribute to human fulfillment and should be instantiated in political and economic structures and enter into the Church's social doctrine. The Church is indebted to the early liberal Catholics not only for restoring to the center of the Church's consciousness the Gospel's assertion that *Christ has set us free,* but also for the insight and analysis that enabled the Church herself to break free of the conservative societal structures in which she had become imprisoned. But the fact that democracy is a legitimate and desirable form of political governance does not make the Lord's own gift of ecclesiastical hierarchy illegitimate, even though it can raise good questions about how power given by God should be used to make his people holy. The primary criterion in judging any idea or form of Church governance remains the Church's fidelity to her Lord.

Instead of understanding Vatican II as a limited accommodation to modernity for the sake of evangelizing the modern world, the liberal project seems often to interpret the Council as a mandate to change whatever in the Church clashes with modern society. The project both for ecclesial renewal and for mission in the world takes its primary cues from the headlines. The Church provides motivation and troops to meet the world's agenda as defined by the world. This is a dead end, because the Church's mission would then have nothing original to contribute to the world's self-understanding. This is not to say that many so-called "Gospel values" or *semina verbi* are not to be found on the editorial pages of the *New York Times,* or even of *USA Today;* it is to say that God's ways are not our ways and that the greatest contribution the Church makes to the world is to preach Gospel truths in ways that, inevitably, will both comfort and confront any society in which she takes up Christ's mission.

Behind the crisis of visible authority or governance in a liberal Church lies a crisis of truth. In a popular liberal society, freedom is the primary value, and the government is not supposed to tell its citizens how to think. The cultural fault line lies in a willingness to sacrifice even the Gospel truth in order to safeguard personal freedom construed as choice. Using sociology of knowledge and the hermeneutics of suspicion, modern liberals interpret dogmas that affront current cultural sensibilities as the creation of celibate males eager to keep a grasp on power rather than as the work of the Holy Spirit guiding the successors of the apostles. The bishops become the successors of the Sanhedrin, and the Church, at best, becomes the body of John the Baptist, pointing to a Jesus not yet risen from the dead and, therefore, a role model or prophet but not a savior. Even Jesus' being both male and celibate is to be forgotten or denied once the Risen Christ can be reworked into whomever or whatever the times demand. Personal experience becomes the criterion for deciding whether or not Jesus is *my* savior, a point where liberal Catholics and conservative Protestants seem to come to agreement, even if they disagree on what salvation really means. Liberal culture discovers victims more easily than it recognizes sinners; and victims don't need a savior so much as they need to claim their rights.

All this is not only a dead end — it is also a betrayal of the Lord, whatever the good intentions of those espousing these convictions. The call to personal conversion, which is at the heart of the Gospel, has been smothered by a pillow of accommodation. The project for a liberal Catholic Church is as unoriginal as the project for a liberal reinterpretation of the Church's mission. A Church, all of whose ministries, construed only functionally, are open to any of the baptized; a Church unwilling to say that all homosexual genital relations are morally wrong; a Church that makes at least some allowance for abortion when necessary to assure a mother's freedom; a Church accepting contraception as moral within marriage and prudent outside of marriage; a Church willing to admit the sacramentally married to a second marriage in complete sacramental communion; a Church whose teaching has to stand the acid test of modern criticism and personal acceptance in order to have not just credibility but legitimacy: there is nothing new in all this. It already exists, but outside the Catholic Church.

Liberal Catholicism, in the too general and somewhat unfair way I have sketched it here, has not sufficiently distinguished between the properly theological warrants necessary to argue convincingly to some of its desiderata and the reasons for ecclesial change that take their strength merely from a liberal culture that tells us, as all cultures do, what to think and how to act. In an apostolic Church, however, the burden of proof for changing established doctrinal and moral teaching rests on those who ask for change. The faith of the apostles and martyrs, of Irenaeus and Augustine, of Brigid of Sweden and Catherine of Siena, of Thomas of Canterbury and Thomas More, of Elizabeth Ann Seton and John Neumann, of Edith Stein and Maximilian Kolbe, of our parents and grandparents, cannot be set aside to make our contemporaries happy or ourselves free of personal responsibility and its consequent guilt. When the apostolic faith is preached in its integrity to the young, to those who have not grown up in a Church that confined them and who have found themselves, instead, trapped in our secularized culture, they take notice. *Here is something different.* They do not always agree, but they are open in ways surprising to those whose own liberating experiences are still bound up with the immediate aftermath of the Second Vatican Council.

As indicated earlier, Alexis de Tocqueville suggested that the centrality of the idea of equal individual rights sets Americans up for the triumph of relativism and individualism. Are these cultural proclivities, which make it hard to hear the Gospel, the immediate result of liberal political institutions? Criticizing John Courtney Murray, David Schindler argues that rules of engagement between faith and culture that prevent the state (which helps to shape a culture) from informing itself religiously inevitably favor worldviews that demand public silence about God. Personally, I tend to think that the practical case for holding our liberal political and economic institutions responsible for the culture that now clashes with the faith is still waiting for adequate elaboration. Nonetheless, these liberal institutions have not prevented the development of a culture that is increasingly hostile to revealed truth or any truth that is not "made true" by personal choice.

One Form of Conservative Catholicism

In response to both a secular liberal culture and its perceived impact on the Church, a certain type of conservative Catholicism picks up the debate on the wrong terms. Seeing that, in a genuine clash between modern or any other culture and the apostolic faith, the faith remains normative, conservative Catholicism in some of its reactions takes refuge in earlier cultural forms of faith expression and absolutizes them for all times and all places. While certain that it differs fundamentally from liberal Catholicism, this conservatism shares the Bellarminian understanding of the Church as society. The hierarchy therefore become central, responsible for all that is good as well as for all ills, able to correct all aberrations by invoking its authority. Though correct in understanding that the Church is essentially conservative in handing on the apostolic faith, contemporary conservative Catholicism can fail to see that the Church is also, for that very reason, radical in its critique of any society. Just as liberal Catholicism is frequently uneasy with the Church's understanding of the gift of human sexuality when her teaching runs up against the popular Freudianism of the sexual revolution, conservative Catholicism is often uneasy with the Church's understanding of a just society when her social teaching draws conclusions about social services and the distribution of wealth from the premise of universal human solidarity.

The neuralgic point, therefore, is the human person. Both conservatism and liberalism, in religion and other fields in America, tend to look on the person as a bundle of desires or dreams, animal impulses and higher aspirations, which are synthesized individually by choice and controlled socially by law. Law therefore is always an imposition — an imposition gladly internalized in some areas by liberals and in others by conservatives. In religion, liberal pastoring assures people that the unconditional love of God means putting aside even moral laws when they get in the way of personal fulfillment; conservative pastoring insists on law without linking it clearly to the truths that Christ reveals about the dignity and freedom of the human person. The human person is the way of the Church, but her understanding of what it means to be human is taken from her belief in who Christ is, a belief born of our living together, in ecclesial communion, Christ's own life.

"Simply" Catholicism

The Church does have power given her by Christ: the power to proclaim the Gospel and celebrate the sacraments and pastor Christ's people. Since any claim to power in a popular liberal culture has to be justified by pointing to it as service or by claiming its popular ratification or reception, the Church in this culture is called to examine constantly her use of power. She cannot reduce the Gospel, however, to what the culture will bear. We are back to "simply Catholicism," which locates power in Christ and in his gift of authority to the Twelve. The Church preaches Jesus Christ, not herself; but Christ cannot be adequately known except from within his body, the Church.

Within the Church, the bishops are the reality check for the apostolic faith. They are not free to change established dogma nor create new doctrines, unless they want to become heretics. In being presented as a revolution rather than a development of doctrine, the Second Vatican Council has left some Catholics with the impression that bishops control rather than preserve the apostolic faith. If bishops won't change, they imagine, it must be fear or willfulness or perhaps stupidity that prevents their being enlightened. It is then up to Catholics with an agenda to force them to change or to make the changes themselves, in a separate peace. But a Church of such factions not only cannot evangelize; it cannot think. That is the greatest practical difficulty, it seems to me, in the use of the terms "liberal" and "conservative." When they are applied now, or even as they were sometimes applied in papal documents in the last century, people stop thinking things through. In thinking things through in the Church, bishops are the verification principle in the development of doctrine.

Pastorally, bishops are ordained to headship, which does not exhaust leadership. Leadership is influence. Sometimes it is based on office, sometimes on charism or purely personal gifts; always, in the Church, it is more obviously from Christ when the leader's friendship with the Lord is evident. When headship and leadership are not adequately distinguished, then either every leader has to become a priest or every priest has to recognize the injustice of co-opting leadership and become just like those who minister only out of the sacraments of baptism and confirmation. In either case, Christ's original gift of the Twelve disappears or is no longer adequately visible.

The Second Vatican Council taught that the bishops' discussions with the world should be "marked by charity of expression as well as by humility and courtesy, so that truth may be combined with charity, and understanding and love. The discussions should likewise be characterized by due prudence allied, however, with sincerity which by promoting friendship is conducive to a union of minds."[3] In other words, the mission of the Church echoes what is in fact the constitution of the Church. The Church is one, holy, catholic, apostolic, and these words also describe the mission. But Church and mission are catholic and so include everyone; no one is counted out. No group is beyond the grace of God, and this truth demands that Catholics reach out in every way possible, even with the experience of having been previously rejected or hated or persecuted. The universal mission, like the Church that carries it, is also apostolic. That means that the Church reaches out not with a cultural accommodation of the Gospel of Jesus Christ, not with a negotiated Gospel, but with the full and authentic Gospel that the Lord Jesus Christ has given us through the apostles. It is futile to reach out to anyone with anything except the authentic Gospel with all its paradoxes and demands, because only that Gospel can convert. To reach out with anything less means there will be no change, no conversion, and the world will not become holy. The purpose of reaching out in catholic universalism with the apostolic faith is to transform the world and convert hearts, to make a change, to make a difference, to make the world holy. Then, catholic and apostolic and holy, the Church will be visibly one in Christ Jesus. That is the sense of mission that is rooted in the nature of the Church, a nature that the Second Vatican Council has made splendidly clear and that effective bishops and priests help lay Catholics to carry out.

I recall that a PBS series on Pope John Paul II raised the question: Is this a pope for our times or against our times? The only adequate answer is: both. That is "simply Catholicism."

Chapter 10

Lay Catholics

The Role of the Lay Faithful in Our Culture Today

AT THE HEIGHT OF the sexual abuse crisis in this country, the bishops of the United States made a number of promises to ourselves and to lay Catholics.[1] A good number of them have already been kept, and a number of others are continuously in the process of being fulfilled. As allegations of sexual abuse of a minor by a priest are judged credible, the priest is taken out of active ministry and sometimes removed from the priesthood itself. Victims are respected and cared for, to the extent that the legal context makes possible. The media say we are doing little or nothing. How is that possible when, from our perspective, we are moving along so resolutely? This clash between the reality and the perception, whether in the newspapers or among some groups or in the general culture, is the context for these reflections.

When we speak about the Church in society, we are speaking in institutional terms of a deeper relationship that we have become accustomed to talking about as the dialogue between faith and culture. I and many other American bishops have talked about the faith and culture dialogue because John Paul II made it a regular theme for over twenty-five years. It is a necessary dialogue because both faith and culture tell us what to do. Culture is a *normative system,* and so is the faith. If the faith and the culture clash or disagree, as they always do to some extent, it is because faith is a gift from

God, and culture is a human construct. There will be tension in us because the faith and the culture are both inside us. Because of our faith, at times there will often be social harassment, sometimes imprisonment, and, if the clash is deadly enough, even martyrdom. We often think about clashes between faith and culture because of what we are called to do or expected to do in ethical or moral matters. We look at practices that the culture legitimates, or at least permits; then we look at the moral demands of the faith; and we see that two normative systems disagree.

But behind the moral issues there is also, more profoundly, a double way of seeing things — a double vision, if you like, a double way of thinking about things, certainly a double way of thinking about God and his creation. These are faith issues much more directly than they are moral issues. They are issues that we do not often think about but that, in fact, form the environment in which we think.

Secularization and the Threat to Religious Claims

One could argue that the most controversial article of the Creed is the one that says, "I believe in God, the Father almighty." Certainly one of the more controversial statements in Holy Scripture is Jesus' proclamation, "All power in heaven and on earth has been given to me" (Matt. 28:18). In a secularized culture, belief in an almighty God, an all-powerful God, seems a threat to human freedom. Since freedom is the primary cultural value in much of the West today, claims that God has power over us are very problematic. Secularization of a culture and of an individual begins when, however subtly, the power of God comes to be seen as a threat to the freedom of man. In the vision of faith, from divine self-revelation, the power of God creates us from nothing and the power of God saves us from sin. God's power constitutes us. There is no way in which the Father of our Lord Jesus Christ can be a threat to our freedom or our salvation or to anything else except sin. But in a secularized culture, God is implicitly, in some sense, a rival, a competitor to human beings, a threat.

Secularization in the form we call modernization began when humans started to clothe themselves with what had been in medieval scholastic theology the attributes of God. First of all, we took over control of nature through technology. Nature, instead of being a gift from God, was tortured in a laboratory and bent through technology to our purposes. We took over not only control of nature but control of history, replacing a provident God with the myth of human progress. Sometimes this has been beneficial, as technology has also had beneficial effects. We have popular governments but, within the history of modern secularization, we have also had the great totalitarian movements that simply took the place of God entirely. Since, for secularists, God is an arbitrary power in the lives of human beings then, in bringing the power of God into human control, they have taken as theirs this arbitrary power rather than the power of God as he lovingly reveals himself in salvation history.

If God is a threat, he has to be done away with. Friedrich Nietzsche "kills" God, and God's existence is explicitly denied in many less spectacular ways. But there is a more subtle way of reducing the threat that God's power might have for us, and that is to tame God. This is the kind of secularization we live with in the United States. This God is a name for everything we cherish, whatever else he might be. This God is like a pet brought out for our enjoyment at times, sometimes an object of fun or even as an accompaniment to our own solemnities, but in any event a construct. This God certainly makes no demands on us, because he has no power. We cannot permit him to have power, lest we lose our freedom. But if God can make no demands, then religion is necessarily a hobby. It is what we do in our leisure time, particularly in the kind of leisure time we have invented with the weekend. When both parents must work very hard for five days, they cherish the two days a week when they can be together with their children. It is leisure time, a time for self-expression. If religion is one form of self-expression, and if you want to express yourself that way, that's fine. If it's not, that's fine too. In any event, neither religion nor Church nor God can make demands on what you do with your free time. Religion is a leisure-time activity, not a way of life. At best, therefore, religion is a set of ideas, now bedeviled with a certain amount of ideological warfare. Religion is useful for celebrating but not for changing anything, because God can have no power. We even have theologies of sacramentality that say that a sacrament is just a name for what is already there. The sacraments do not cause something; they are not powerful.

What religion cannot do in this situation is to make truth claims. In a postmodern situation, any objective truth claim is illegitimate, a threat to subjective freedom. Religious truth claims, and therefore the exercise of religious authority or power, are particularly offensive. They are threats to subjective freedom and must be controlled. If they cannot be controlled, they must be ridiculed. If they cannot be ridiculed, then they have to be contained. If God has no power because otherwise we cannot be free, then bishops certainly can have no authority. Any exercise of religious authority is, therefore, a form of usurpation. The crisis of faith in this kind of culture is not limited. It is not a crisis of belief in a particular dogma or in the moral teaching of Christ. It is a crisis of belief in the all-powerful God. It is a loss of the conviction that spirit has power. Spirit is at best an epiphenomenon of matter. Only matter is powerful, and to make claims that spirit has power independently of matter is to indulge in superstition and to give oneself to a kind of religious enslavement.

Consequences of Secularization

There are at least two consequences to this phenomenon of "soft" secularization, of taming God by rendering him powerless and turning religion into a hobby. The first is that nothing can be really new. If, in fact, the world is in our hands, both in our destiny and in the present, then anything that is unintended is an affront, and we must seek to insulate ourselves against it. A primary example we have lived with for a generation now is that of an "unwanted" child. In current perspective, children are not inherently worthy of dignity: it is the wanting by another that makes a child valuable. An unwanted child, then, is an affront and somehow must be done away with.

As in intercourse and pregnancy, so in all our experiences, there can be no unintended consequences, no accidents that cannot be righted. After every kind of incident or tragedy, the first thing the authorities are expected to do is to reassure people, not only that things will be all right but that everything will be restored to the way it was before. In this kind of social economy, devoted to keeping us safe from all forms of disruption, a high percentage of our assets is exhausted in insurance, litigation, the upkeep of prisons, and the development of homeland security in its many forms until, finally, we all end up living in prisons constructed by ourselves. This is to embrace despair.

Since there can be nothing that is truly new, the present is made tolerable only by expensive distractions and frivolities which, in fact, change nothing. They are designed to change nothing and to reinforce a sense of determinism. Because of the particular kind of secularized Calvinism in which we live, our rhetoric is always full of imminent warnings; but fundamentally, nothing changes. Every change that is not willed is considered wrong, and somebody has to pay.

But if there is nothing new, then nothing can be forgiven. For every genuine act of forgiveness means that a new beginning is possible, and there can be no truly new beginning. We see this in the tragedy of the priestly sex abuse scandal, where healing cannot begin without an act of forgiveness on the part of one whose life has been badly harmed, sometimes ruined, because of sexual abuse. Yet in this secular culture, the one thing that cannot be done is to forgive. To forgive is to lose, in many people's minds. The culture is bizarre in its insistence that we should try everything, "just do it," and that "you can be whatever you want to be"; but the sometime negative effects of our actions cannot be admitted or adequately dealt with to arrive at a new beginning. Everything is possible, but nothing can be forgiven.

Faith, by contrast, says that many things cannot be done. Jesus says, "If you love me, keep my commandments." There is much activity that is forbidden. But in the end, everything can be forgiven. Perhaps that is the clue to the crisis of the sacrament of reconciliation: the sense of sin has not been lost so much as the conviction that a new beginning is possible and that forgiveness is available through the power of our risen Lord.

One religious response to this kind of society is to institutionalize schools and hospitals and works of mercy, charity, and justice in such a way that we contribute to the culture, but on the culture's own terms. This response, which assumes that it is a good thing to be socialized according to the patterns of this culture, has exhausted many of the resources of the Catholic Church in the United States. For good and ill, our Catholic universities are American universities, and our Catholic hospitals are American hospitals. Have our institutions, which have been our best hope for taking the children of immigrants and keeping them Catholic while making them Americans, demanded too high a price? Have we formed very fine professionals, but not formed disciples?

The Church in this kind of culture becomes one more voluntary association, a spiritual club. The emphasis is upon belonging. Even the theology of communion is permitted to emphasize only the relationships that unite us to Christ and to one another. Of course, if we are to be visibly in Christ, we must belong. But good ecclesiology moves between two poles, that of belonging and that of converting. Catholics may not have spoken often enough about the need for conversion in order to belong. The evangelicals are very good at this, but without an adequate ecclesiology. For them, without a subjective experience of conversion, one cannot make a claim to belong to Christ. Catholics can belong to the Church as we belong to a family, before we have personal experience. But we have to be led, particularly through receiving the sacraments and through good preaching and catechesis, to the experience of conversion, of having ourselves turned inside out so that Christ is at the center of our life, not ourselves. The cry "We are Church" is often a claim that, if there is a clash between our personal culture and the Catholic faith, it is the faith that must change, not us. That is new. In earlier years, largely through parochial missions and in hearing Sunday sermons, Catholics assumed that if they were in disagreement with the Church, it was they who were wrong, or sinful, and eventually had to change. The Church had the right to call them to conversion. With the weakening of Catholicism as a way of life, we have lost the regular common life of fasting, prayer, and devotions that reminded people hour after hour throughout the day and the night that the Church could make demands on them, that God could make demands on them, that Catholicism is a way of discipleship. All that seems to have largely disappeared and, with it, the automatic assumption that the Church has the right to call anybody to conversion as a necessity for belonging. If, in fact, we have focused too much on belonging and not enough on conversion, then to respond adequately to our situation today it is not enough to change the institutions and structures of the Church. Rather, in all of our life and ministries, and in the way we think about things, we must focus again on real change, real novelty, on an alternative way of life that gives hope.

I would argue that the primary crisis at this moment, and always, is a crisis of discipleship, of conversion to Jesus Christ individually and socially within his body, the Church. Next, there is a crisis of marriage for life and for the sake of family. Only in the wake of these two crises is there a crisis of vocations to the priesthood and the consecrated life. If we could solve the first two, we could easily solve the third. It is a mistake to begin with the third. We have to go back and ask again about Vatican II's purpose as it was envisioned by Blessed Pope John XXIII. The purpose of the Council was to strengthen the mission of the Church in order to change the world. The purpose of calling the Council was to make vigorous the mission of the universal Church in order to help the world come to the discovery that we are brothers and sisters in Christ, to bring all Christians together through the ecumenical movement, to heal the sins of racism, to engage in interfaith dialogue, and to address the world in terms of social justice and universal charity. This conciliar program, all of it rooted in the Gospel and Christ's will for unity among his people, was brought forward precisely because the world was in need of change. The Church was also in need of change, but only to the extent that she needed to look again at how she could most effectively change the world. We have allowed a missionary council to be domesticated.

The greatest failure of the post–Vatican II Church is the failure to call forth and to form a laity engaged in the world politically, economically, culturally, and socially, on faith's terms rather than on the world's terms. If perhaps we paid less attention to ministries and to expertise and to functions, necessary though all of that is, and more to mission or purpose, then we might recapture the sense of what should be genuinely new as a result of the Council. The novelty, the change sought, was in the world, and only secondarily in the Church. Not that the Church does not have to change. Of course, the Church must constantly change to be obedient to the Lord who calls her, as a Church, to constant conversion. But the purpose of the Church herself is not just to counsel individuals, celebrate events, or be a voluntary association for people who like to spend their leisure time in that way and do good things together.

The purpose of the Church is to tell the world with one united voice that an alternative way of life is possible, that we do not have to live in the despair that more and more marks our society. The purpose of the Church is to be the instrument of Christ's judgment and redemption of the world.

This means that we have to recognize what we are up against. The world is both friendly and unfriendly, both holy and demonic. The world will welcome some of our criticisms and will do everything it can to contest others. When we hear the demands of the world, which we have to hear, lest we fail to attend to the signs of the times, the great missionary challenge is then to discern what the Church must adapt to and what is incompatible with the faith. The call of Christ himself, in the liturgy, in public devotion, in private prayer, has to be heard by every Catholic as a call to conversion. We cannot allow anyone's fear of the mission Christ gave his Church to distract us or paralyze us from moving ahead together.

Next Steps

What should we do now?

We should pray for courage. There are good reasons to be afraid. The present challenges are very difficult. At the time that the United States began to invade Iraq, I received a letter from a man on the northwest side of Chicago, not far from where I was raised. He returned his baptismal certificate to me because he said he was ashamed of the Holy Father's opposition to the war. The Holy Father did not understand why America had this mission to bring freedom to the Iraqi people. I wrote back to tell him that the Holy Father truly must constantly plead for peace because war, even if justified, is always a failure for the human race. The Holy Father went on to plead for peace even after the warfare began, without condemning the actions of those who were going to war. The pope's message and the situation of Iraq were both far more complicated than this man had been led to believe. At the end of the letter, I said, "No matter what you accept or don't accept of what I've written, I see by your baptismal certificate that you are sixty-five years old. In a very few years, you will appear before the Lord Jesus Christ. He's not going to ask for your U.S. passport, but he will be interested in knowing that you were baptized."

The culture is strong and very much able to fight. It has something to teach us as well. The conflict is not between a demonic culture and a holy faith. It is much more complicated than that. Nonetheless, despite the complications, Christ needs lay disciples who can take up the challenge of the Council and transform the world. We have to pay attention to helping people understand the common good in a social system that is seen as a collection of interest groups and interested individuals. We have not paid enough attention to the way in which our kind of culture is fundamentally based upon conflict, needs conflict. The legal system is based upon conflict. The political system is based upon conflict. The economic system is based upon conflict, or at least competition. The media are based upon conflict: there must be a difference of opinion and a clash of personalities. The conflict that is part of our cultural formation makes it very difficult for us to think beyond a particular interest to the common good; but it is possible. Many good people do think about the common good first. We meet them in our presbyterates, in our schools and convents, and in our parishes every day.

We have to form people with a genuine love of today's city and love of our culture itself. Even with its demonic elements, the culture must be loved, because you cannot evangelize what you do not love. We have to love the city — not to possess it, but to perfect it for Christ in order finally to deliver it to him when he comes again in glory. That is a particular kind of disinterested love far removed from the love of possession, which is the primary sense of love in our culture.

We have to develop people who have a distinctive way of life. We had a Catholic subculture, but it could not endure with the changes in the dominant culture. It is not a question of returning to the 1940s or 1950s. Even if somebody wanted to, that is impossible; and I do not believe it is desirable. But there is a way of life that is bound up with being a disciple of Christ in his Church, a common way of life not constructed by individual choice. It has a common calendar, penitential practices, prayer. It has common devotions and a common vocabulary. It is a way of life which tells me every moment of my life that the Church can and must make demands upon me, because she is the body of Jesus Christ, to whom all authority has been given in heaven and on earth.

We have to form people who look to the poor not merely as objects of concern but rather as guides. Poor people are closer to the necessities and basics of life than many wealthy or middle-class people are. In this country, even our problems are luxuries that most of the world cannot afford. The poor cannot afford the illusion of personal independence. They therefore sometimes have a more immediate sense of dependence on God. At the time of the Second Vatican Council, Yves Congar and others spoke about a Church of the poor. Of course, no one should romanticize the poor; the poor are as sinful as anybody else. Catholics here have remembered what it was to be poor in the Great Depression and in the first generations of immigrants. Who wants to be poor? Involuntary poverty is certainly not an ideal in the sociological sense, but voluntary poverty is an evangelical ideal. The proclamation that the poor are the ones who are favored in the kingdom and that it is likely that the rich will go to hell is a sobering warning in the Gospels. Without conversion, we will collapse into the ways of those whom Jesus warned would lose eternal life. There is nothing wrong with being wealthy or middle class. It is the way of responsibility, the way of doing many generous and good things. The middle class exists in order to set people free, including the poor; but if wealth is not dedicated to the well-being of the poor, and put to work in cooperation with them, then wealth becomes a road to condemnation.

We have to make the Church more clearly the way of freedom. If God is not a threat, but is someone who makes us free, then, especially for the young, the Church can be the way of freedom, because the young know the world is a trap. The openness to the world that was rightly called for in *Gaudium et spes* was, at times, confused with self-secularization, seeing the world as the primary way of grace. The Church had to "catch up" to the world, so it was assumed, and the better she was conformed to the world, the more she would be truly renewed.

We have to speak about freedom. Freedom is a Gospel virtue. True freedom is what we are all about. We should speak about freedom before we speak about anything else. Freedom is a gift, however, not something won by conquest. Discipleship means knowing how to wait in order to be set free by Almighty God. I was once with some young people in Chicago in a tavern near Wrigley Field at something called YACHT (Young Adult Catholics Hanging Together). It is an extension of the well-known "Theology on Tap." There were about three hundred young people there. Shortly after the conversation began, they asked, "Cardinal, why should I be Catholic?" I said, "You should be Catholic because God wants you to be Catholic. God is active in the world. God is powerful. God sets us free, and God wants you to be Catholic." Then they asked, "What about my Buddhist roommate?" and other very good questions. None of them, however, contested the truth claim that God wants you to be Catholic. They were open to hearing that call and had a sense of it, though they were not all convinced. That is what we have to proclaim: "Dear brothers and sisters, in this culture, God wants us all to be Catholic. Here's how you go about it. If you do so, God will free you and those you love. God is doing wonderful things here. Why shouldn't he? He is God, and we are not." If we proclaim the Gospel well, then bishops can trust the laity to work it out in the world and, in the name of Christ and with his authority, hold them accountable in this world, as Christ will in the next.

Chapter 11

Receiving Identity
from the Risen Christ

*Ordained Priesthood and Leadership
in the Catholic Church*

ESUS HAS RISEN from the dead and is freed from the bonds of death.[1] In his risen body, he passes through locked doors. His is a human body without bodily limitations. The laws of space and time no longer apply to him, although his body is truly his own, born of the Virgin Mary, bearing still the marks of the crucifixion in his hands, feet, and side. Perfectly free, he wants to be with us and, because he is free to send the Spirit, he shapes the Church to his own liking and design. He acts freely in the Church in the sacramental rites, which are actions of the Risen Lord. He governs his people personally through the pastors he ordains for them. He teaches in the Church personally through the proclamation of the Gospel and its explication in the doctrines of the Church. That identity between Christ and the Church is clear in his own teaching: *What you do to the least of my brothers and sisters you do to me* (Matt. 25:40). It is clear in the history of his calling of the great missionary Paul. Struck by the Risen Christ, which is the only Christ that Paul knew, just as it is the only Christ we know, blinded by a light in which he heard a voice, "Saul, why do you persecute *me?*" Paul learned of the body of Christ that is the Church. The

Church makes visible the life of the Risen Christ, acting in every age until he returns in glory at the end of the ages. The Church lives by Christ's life, the life of the Holy Spirit. The hidden dynamic of the actions and the movements of the Risen Christ are made available in the mission and ministry of the Church. This is the mystery of the Church taught with compelling clarity in *Lumen gentium*, the Second Vatican Council's Constitution on the Church.

Warrants for Leading

If all this is true, then it is a mistake to allow a discussion of leadership in the Church to be reduced to an analysis of those in holy orders. To be sure, the sacrament of holy orders does make visible the Mystery of Christ precisely as head of his body the Church. At the end of the first century, St. Ignatius of Antioch, continuing a theme from the pastoral epistles of St. Paul, makes clear that nothing in a particular local church or a diocese is to take place apart from the bishop. But because nothing can take place in the body without the head coordinating it in some manner, it does not follow that the bishop, or the ordained priests with him, are the only leaders in the Church. They lead, but they lead as pastors, as those who must constantly be concerned with keeping everyone together around Christ. Their authority to pastor the people as Christ would govern them, to love the people as Christ loves them, comes from Christ himself directly through the sacrament of holy orders. But there are other bases for leadership among Christ's people. There is *expertise,* which gives a certain claim to rightful influence. There are *charismatic graces,* sent by the Spirit to meet the needs of a particular moment; these can be a claim to leadership if they are properly discerned. Finally, *holiness of life* is the first title to leadership among a people made holy by Christ's self-sacrifice.

Think back to the thirteenth century. Innocent III was a remarkably strong pope in the history of that office, but the other dominant figure of that time was St. Francis of Assisi, whom the pope knew and approved of. In the long run, it was St. Francis of Assisi's leadership that shaped the Church far more than did the ministry of Innocent III. In our own day, John Paul II recognized a similar importance in Mother Teresa. Curial cardinals said he wanted his twenty-fifth anniversary celebration as Pontiff, as bishop of Rome, to coincide with the beatification of Mother Teresa. They told him, "No, you have to have two separate celebrations." And in the end, he accepted, and celebrated and enjoyed both. But he clearly wanted to say that the meaning of his ministry as bishop of Rome, as pope, is to be found in what Mother Teresa did, because she exemplified the meaning of the Church's mission in the world according to the Second Vatican Council.

The spirituality of the Council is the spirituality of the Good Samaritan, as Pope Paul VI said in the Council's closing homily. This means that the Church, the body of Christ, from the strength of her own unity is to heal the wounds of a divided and broken world. In this understanding of the Church's reason for being in the world, of her mission in the world, it is a sin of clericalism to allow ordained priesthood to monopolize leadership. There are many ways that the Church heals the sins of a divided world and, if that is her mission, it is surely as much or more in the hands of the laity as it is in the hands of the ordained.

Pastoral Leadership

That said, let us examine the specific leadership role of pastors, which is always indispensably necessary for the Church. In every age, the Church must be formed into Christ's body by sharing his gifts for the sanctification of the laity, who are called to make the world holy by means of lives dedicated to the pursuit of charity and justice. In a culture historically Protestant such as that of the United States, holy orders and the hierarchy it establishes puzzles or angers people, because the apostolic office of the bishop was explicitly rejected by the reformers of the sixteenth century. For the reformers, the head of the Church was, of course, Christ. And that is true for us Catholics well. But Christ is now invisible, and for the reformers the participation of that headship is now functionally, not sacramentally founded. The reformers considered the sacrament of holy orders as church-instituted and not willed by Christ. For many Protestants, therefore, the hierarchy of the Catholic Church is at best an anachronism, and at worst a danger to the freedom of Christians who see themselves directly inspired by the Spirit in the study of Scripture. For secularists, the hierarchy poses a danger to democratic freedoms that accept directions only from leadership elected by the people.

Ours is a post-Protestant culture, even though Protestantism, Catholicism, and other religions are still quite influential. Classical Protestantism is our ally against secularization of the society, despite the divisions that weaken all of us. When we face irreligious secularism, we face a phenomenon that feeds on two convictions, sincerely held by many people, both of which assert that religion is a threat to personal freedom and societal harmony. First, if God is almighty, and if others can tell us in his name what we can and cannot do, we are less free than we could be if we were governed only by our own choices. Second, since 9/11, religion is also regarded as a primary cause of social violence. If religious people in the name of the God of Abraham can destroy people's lives as the terrorists did, then for the sake of peace it would be better not to have religion at all. This secularist take on religion does not recognize the way in which God himself sets us free; nor does it notice the many ways in which religion is an instrument for peace; yet this vision seems to have growing influence in our culture today. If it becomes the dominant vision of who we are as a people, religious authority will of necessity be steadily weakened, if not eliminated. The only safe religion would be one that, however personally comforting and charitable, makes no claim to teach truths in God's name nor to shape lives by moral norms that do not admit of exceptions freely chosen.

The priestly sex abuse scandal has been transformed into a scandal of Church leadership, of Church authority. Deservedly so, for bishops have failed, but also deliberately so. Anyone who followed the opinion columns in the *New York Times* saw that when the scandals began to become highly publicized, particularly in the Archdiocese of Boston, the first articles decried the immorality of individual priests. Those that followed talked about the irresponsibility of bishops and said that the anger of the people would not be turned against priests in general. *We can sympathize with sinners,* according to this view, *especially sinners weak sexually, but we cannot forgive those who should have made certain that children were not abused.* And, having separated laity from bishops, articles began to discuss separating the Catholic Church in the United States from the Roman Apostolic See. Priestly abuse of children and young people is a great tragedy of unbounded proportions and bishops must take responsibility for it; but it is also an occasion to unleash the anti-Catholicism that has never been far beneath the surface in U.S. history. For some, the only safe Catholic, the only good Catholic, is a Catholic who is at odds with the bishops. In that sense, it is somewhat ironic that the self-styled prophetic voices in the Church today are those that give loudest voice to the dominant culture. It takes no enormous courage to be pro-abortion, pro-contraception, pro-divorce, pro–gay marriage — pro any of the other items on the long list of sexual and cultural freedoms claimed today. That is the voice of the dominant culture, and those who speak it receive their reward, at least in the opinion pages of the *New York Times.*

In this cultural atmosphere, the failure of bishops and priests to protect victims of sexual abuse has stirred many voices for reform of the Church, especially reform of her structures and hierarchy. Such voices should be listened to carefully because they are often thoughtful. I think they are usually also sincere, and there is the distinct possibility that the Spirit is reminding us always to be attentive to the voice of all who are baptized in Christ. But finally, the reform of the Church will not come from management theory. It will come from holiness. St. Francis of Assisi, Blessed Mother Teresa, St. Catherine of Siena are the reformers we look for, even we bishops. The management problem, though important, depends on holiness to point the way to serious institutional change. But then we need to ask: What changes? Benedict XVI made several pointed suggestions on his journey to the United States, even before his plane landed, underscoring his own view of the seriousness of the situation.[2]

Ecclesial Lay Leadership

One of the most thoroughgoing analyses of the present situation with suggestions for reform of leadership structures in the Church has been offered by Peter Steinfels in an important book, *A People Adrift: The Crisis of the Roman Catholic Church in America*. Peter Steinfels's reflections carry the credibility born of his many years of commenting carefully and incisively on Catholic issues. They reflect as well the opinion of many dedicated and well-educated Catholic laypersons.

In many ways, Steinfels's work is a tour de force of reportage. Anyone seeking a portrait of American Catholicism almost fifty years after the Second Vatican Council should read it. He examines in a generally balanced way issues ranging from the Catholic identity of universities and hospitals and the role of women in the Church to the acceptance (or nonacceptance) of official Church teaching on sexuality and ecclesial leadership. What he proposes on this last question is inconsistent with Catholic ecclesiology and with the Catholic understanding of ordained priesthood. But his point is argued well, and it has to be attended to.

As noted above, when we talk about leadership in the Church, we cannot pay attention only to those in holy orders. To limit leadership solely to bishops and priests is clericalism, which is a sin. We cannot make the opposite error, however, and say that ordained pastoral leadership is not intrinsic to the very nature of the Church. Leadership has to be examined and perhaps even exercised in different ways, particularly because of this crisis. Bishops have to be open to asking people who are critical of the present situation what it is that they want. But we also have to determine whether what they want is in harmony with our faith.

Steinfels addresses the issue of Church leadership in the final chapter of his book, called "At the Helm." He begins provocatively. "The leadership throughout American Catholicism is changing," he writes. "Nothing can stop that. Leadership by priests and nuns is giving way to leadership by lay people."[3] The rest of the chapter is an empirically based defense of this claim and a frank celebration of it. His presentation proceeds in three stages. First, he shows that the moral authority of bishops has been irredeemably undermined. Second, he tries to demonstrate that the priesthood as we know it is fading away. And finally, he points with great satisfaction to the emergence of a new coterie of leadership in the Church — ecclesial lay ministers.

The sex abuse scandal, he argues, has revealed a massive failure on the part of bishops in the face of the greatest crisis the Church in America has ever faced. They were indecisive, unfocused, defensive, self-protective, and indifferent to the victims. He is convinced that the majority of these men were not malevolent, but he insists that they were mediocre, and their leadership clearly inadequate. In light of these failures, it is difficult for bishops, Steinfels thinks, to claim an unquestioned moral and spiritual authority. Next, he turns his attention to priests, following Father Andrew

Greeley's insight that though bishops officially enjoy the highest status, most of the faithful take their doctrinal and ethical cues from their local pastor. On this point, he is just as dispiriting, like many other commentators on both the left and the right. Steinfels recounts the statistics on what appears to be the irrevocably declining number of priests in this country. He shows for instance that the number of annual ordinations had dipped from nearly one thousand in 1965 to fewer than five hundred today, and that for every one hundred American priests who die, only thirty-five new ones are ordained. The call by many conservatives to reverse this trend through a reintroduction of a more heroic and demanding vision of the priesthood Steinfels sees as a hopeless strategy. Might heroism and distinctiveness, he wonders, simply be masks covering up psychological insecurity and a grasping at power and office? Furthermore, the so-called John Paul II priests cultivated at a handful of conservative seminaries will never be able to lead effectively, he claims, since they so often stand at odds with the vast majority of the laity, especially women, on a wide variety of issues. Steinfels's conclusion is clear: "Recruit as energetically as possible, define the priesthood or religious life in whatever unambiguous, privileged, or heroic terms one chooses, and still the most that can be expected is a leveling off of the declining numbers."[4]

According to this diagnosis, bishops lack spiritual authority, and priests, from whose ranks the bishops are chosen, are fast disappearing from the scene. In delineating what stands behind this decline, Steinfels develops one of the most provocative arguments in his book. The Second Vatican Council celebrated the goodness of the world, the positive dimensions of secular culture, the beauty of the human body, and the spiritual quality of human sexuality, he notes. Though these affirmations have been made sporadically throughout the history of the Church, they were given a particularly strong and unambiguous emphasis at the Council. And nowhere is the triumph of this perspective clearer than in the writings of Pope John

Paul II himself, especially in his lyrical evocations of the spirituality of the human body. What follows from this shift, argues Steinfels, is the abandonment of the dualistic flight from the world, an attitude that held sway within Catholicism for centuries and that had effectively undergirded the practice of celibacy in religious life. As long as the physical and the sexual were perceived as, at the very least, spiritually ambiguous, it made good sense for those who aspired to a higher, more perfect life to turn from them and embrace a celibate lifestyle. But once sexuality and married life were appreciated as altogether valid paths to holiness, Catholics began to wonder why celibacy, with all of its rigors, was desirable. Steinfels concludes, "But the status that celibacy once enjoyed as *the* model of holiness to be routinely required of every parish priest and Eucharistic minister, is simply incompatible with the Church's currently affirmed Catholic humanism."[5] But, Steinfels says, none of this should fill us with alarm, for just as the priesthood is falling into the shadows, a new form of ecclesial leadership is coming into the light: lay ministry. Before the 1960s, parishes were staffed almost exclusively by priests, while lay people functioned as volunteer cooks, cleaners, organists, and directors of choirs. Today, Steinfels reminds us, "there are over thirty thousand lay parish ministers, paid for at least twenty hours a week, working in over 60 percent of the nation's parishes."[6]

More to the point, in 1997, for the first time, the number of ecclesial lay ministers surpassed the number of parish priests. This seismic shift, which has produced difficulties both practical and theoretical, is comparable, Steinfels maintains, to the transition that occurred in the thirteenth century when the mendicant orders (Franciscans, Dominicans, Augustinians, and Carmelites) emerged and challenged the ecclesial status quo. The Church made adjustments and learned to assimilate the new forms then; it will do so now. Steinfels is impatient with the two standard arguments marshaled against lay ministry. The first argument maintains that bringing the nonordained into the formal ministry of the Church deemphasizes the apostolate of the laity in the world, their distinctive contribution to the transformation of society so often present in the Vatican II documents. But Steinfels answers that empirical studies have demonstrated that lay ministers actually serve to awaken in parishioners a deeper sense of their spiritual obligations in the world. The second argument claims that the presence of lay parish ministers will blur the distinction between the ordained and the nonordained. But Steinfels finds this concern fussy and ungrounded, born of clerical defensiveness. In fact, he wants to preserve the distinction though, interestingly, not so much to protect priesthood as to protect the integrity of lay ministry. Lay ministers should not be seen as substitutes for priests, but rather as full-fledged leaders in their own right. This observation leads him to the telling conclusion that "the number of priests is not the primary issue. Leadership is, and a certain kind of leadership: American Catholicism needs priest leaders for a church of lay leaders."[7]

We notice here something of great importance to which we shall return, namely, Steinfels's tendency to conflate priesthood and lay ministry under the generic heading of "ecclesial leadership," overlooking the qualitative difference between the two forms of life insisted upon in the documents of Vatican II itself. The argument having been made, we can then ask — what should this collaborative priesthood of the future look like?

Cooperation between Lay and Priests in Leading

Priests, Steinfels claims, must first have the theological capacity to make the sacraments, the Word of God, and ordinary daily experience deeply meaningful to their parishioners. Second, they must be able to empower and animate others in their legitimate leadership roles. This means that future priests might function in a parish in a more or less episcopal way, overseeing and coordinating the various

works of lay ministers. And third, priests will have to be accountable not only to the bishop but to the people whom they serve.
For too long, he argues, ordination has been "a lifetime license
to preach, teach, instruct, counsel, and run parishes — perhaps
superbly, perhaps indifferently, perhaps terribly — with little like-
lihood of any regular measurement of performance."[8] Accordingly,
Steinfels calls for monitoring of priests by fellow clergy and pastors, but also by outside boards of lay people along the lines of the
procedures used in academic accreditation.

Also, laity ought to serve on diocesan personnel committees,
which play a key role in advising bishops as to the assignment
and reassignment of ordained priests. More radically, Steinfels suggests that the Church might consider ordaining married men to
the priesthood or allowing diocesan priests to make a promise
of celibacy for a limited time, after which they would be free to
marry, continuing to serve the Church perhaps as deacons. We
might entertain the possibility of a ministry of lay preaching involving gifted public speakers, lawyers, teachers, and politicians found
in the ranks of the faithful. Enabling these men and women to
preach on a semi-regular basis would free priests for an ever more
demanding sacramental ministry.

Finally, Steinfels calls for a basic reform of the manner in which
bishops are chosen and monitored. He is particularly bothered by
the bureaucratic, hyper-careful style the American bishops have
adopted in the interests, he says, of placating Roman authorities.
Even staunchly pro-Vatican bishops of an earlier time, like Richard
James Cardinal Cushing and Francis Cardinal Spellman, he argues,
had a keen sense of their own authority and did not cower at the
slightest sign of Roman displeasure. Today's American bishops, in
his telling, seem to lack the spine to resist even the most insulting
and unreasonable of Vatican demands. Further, the selection process for bishops is narrow, secretive, and almost exclusively clerical.

It should be opened up so as to include the input of diocesan councils of both priests and laity and perhaps even a wide constituency of the faithful. Only when these reforms are instituted will the priesthood and the episcopacy be fit to collaborate creatively with the emerging Church in the United States.

Leadership Rooted in Sacramental Distinctiveness

Let us turn now to the difference between priestly ministry and lay ministry as the Church understands their respective relationship to leadership in the Church. I would like to begin a response to Steinfels's proposal by briefly considering a hypothetical scenario he himself presents in the course of his discussion of lay ministry. He imagines an elderly woman in a hospital who is ministered to very effectively by a dedicated lay person. The lady is extremely grateful, but deep down she is disappointed that a priest did not come to see her. Steinfels regrets this scenario and is sorry for the woman and people like her, suggesting that they adjust their expectations and accept the legitimacy of lay ministers who may, in many cases, be just as effective or more so than the sometimes bumbling priest.

Despite Steinfels's lament, I think this hypothetical parishioner senses something altogether essential, something that Steinfels consistently tends to miss: the quality of the priesthood grounded sacramentally in holy orders. In longing for the presence of the priest, that lady was not looking primarily for psychological comfort, companionship, or counseling — as important as those are and as ministerial as they can be. She was looking for Christ sacramentally present in the one particularly conformed to his person through orders. In his novel *The Power and the Glory* Graham Greene tells the story of a whiskey priest, a sad, battered, and deeply flawed man who wanders from village to village in the rural Mexico of the 1920s trying desperately to avoid capture by the fierce anticlerical government that would put him to death. The towns-people whom he encounters know full well that he is anything but a saint. Yet they revere him as a priest — someone who can bring the Eucharist and the forgiveness of sins. Therefore they consider his arrival an occasion for joy.

In the religious subjectivism of the American mind, this sacramental objectivism of Catholicism, this quality that explains the essential difference between the ordained priesthood and that of the baptized, is not appreciated and, in fact, is often resented. Throughout his discussion, Steinfels has assumed that the priest and lay minister are subsumable together under the generic heading of church leader, that they are both functionaries who, whatever their distinct roles, minister in the Church in fundamentally similar and hence interchangeable ways. This functionalistic approach misses the heart of the matter. The constitution *Lumen gentium,* from the Second Vatican Council, states that the difference between the common priesthood of the faithful and the ministerial or ordained priesthood is one of kind and not merely of degree. How to explain this difference of kind? The priestly leadership of the Church comes not from below through the consent of the faithful, but from above through the choice by Jesus Christ of a man to represent him as head of his body the Church.

In his postsynodal exhortation on the ministry of bishops, *Pastores gregis,* John Paul II reminded us that Jesus, in the course of his ministry, called men and women to be his disciples, but that from this group he chose twelve, symbolic of the twelve Tribes of the old Israel, to be with him in a unique way. These twelve apostles were invited into an intimate and a specific communion with Jesus himself. In the Gospel according to St. John, two disciples of John the Baptist come to Jesus, and the Lord asks them what they are seeking. "Where do you stay?" they respond. And Jesus says, "Come and see." Then the Gospel tells us they stayed with him that day. This particular form of *staying with Jesus* is the crucial element in the formation of the apostles. They are not simply learning doctrines from Jesus, nor are they being prepared for a function. They are being radically transformed, converted through a mystical participation in the person of Christ himself made possible generation after generation because the Risen Christ is free to do so.

Staying with Jesus for the baptized is to live with Christ as a son or daughter of the Father, staying for our own salvation. That is how we are given sanctifying grace and made holy, by having through adoption the same relationship to the Father that Jesus has of his own nature. But to stay with him as an ordained priest is to live with Christ precisely as head of his body the Church for the salvation not of the priest, but of others. Confidence in Jesus' providential guidance of his Church inspired the apostles to choose successors, men who would enjoy the same apostolic intimacy with the Lord and would carry on the same apostolic work. And, through the laying on of hands, these early bishops in turn chose to consecrate certain co-workers who would share in their authority and power. In this way, John Paul II told us in *Pastores gregis,* "the spiritual gift given in the beginning has come down to our own day through the imposition of hands, in other words, by episcopal consecration, which confers the fullness of the sacrament of Orders, the high priesthood and the totality of the sacred ministry. Thus, through the bishops and the priests, their co-workers, the Lord Jesus Christ, seated at the right hand of God the Father, remains present in the midst of believers. In every time and place it is he who proclaims the word of God to all peoples, administers the sacraments of faith to believers, and guides the people of the New Testament on their pilgrimage to eternal happiness."[9]

This is why the suggestion made by Steinfels that the leadership of the Church is simply shifting from priests to the laity is deeply problematic. A Church that is not hierarchical, which is to say led by ordained bishops and priests, is no longer the Church willed by Jesus Christ. This apostolic order is not something we can arbitrarily change according to the reigning values of contemporary culture, although we can change the way in which it is exercised. And in fact, it has changed over the years. In the United States, each diocese is incorporated, and we have taken into our ministry many of the trappings of a business enterprise. This is because we take on the forms of the society wherever the Church is implanted; this is only natural and necessary. But behind every change and functional adaptation there is an element of mystery, of the structure of the Church willed by Christ himself; that is the reason for everything we do. Ordination to the priesthood confers on the ordained a new relationship to Christ for the sake of the Church.

Leading as Priest, Prophet, and King

We can specify the distinctive nature of this ordained priesthood by appealing to the *triplex munus,* the threefold office of the bishop and priest that is described in a whole range of ecclesial documents. Bishops and priests are, first, prophets, that is to say, teachers of the faith. They participate in the authoritative teaching office of Jesus himself, acting as preachers, catechists, and theologians. Second, they are priests or life-givers, sanctifiers of the people of God, participating in Jesus' mission to make the world holy by making his followers holy. And third, they are kings or rulers, shepherds of the Church charged with the task of ordering all the charisms of the faithful so as to direct the body of Christ toward its ultimate end. In this they share in the kingly work of Jesus the Shepherd who in a preeminent way governs his people. Because all these flow from a participation in the one Christ, these offices are interdependent, inseparable, and imply one another, which means there cannot be a division of powers in the governance of the Church. When one teaches effectively one ipso facto sanctifies and governs. When one sanctifies authentically, one simultaneously teaches and governs. When one governs properly, one necessarily teaches and sanctifies.

The three *munera,* in the words of John Paul II, exist in a sort of practical *circumincessio.* This is most visible when the bishop is in the cathedral surrounded by his priests, deacons, and people, preaching on the occasion of a Eucharistic celebration. At that point, it all comes together. Someone might object that the three-fold office cannot be the distinctive mark of the ordained priest since, as *Lumen gentium* also says, all of the baptized are priests, prophets, and kings. And lay people do certainly share in these offices inasmuch as they participate in the life of Christ through baptism and confirmation. But they exercise their office, according to Vatican II, not so much officially in the Church as through their apostolate in the world. A baptized conscientious lawyer who plies his trade and consciously works for justice is making society holy. A Catholic mother who instructs her children in the faith is teaching as Christ would teach. And a believing senator who enacts laws in line with the principles of the Gospel is exercising a kingly office.

The ordained priest's characteristic role is to root all of these activities clearly in the paschal mystery through the sacraments and the preaching of God's word. But couldn't we then press the argument in favor of ecclesial lay ministers? Are these people not exercising a teaching, sanctifying, and governing role as they do their work officially in and on behalf of the Church? Are they not then, as Steinfels seems to suggest, ecclesial leaders to the same degree as priests? In fact, the Vatican II documents do not consider this to be a middle case, and today we struggle to create an adequate theology of lay ministry.[10] Certainly theirs is a functional participation in the pastoring of the baptized, and so they are truly called ecclesial lay ministers. Their relationship to the Church, however, is not directly that of headship but of ministerial service.

Leadership and Eucharist

The distinctive and indispensable manner in which the ordained bishop or priest carries out the threefold office flows from his relationship to the Eucharistic Christ. Thomas Aquinas identifies the character that comes from ordination as a *potentia activa,* an active potency or force, a power to consecrate bread and wine, changing them into the Body and Blood of the Risen Lord. Through the laying on of hands, a man becomes a Eucharistic person uniquely conformed to Christ, sacrificed for his people so as to act in Christ's name and through Christ's power to affect his real presence. This must not be seen as incidental to the life of the priest, a capacity that he exercises for only a few moments every day, but rather as the all-determining quality of the priest's life and ministry. It is the primary way in which he stays with the Lord, participating in the intimacy with Christ enjoyed by the original twelve apostles. This active power, this *potentia activa* in all its mystical implications, is what the villagers in *The Power and the Glory* sensed beneath the unsavory veneer of the whiskey priest and what Steinfels's hypothetical parishioner longed for when she was dying. It is also what priests tell you when you ask them, "What is the most important part of your existence? What do you want to do and enjoy doing more than anything else?" Invariably, in my experience listening to them and from my own experience, the answer comes, "Celebrating the Holy Eucharist." Without this explicitly Eucharistic orientation, ecclesial governance devolves into a secular and bureaucratic exercise of power. The priest governs the mystical body of Christ in the same dynamic by which he enters into the administration of the sacramental body of Christ.

Perhaps now we are in a better position to understand *Lumen gentium*'s claim that the ordained priest's manner of teaching, sanctifying, and ruling is qualitatively different from that of the baptized lay person. The *potentia activa* to confect the Eucharist is a character that marks the ministerial priest at the core of his existence, conforming him uniquely to Christ and shaping definitively his act of bearing the mysteries of salvation. This sacramental identity grounded in Christ's own election of the priest is peculiar to the ordained person and indispensable to the life of Christ's body. Though lay ministry in its various modes is crucial to the Church's ability to serve her people today, and will be in the future, it can never be seen as a substitute for the ordained priesthood. They are complementary.

The various experiences of being anointed with chrism in the sacramental life of the Church to conform us to Christ, the anointed one of God, shows how our relationships are distinctively changed. A little baby is brought into church as a creature of God and, after baptism and the anointing, there is a new relationship in his or her whole being, in their inner self. He or she leaves that church as a true son or daughter, a child of God, not just a creature. When confirmed, that same baptized child receives with chrism the mark of the cross on the forehead. There is a new relationship to the world. With the sealing of their baptism, the young disciple is given a power to witness courageously to the entire world that Jesus is risen from the dead. When a priest is ordained, his hands are consecrated with chrism because the care of the Church is now in his hands. He is to love the Church as Christ himself loves her. When a bishop is ordained, his head is anointed with chrism to indicate, as the mitre does, that here is headship, here is the linchpin for all the rest, not to control everything but to coordinate all so that everything is oriented toward the purpose of the Church, which is the holiness of her members and the sanctification of the world.

Episcopal Leadership

With all this, of course, there remain Steinfels's particular objections. There is the argument about celibacy; it is important to review the entire history of the creation of celibacy as a spiritual path, one that from apostolic times was associated in different ways with the apostolic office of priest and bishop. His concern about the monitoring of bishops is certainly legitimate, and bishops themselves have taken to being part of one another's ministry in ways that would not have been imagined ten years ago. For example, financially we now have to share our balance sheets within an ecclesiastical province. And whenever the bishops of our Province of Chicago, which is the state of Illinois, get together, we always put as the first question on our agenda: How are you helping victims? How are you protecting children? How are you taking care of priests? We would not have opened our ministry to one another's inspection in the same way just a few years back, and I expect this practice will continue. That, of course, does not answer all of Steinfels's objections, and we have to examine them, but without ever surrendering juridical executive authority to a governing agency external to the bishops themselves. Nor is this a hypothetical fear; there is some danger of this as the state now begins to encroach on the freedom of the Church in ways that also would not have been thought possible a decade ago.

Finally, Steinfels talks much about the selection of bishops and a democratizing of the process. Some history of the way in which the selection of a bishop was gradually separated from secular authority must come into that discussion, because it judges situations like that of the Church in China today. Of course, consultation of lay people can be part of the process, and in fact already is so. Whenever I am asked if someone should be a bishop, on the list of names I prepare of people who should be consulted, I include the names of lay men and women, to be sure that the apostolic nuncio expands the consultation. I know that many other bishops do the same. In the end, however, bishops choose bishops, as has been the case wherever the Church is free to be herself.

Leadership and Freedom for Mission

A final consideration about the importance of the topic of Church leadership today arises from the central importance of the Church's mission in establishing her identity. Why do we have leaders at all? The Church needs leaders because she must be able to heal the world as the Good Samaritan would and to make people holy for the next world. She needs ordained ministers to make her really one in Christ, because anyone of two minds is paralyzed. When arguments are equally strong on both sides, action cannot be taken. Major internal divisions destroy the Church's mission to the world. The tragedy today is that the very sources of our unity in Christ, the gifts that he has given us to be sure that we remain united so that we can be effective in mission — the Holy Eucharist and the apostolic office — have become occasions for division in the Church.

In 1994, Joseph Cardinal Bernardin and I were both at a Synod on Consecrated Life in Rome, staying at the North American College. We found ourselves together one evening close to midnight in the kitchen of that seminary, each of us looking for some milk before we went to bed. Cardinal Bernardin was a man keenly attuned to the dynamics of gatherings, particularly gatherings of bishops, including the synods in Rome. Since this was my first synod, I asked him what was going on, because I recognized that he would know far better than I. And he did. He explained to me where the currents were, what was coming along, what was probably going to happen. It was fascinating. And then, because he knew I had been born in Chicago, we began to talk a little bit about Chicago, neither one of us ever imagining that I would be his successor. He started to paint a picture of division in the Archdiocese of Chicago and of his great difficulties in trying, as bishop, to keep everything together. I kept listening. I had been in and out of Chicago frequently visiting family, but I had never paid much attention to the governance of the Church in the archdiocese, since

I had left Chicago when I was twenty. Finally at the end I said, "Well, this is really disconcerting. What's going to happen?" And he stopped then, looked at me with a smile born of faith in God's providence, and said, "Well, you know, Francis, Chicago is sometimes ungovernable."

That statement comes back to me again and again at odd moments! In fact, in the Church today, there are voices on the left that resent the Church's teaching about many issues, particularly sexual morality, and therefore resent the bishops who uphold it. There are voices on the right that say they embrace the teaching but resent bishops who do not govern the Church exactly as they insist bishops should. But the nature of episcopacy is to be free to act in Christ's name as pastors of the Church. Bishops cannot be co-opted by state authority or political power, nor by pressure groups within the Church, lest the bishops fail in their office. That is why bishops often pose the question to themselves: "What went wrong that the office was not properly exercised and we did not oversee priests as we should have?" On this score, some of Steinfels's remarks about an ingrown clerical culture are quite accurate and have to be taken to heart.

There has been throughout the history of the Church constant tension between the state and the Church, because separation of church and state is part of our faith. It is not merely an American constitutional device. In the Catholic faith, the king is never a priest. There has been separation of the state and the Church from the very beginning. That is the nature of things. It can work itself out institutionally, constitutionally, as we do it in this country. It can work itself out otherwise in other forms of government. But there is a separation and therefore a tension. The state constantly throughout the centuries, and increasingly today in the United States, tries to make inroads on the freedom of the Church, particularly in the exercise of episcopal authority and ministry. Today, that tension is also reflected in the deterioration of trust between laity and bishop. Parish priests attest to this and often feel trapped in it, as do ecclesial lay ministers. But that is no reason to lose courage, nor even to be dismayed. We are here, precisely because Jesus Christ has risen from the dead and, himself free, gives us freedom as a gift from him, not freedom to be a slave to our own desires but freedom rather to follow him, to be his disciples on his terms, not ours. The great sin against the Holy Spirit is self-righteousness. For the self-righteous on either the left or right do not need a Savior, not even one who has risen from the dead to set us free.

Chapter 12

To Reveal the Father's Love

The Mission of Priests

OUR IDENTITY as Christ's people begins with our relationship to him as disciples and our exercise of various ministries and services to one another in his name.[1] The ministry and lives of bishops, priests, and all disciples of Jesus unfold now in a period of great grace and also great turbulence, of hope and danger. Perhaps every age is that way, but both the grace and the danger are in high profile in our time. Think of the grace identified in John Paul II's reflections on the Great Jubilee in *Novo millennio ineunte*, written near the turn of the millennium. He recognized the great gifts that God is always bestowing on the Church. In a particular way, he pointed to the renewal initiated by the Second Vatican Council. He wrote later, "Now that the Jubilee has ended, I feel more than ever in duty bound to point to the Council as *the great grace bestowed on the Church in the twentieth century:* there we find a sure compass by which to take our bearings in the century now beginning" (no. 57).

At the same time, while thankful for the grace, we are also aware of the turbulence and danger born of the infidelity and weakness that mark our life in the Church at this moment. The world suffers as well from the troubles of war, political instability, and inequities among the world's peoples. In this complex season of our human history — a history the Church always shares, for she is for the world — we may be tempted by dint of our own efforts to marshal our human resources, to develop our own clever strategies, and to attempt to master the situation with the aim of controlling it entirely. For those of us ordained priests for the service of the Gospel in the Church for the salvation of the world, succumbing to that temptation to get it all under control would be a tragic mistake, not to mention an impossibility. Reliance on our own resources will only intensify the turbulence and the dangers that beset us. This particular moment for the Church in the history of the world summons us to recenter ourselves in the grace of God, who makes all things work for the good of those who love him (Rom. 8:28).

The bishops of the United States in collaboration with the Holy See have struggled to find structural and canonical remedies to address the difficulties in the Church concerning clerical misconduct and the failure of bishops' oversight of priests. We have taken painful but necessary steps, and we have adapted some important provisions; but these attempts to create a stable juridical framework for answering a problem that is far more than juridical, while necessary, do not guarantee our fidelity to the mission entrusted to us. In fact, that assurance only comes from the proper spiritual formation of priests and from their identity as Fathers in the Church. In reclaiming authentic priestly identity and recommitting ourselves to serve Christ's mission through the Church, we renew God's grace at work in us and receive the means to calm the turbulence and circumnavigate the dangers that afflict the Church and the world.

A priest's identity obviously has Trinitarian roots. In *Pastores dabo vobis,* the late Pope John Paul II wrote: "The priest's identity...like every Christian's identity, has its source in the Blessed Trinity, which is revealed and communicated to people in Christ" (no. 12). This communion of the life of the divine Persons in the Trinity finds its reflection in the living communion of God's sons and daughters in the Church. Priests can claim no better title than "Father," which expresses their sacramental existence in the Church as effective signs revealing through Christ, in the power of the Holy Spirit, the Father of mercies who gives us eternal life. The priest is rightly called father because he is a life-giver in the Church.

For this reason, the Second Vatican Council's Decree on Priestly Formation, *Optatam totius,* synthesized with remarkable effectiveness the whole scope of spiritual formation in these words: "Spiritual formation ... should be conducted in such a way that the students may learn to live in intimate and unceasing union with God the Father through the Son Jesus Christ, in the Holy Spirit" (no. 8). This Trinitarian vision of priestly spirituality grounds and animates the priest's mission — founded in Christ, empowered by the Spirit — to reveal the Father.

How does Jesus Christ reveal the Father, and what does this mean for the lived spirituality of priests and seminarians? Self-giving in generative love is the central theme for any reflection on this subject: first, in the Blessed Trinity; second, in the paschal mystery, the revelation of who Christ is and therefore who the Father is in the power of the Spirit; third, in the sacraments, which are our access to this self-giving generative love of the Father revealed in the Son, particularly in the Eucharist, penance, and marriage. Then we need to consider the way in which priests themselves reveal the Father in their own sacrament of holy orders. Finally, there is priestly life: its integrity, its integration, its transparency, and in particular the virtues that are necessary to preserve priestly identity and priestly ministry.

Self-Giving in Generative Love in the Blessed Trinity

When we are watching broadcasts of football games, we frequently see "John 3:16" flashed on signs and written on banners, usually held by our evangelical brothers and sisters. The verse itself can become almost a commonplace, perhaps its power muted, its spiritually revolutionary significance dulled. But even at football games it is good to see that reference because these are the words drawn from Jesus' nighttime conversation with Nicodemus. Set near the beginning of John's Gospel, the text describes the Son's revelation of the Father already anticipated at the end of the prologue to the Gospel according to St. John: "No one has ever seen God. The only Son, God, who is at the Father's side, has revealed him" (John 1:18). Then in John 3:16, speaking to Nicodemus, Jesus says: "For God so loved the world that he gave his only Son, so that everyone who believes in him might not perish but might have eternal life."

Jesus reveals the Father as the one who gives neither *some thing*, nor some portion of divinity (which would be impossible in any case because of divine simplicity). "He does not ration his gift of the Spirit," as we read in the third chapter of the Gospel according to St. John. Rather, the Father gives himself entirely in giving his only Son. And just as the gift is simple and singular — the gift of self, of divine personhood — the motive is likewise simple and singular. It is love. "For God so loved the world..." This is no surprise, for just as the giver and the gift are one, so is the motivation of love: "God is love" (1 John 4:7). And what is the result of the Father's gift of himself in the Incarnate Son, the word made flesh, the gift that stems from pure love? The result, of course, is life, for in the Godhead life and love are never separate, from the Book of Genesis to the very end of the Book of Revelation. The regeneration of those who believe takes place in their being born again in the very life of God, which is eternal life, "so that everyone who believes in him might not perish but might have eternal life."

In these words to Nicodemus in the third chapter of the Gospel according to St. John, Jesus reveals the Father as the one who makes the gift of his eternal self to the world and therefore makes the gift of his very self in generative love, for it is his Son that he sends. "For God so loved the world that he gave his only Son, so that everyone who believes in him might not perish but might have eternal life." Compressed in these words is the revelation of the Father, in the

Word made flesh, the revelation of the Father who is absolute self-giving, for Father and Son are one in life-giving love, and the gift of the Son is for the sharing of divine love with the world.

In the Paschal Mystery

Looking to the life of the Trinity as it is revealed in the Incarnation, we see Trinitarian self-giving and generative love brought to full visibility and full effectiveness in the paschal mystery of Jesus Christ. In Renaissance depictions of the Annunciation by the angel Gabriel to the Blessed Virgin Mary that she is to be the mother of the Messiah, there is often (usually at the bottom of the painting) a small tomb. This reminds the viewer that the same body that was conceived in the womb of the Virgin Mary rose from the tomb on the third day after his crucifixion. This is the sense of the letter to the Hebrews, which puts the words of Psalm 40 in the mouth of Jesus: "When he came into the world, he said: 'Sacrifice and offering you did not desire, but a body you prepared for me; holocausts and sin offerings you take no delight in. Then I said, "As is written of me in the scroll, Behold, I come to do your will, O God...."'" "By this 'will,' we have been consecrated," says the author of the Epistle to the Hebrews, "through the offering of the body of Jesus Christ once and for all" (Heb. 10:5–7, 10).

The paschal mystery of Christ with its foundation and beginning in the mystery of the Incarnation is the great act of Jesus' self-giving in generative love. Jesus' sense of his own identity is heard in the Good Shepherd discourse: "I am the good shepherd, and I know mine and mine know me, just as the Father knows me and I know the Father; and I will lay down my life for the sheep.... That is why the Father loves me, because I lay down my life in order to take it up again" (John 10:14–15, 17). In his death and resurrection, Christ is the Good Shepherd who gives the gift of himself, lays down his life, out of love for the sheep, "so that they might have life and have it more abundantly" (John 10:10). But then, unlike anyone else who surrenders himself in death, Jesus takes his life back again as the eternal Son of the Father. What Jesus reveals of the Father, he also reveals of himself: and he lives this identity out in his paschal mystery, his self-sacrifice, his self-gift in generative love. What is most clearly expressed in the Johannine literature also exists in the Synoptics. The clear teaching about Jesus' identity in the Synoptic Gospels is just what it is in the Gospel according to St. John and in his epistles.

The service of Jesus is never anything less than the giving of himself in generative love: "to give his life as a ransom for the many" (Matt. 20:28). His passion is not to please others, such as his disciples James and John, by acceding to their requests. His passion, rather, is to love them. He expresses this love by giving his life, so that they are ransomed from sin and death and can enter into the fullness of life, even in ways that they themselves would not choose, and did not think they were choosing, when they entered into the community of Christ's disciples. But receiving life from Christ is always receiving his life on his terms, not on ours, so that we can be fully delivered from the sins and the death of our life and enter into his. Our entry into that life in this world is through the sacraments, and so I would like to pass now to the third form of Jesus Christ's revelatory self-gift in generative love made present and operative in the sacraments of the Church.

In the Sacraments

The first time I heard an evangelical Christian ask, "Have you been saved?" was when I was visiting the Oblates of Mary Immaculate in Argentina. I found myself on a plane with an American evangelical missionary. She was obviously a person who loved the Lord. She was a convinced disciple of Christ and very concerned about the Catholics of Argentina because she could not understand a number of things. She could not grasp the width, the expansion, of the act of faith in the Catholic Church, which is so much more inclusive than simply a faith that Jesus is our personal savior. Our faith includes also our understanding of the Church herself as part of divine revelation. Nor could she understand, as she saw it, the formalism of the Catholic way of being disciples, even though she recognized the good will of the people to whom she had very generously come to share her faith. She was puzzled by it.

She had never asked anyone in Argentina, "Have you been saved?" But perhaps because we were both Americans and that gave her courage, she put that question to me. She asked me sincerely, not as a way to trap me nor as a way to put me down, but because she was concerned about my salvation. I thought for a moment, because I had never been asked that question directly before, and I said simply, "Yes, I've been saved by Christ, but from within a sacramental system that demands my free participation." The use of the word "sacraments" caught her by surprise, and it began another discussion.

The sacraments are the effective and transforming means that give believers access to the saving mysteries of Jesus Christ. The sacraments do so objectively. They are acts of Christ. The Risen Christ acts now through the sacraments because he is totally free, not bound by space and time. He passes through a rock sealing a tomb and through closed doors: now you see him, now you don't. He is no longer restricted in any way, having passed through the great limitation of death itself, he now exists in a way that gives him total freedom. He can be anywhere he wants to be, and he wants to be with us. He is with us objectively and truly, no matter our own subjective weakness, through the sacraments of the Church. Across time and space, the sacraments make Christ's action in his paschal mystery present to believers who come to know in them that his redeeming and transforming grace is available to them.

Sacramental life is the will of the Father, the work of the Son, done in the power of the Holy Spirit.

While we commonly profess our faith that the sacraments effect what they signify, we can also say that they reveal what they effect. They make present Jesus' self-gift in generative love, his self-sacrifice for our salvation, and, simultaneously, they reveal in his self-gift his own disclosure of the Father as the absolute mystery for us of self-gift in generative love.

The effective presence and revelation of self-gift in generative love is most evident in the sacrament of the Holy Eucharist, in the Sacrifice of the Mass. The very earliest New Testament accounts of the words of institution indicate this. St. Paul draws on an ancient rabbinical formula to frame his account with reliability in his first letter to the Corinthians: "For I received from the Lord what I also handed on to you, that the Lord Jesus, on the night he was handed over, took bread, and, after he had given thanks, broke it and said, 'This is my body that is *for you*'" (1 Cor. 11:23–24). Similarly, in the Gospel according to St. Mark, we read: "While they were eating, he took bread, said the blessing, broke it, and gave it to them, and said, 'Take it; this is my body.... This is my blood of the covenant, which will be shed *for the many*'" (Mark 14:22, 24). The Eucharist reveals the self-sacrificing, self-giving generative love of Jesus Christ and makes this gift available to believers at all times and in all places. The meaning of Holy Thursday is Good Friday. The reality of the Eucharistic meal is the sacrifice on the cross.

The effective presence and revelation of Christ's gift of himself in generative love is also present, though not always seen in that way, in the sacrament of penance. Think of the scene from the Gospel according to St. John when the apostles were gathered in the upper room on Easter evening: "Jesus said to them again, 'Peace be with you. As the Father has sent me, so I send you.' And when he had said this, he breathed on them and said to them, 'Receive the Holy Spirit. Whose sins you forgive, they are forgiven them, and whose sins you retain, they are retained' " (John 20:21–23). In the mystery of Trinitarian communion, when Jesus breathes on the apostles and says "Receive the Holy Spirit," he makes the gift of himself. This gift of the Spirit with the gift of himself echoes the moment of Jesus' death on the cross. "When Jesus had taken the wine, he said, 'It is finished.' And bowing his head, *he handed over the spirit*" (John 19:30). Of course, this gift of the Spirit in love for the forgiveness of sins has a regenerating, a life-giving, purpose: to release the death-dealing bonds of sin and to enable repentant sinners to live born again in God's love.

In the sacramental economy, the presence and revelation of Christ's self-sacrifice, his self-gift in generative love, is also made manifest in the primordial sacrament of the Church herself and, more particularly, within the Church in the sacrament of marriage. This is evident in the letter to the Ephesians: "Husbands, love your wives, even as Christ loved the church and handed himself over for her to sanctify her, cleansing her by the bath of water with the word, that he might present to himself the church in splendor.... This is a great mystery, but I speak in reference to Christ and the church" (Eph. 5:25–27, 32). Christ, especially as depicted in the captivity epistles, is the bridegroom of the Church. He gives himself without reserve to her. He gives himself in love so that the Church may bring forth children for this life and the next. Husbands and wives in marriage mirror and sacramentally make present the relationship of Christ in his body the Church. They do so when they make the unqualified gift of self to one another in life-giving love.

These relationships and realities of Church and marriage indicate the critical importance of strengthening and protecting authentic life-long and life-giving married love. What is at issue is our acceptance in faith of Jesus' revelation of the Father, our participation in Christ's paschal mystery, and our life in the Church. The thread connecting these three dimensions of faith is always self-gift in generative love, self-sacrifice for others. These relationships underscore the critical importance of Pope Paul VI's encyclical letter *Humanae vitae* as an affirmation of the authentic meaning of Christian marriage. The pope wrote: Married love particularly reveals its true nature and nobility when we realize that it takes its origin from God, who "is love." ... Marriage ... is in reality the wise and provident institution of God the Creator, whose purpose was to effect in man His loving design. As a consequence, husband and wife, through that mutual gift of themselves, which is specific and exclusive to them alone, develop that union of two persons in which they perfect one another, cooperating with God in the generation and rearing of new lives (*Humanae vitae,* 8). When that unity begins to unravel in even a very small way, it ends in complete dissolution. Despite initial scoffing that the document's warnings were hyperbolic, all the aberrations and the defections from the Church's moral teaching foretold in *Humanae vitae* have, in fact, proven to be the case, even in some schools of Catholic moral theology. Practices and beliefs that were unthinkable forty years ago are now taught as morally possible and even desirable.

The sacramental economy in the Catholic Church is suffused with the mystery of Christ's paschal gift of himself in generative love, the gift that reveals the mystery of the Father for us as absolute self-giving and life-giving love. All the baptized participate in this holy mystery, and all are called to live it out in the self-sacrificing and life-giving love of Jesus Christ that reveals who the Father is. This is the sense of St. Paul's plea to the Christians in Rome: "I urge you, therefore, by the mercies of God, to offer your bodies as a living sacrifice, holy and pleasing to God, your spiritual worship" (Rom. 12:1). While Paul recommends this gift of self in generative love to all Christians, it has a particular resonance for priests, both for their identity, which conforms them to Christ as head of the Church, and in their mission and ministry, which bring forth life in their love for the Church.

In Holy Orders

We now move to a fourth set of reflections: how priests reveal the Father's love. By their ordination, priests are sacramentally conformed to Jesus Christ as Head and Shepherd of the Church. That is the distinctive relationship that becomes real, the ontological change that takes place in one who is ordained, different from the relationship that becomes real when we are baptized. The relationship to the Father, which is what sanctifies us in ourselves and is necessary for our salvation, is given in baptism. In holy orders, a new relationship is given, a relationship not to the Father but to the Church. Priests' sacramental conformity to Christ as head of the Church enables ordained priests to act in the name and person of Jesus Christ, not only to act on his behalf in the Church but also to stand sacramentally for him within the Church at the head of the body. The existence and presence of priests enable the Church to encounter her Lord and, through their ministry, to experience his transforming power and become both fruitful and faithful.

This is the synthesis offered by Pope John Paul II in *Pastores dabo vobis:*

> In the Church and on behalf of the Church, priests are a sacramental representation of Jesus Christ, the Head and Shepherd, authoritatively proclaiming his Word, repeating his acts of forgiveness and his offer of salvation, particularly in Baptism, Penance, and the Eucharist, showing his loving concern to the point of a total gift of self for the flock, which they gather into unity and lead to the Father through Christ and in the Spirit. In a word, priests exist and act in order to proclaim the Gospel to the world and to build up the Church in the name and person of Christ the Head and Shepherd. (no. 15)

Who priests are (their identity) and what they do (their ministry) are intimately attached to priesthood's purpose: their mission. As the pope said again in *Pastores dabo vobis,* "Their mission is not theirs but is the same mission of Jesus." His mission, his being sent, is both to reveal and to effect the Father's plan of regenerating love. Priests reveal, as Christ revealed, the Father as the source of all life, all holiness, all love. This is well summarized in the introductory prayer of the third canon of the Mass. Priests reveal the Father as absolute self-giving and life-giving love that heals and transforms us and draws all to share in the very life of the Triune God: Father, Son, and Holy Spirit. As sacramental signs of Jesus Christ and therefore as revealers of the Father, priests share in a spiritual fatherhood. What kind of life is the life of priests? Let us consider its integrity, its unity, its integration, and its transparency.

In Priestly Life and Ministry

Because ordained priests share in and continue the mission of Christ to reveal the Father, they also share in spiritual fatherhood. This is St. Paul's conviction when he speaks to his beloved and troubled Corinthian community: "Even if you should have countless guides to Christ, yet you do not have many fathers, for I became your father in Christ Jesus through the gospel" (1 Cor. 4:15).

Integrity of Life and Priestly Virtues

People come to priests not because priests are sinless. If ever anybody imagined that to be the case, they know differently now. If there was a kind of hubris attached to priesthood, and if that disappears now, that will be a purification and will be beneficial for the Church and for priests themselves. But people will continue to come to priests because they know they must gather around them if they are to be visibly one in Christ. It is in the ordained priesthood that Christ's authority for the salvation of his people is exercised and made visible. Authority is given to priests to give life to others: God's own life for the salvation of the world. That means that in a priest's life there must be a certain integrity. I think of my father's first, less than enthusiastic response when I told him I wanted to be a priest. "Well," he said, "if you're going to be a priest, at least be a good one." Had he met bad ones, priests wanting in integrity? The integrity of any Christian life is protected by virtues, which are habits of life that enable us without a constant struggle to live fittingly with the grace that Christ wants to give us in this life so that we may have its fulfillment in the life to come.

Since the Second Vatican Council, we have spoken about the primary virtue of ordained priests as pastoral charity. Before the Council, the primary virtue of priests was usually described as zeal. *A good priest is a zealous priest.* That remains true. A priest is zealous for the salvation of the world. But the reinterpretation of zeal as pastoral charity in the documents on priesthood in the Council and since the Council is an advance in understanding of what habits a priest needs to live his life with integrity. Pastoral charity indicates not only zeal for the salvation of the world but also love for the world. One cannot evangelize anyone he doesn't love. One cannot speak of evangelizing a culture unless one is able to participate in it and show that he loves it. A zealot is not an evangelizer. Only someone whose life is marked by love has the ability to reveal the Father's self-giving in generative love for the world. There is in pastoral charity not a general love but an ascetic love. If a priest is truly pastoral, he is sacrificing himself for the people. The type of availability to the people that is intrinsic, that is integral, to priestly ministry is a form of spiritual ascesis, a form of penance and self-discipline. Pastoral charity is a self-sacrificing love. That is the primary virtue that should inform the life of priests. But it has to be protected by other priestly virtues that help ensure that pastoral charity is always vital. Let us look at three of these virtues: faith, obedience, and chastity.

FAITH

All priestly virtue is a habit of surrendering oneself to Christ for the sake of his people. In the virtue of faith there is a surrender of one's mind. Faith is a virtue that is infused and also one that grows as we come to study and understand the contents of the act of faith in a more explicit fashion. It is a great tragedy when the Creed, which is a proclamation of praise and thanksgiving because God has revealed the truths that make us free, is interpreted as a loyalty oath. It tells us that some do not understand the connection between freedom and truth. Without an understanding of the intrinsic connection between freedom and truth, the Christian anthropology that undergirds the Council's teaching and that was explicit in Pope John Paul II's magisterium cannot be understood. If freedom is simply the expression of individual autonomous choice and if truth is at best regulative, then it is important to know the truth only so that you don't make too many mistakes in your choices. What is lost in this analysis is the sense in which truth is perfective of the person who knows the truth. Truth makes us free because we ourselves are less than what we should be if we live in falsehood. Truth is not just a question of conforming our mind to a particular reality; it's a question of perfecting our very selves. In discovering who we are, we become truly free. Without knowing the truth about ourselves, we are enslaved to falsehood. The intrinsic connection between freedom and truth, however, is not easy to establish in the kind of society in which we live now. In order to find the connection between truth and freedom, we have to surrender our minds to Christ in faith; we have to surrender our intelligence to what God has revealed in Christ and what is handed on in the Church.

Is the priest, then, not supposed to question? Questioning is necessary for a deeper understanding of revealed mysteries. As Cardinal Newman said, "A thousand difficulties do not make a doubt." If one has never had any difficulty, he doesn't understand the faith very well, because God's mind is not ours. To get our puny minds around revealed truth means facing difficulties in understanding. A priest's life is marked by faith, given in the surrender of his mind to God's self-revelation in Christ Jesus, as that is handed on in the Church's definitive teaching.

OBEDIENCE

Besides the virtue of faith, the virtue of obedience is also necessary to have an integrated priestly life. The virtue of obedience also enjoins a specific surrender, a surrender of will, a surrender of one's self-purpose, an acceptance of the plan of one's life as a mission, as something given us by another. If that surrender of will is not part of a priest's life, eventually, even his very effective pastoral ministry will divide the Church. In the Church, the mission is Christ's, and the purity of mission is protected by the virtue of obedience, by a surrender of one's will.

CHASTITY

Besides faith and obedience, there is the virtue of chastity. Chastity is a matter of priestly integrity, and in the Latin Rite in the Western Church, chastity is lived in celibacy. The Latin Church calls to ordained priesthood those who accept the gift of celibacy for the sake of the kingdom of heaven. It is from this group of men who have experienced the call to celibacy that the Church in normal practice chooses those who will be ordained priests. In the Latin Church, normal discussion of a priestly vocation begins with this understanding. Celibacy becomes a burden if it is only extrinsically attached to what one really wants, namely, to be an ordained priest. Then there is a constant struggle and, often, resentment shapes one's life. The priest lives with the conviction that "the Church has imposed this condition on me." One cannot be the revelation of the Father's love, one cannot give his life for the sake of generating new children in the Church, if his life is mired in resentment. Priestly resentment will destroy the Church as well as the priest. Pope John Paul II, again in *Pastores dabo vobis,* spoke of celibacy as something to be "welcomed and continually renewed with a free and loving decision as a priceless gift from God, as an 'incentive to pastoral charity,' as a singular sharing in God's fatherhood and in the fruitfulness of the Church, and as a witness to the world of the eschatological Kingdom" (no. 29). Celibacy is "a singular sharing in God's fatherhood."

Samuel Cardinal Stritch was the archbishop of Chicago when I was a very young boy. He was a kind man, a truly fatherly man. Toward the end of his life, he was named by Pope Pius XII to be head of the Congregation for the Evangelization of Peoples as it is called now, Propaganda Fide as it was called then. It seems he didn't want to leave Chicago; perhaps he knew that he wasn't well. But he went in obedience, and he lasted about a month in Rome before he died. On the boat across the Atlantic, he must have suffered a stroke. The blood to his arm was cut off. When he arrived in Naples, they took him immediately to Rome, and the doctors decided that they were going to have to remove his arm in order to save his life. There was some concern among the physicians about how Cardinal Stritch would react to the news. They told his secretary, Msgr. James Hardiman, that he was going to have to tell the cardinal that he had to lose his arm. Msgr. Hardiman went in to the cardinal's sick room and said, "Your Eminence, you know that you're not well. The surgeons have said that, in order to save your life, they need to cut off your arm." The cardinal replied, "Father, tell the surgeons not to worry. When I became a subdeacon, I surrendered my body to Christ. Let the surgeons do what they have to do." So his arm was taken off and brought back to Chicago. A month later the rest of his body was brought back to Chicago and buried there.

Here is a revelation of what celibacy means for a priest: it is a surrender of your body so that it is no longer yours; it is in the hands of the Lord to whom we give ourselves for the sake of the Church.

Through their practice of celibacy, priests live out the "nuptial meaning" of the body, as Pope John Paul II has identified it, that is, understanding the body as a way of communion and an instrument of the self-giving that animates all authentic human sexuality. Additionally, a celibate priest, precisely through his celibacy, his gift of self in generative love, awaits "in a bodily way, the eschatological marriage of Christ with the Church, giving himself... completely to the Church in the hope that Christ may give himself to the Church in the full truth of eternal life" (*Pastores dabo vobis,* 29). Celibacy is then, at one and the same time, self-gift in generative love to Jesus and a revelation of Jesus' own gift of self in generative love to the Church which, in turn, reveals the saving love of the Father for the salvation of the world.

The popular conception of celibacy as a form of asexuality entirely misses the mark. For a diocesan priest, celibacy is the practical and real way that he lives his existence as a sexual being. If sexuality involves connection, celibacy is a path of communion. If sexuality involves generativity, celibacy is a path of giving spiritual life. If sexuality is sacramental in the sense of being disclosive of the divine, celibacy is a path par excellence of revealing Jesus and the Father who sent him. Celibacy for priests is a way of being married to the Church. It's not to be a way of life that would leave priests ecclesiastical bachelors. Much contemporary writing on sexuality and celibacy focuses on the relational dimensions of celibate living. In our kind of culture, sexuality is a means of forming relationships. What is sacrificed in celibacy is intimacy more than anything else. In other cultures, particularly among tribal peoples, it's not intimacy that is sacrificed with celibacy; it's children. In our culture, if you are not having sex with someone, somehow you are not adult.

In other cultures, if you are not bringing forth children, you are not a man. In our kind of culture, the crisis of celibacy arises from a lack of genital relationship, and we speak about a fear of loneliness, a loss of intimacy.

All of us, in whatever state of life we are called to, are destined to be both persons of communion and persons who want progeny. How is it that celibacy connects? How is it that celibacy gives life or makes someone a life-giver? Paul VI's encyclical *Humanae vitae* linked the unitive and procreative dimensions of conjugal love. This vision, however, can be expanded across a wider range of experience to include celibate sexuality, both as communion and as generativity.

The virtue of celibacy is most frequently brought into contention when the future of the priesthood is discussed in our society. But chastity as a priest, that is, celibacy for the sake of the kingdom, along with obedience and faith, are all forms of surrender in order to make pastoral charity the central virtue of our lives. It is pastoral charity that integrates our life. A few words about integration and transparency will complete these reflections on priestly life.

Integration of Priestly Life

If a priest's spiritual fatherhood is to be lived out authentically, he must be committed to a process that constantly, through ongoing formation and transformation, brings his life together in integrated ways. Again in *Pastores dabo vobis,* the continuing integration of priestly identity and functions or services for the sake of mission in communion with Christ and the Church signals movement toward unity of life. Integration of life draws together and dynamically relates who we are, what we do, and what we are about: our identity, our ministry, and our mission. These have to come together in a unity around the one thing that is necessary: the Gospel and God's self-generative love for our salvation. If a priest is to be at his ease as a spiritual father in the Church, he must have an increasingly clear sense of himself as spiritual father and link that identity explicitly to the particular ways that he serves: the proclamation of the Word, the celebration of the sacraments, the giving of a shepherd's care to a community, the fostering of the unity of the Church, and the tending to the Church's fidelity to her apostolic foundations.

Among the means for cultivating this integrated sense of spiritual fatherhood are prayer, reflection, spiritual direction, holy conversation, and priestly fraternity. These are the necessary means that enable us to unify our life not just as individuals but as members of the presbyterate. The priestly charity that we spoke of as the foundational virtue of priestly life is impossible without priestly fraternity. The pastoral charity that we exercise with our people has to be exercised within a priestly fraternity. Nobody ministers alone in the Church, just as nobody goes to Christ alone. We always come to him together, as his body; and priests always minister together as a presbyterate, as a priestly fraternity. The ways that are available to a priest to increase prayer, to deepen it, to have moments of reflection, to have good spiritual direction, and to strengthen the bonds of priestly fraternity are all necessary to virtuous priestly life.

This approach to spiritual fatherhood moves in a direction that is not always understood, because we Americans are a very functional, pragmatic people. Life is divided into different sections. We have "how-to" books on how to be a good father, and they usually reduce fatherhood to functions rather than understanding it as a relationship. Priestly life, too, can be reduced to functions, to ministry, instead of seeing priesthood as a relationship that permeates everything, including one's "free" time.

Transparency of Priestly Life

A generation ago, Jean Laplace, a French spiritual writer, wrote about the transparency of spiritual fatherhood in this way: "[The spiritual father's] fatherhood is the more real as it becomes a pure transparency for the unique Fatherhood of God and knows its dependence on the one Spirit who alone guides our hearts."[2]

Laplace held that, in order to maintain this authentic sense of fatherhood by participation in God's fatherhood, the priest has to practice detachment. Of course, detachment is necessary to undergo the surrender that characterizes the life of virtue. Like John the Baptist, who was the bearer of the Father's word announcing the coming of the Word made flesh, those who share spiritual fatherhood must be completely invested, as any good father is, and also thoroughly detached, as is any created representative of God.

Think of how a married man works out his salvation. He leads his own life, he does his own thing, he's attracted to a woman, he eventually comes to love her, to know that his own identity is bound up with his relationship to her. Then in marriage he sacrifices himself for the good of his wife and for the good of their children.

This integration and the transparency that are internal to married life are not characteristic of professional life as such. Married life is not a profession, and neither is priestly life. I make this point because, in trying to renew priestly life, we've sometimes been tempted to model it after other professions. Being a priest is then understood as similar to being a doctor or lawyer. But ordained priesthood is a vocation. Like a professional, the priest serves, but the service of a professional person is on the profession's own terms. In the medical profession, one speaks about quality control or scientific control. Controlling, even for the sake of service, marks a profession. Priestly life, however, is marked by a surrender for the sake of service. In other words, what you do is not done on your own terms. You work for the good of others, as does a professional, but on someone else's terms. Your identity is given you on Christ's terms — it's a received identity — and your ministry is on the Church's terms. You don't control the people you serve. You set them free. You surrender your life to them on their terms and on

Christ's terms, not on your own. In that sense, priesthood is not a profession, and we are ill-served by taking too closely the professional model as a way to priestly renewal. Not that priesthood does not have elements of a profession. There is control of a body of knowledge, of the theology that explains the faith. Being a learned group of men is all part of our life. But none of that is most basic. What's most basic is the surrender that we've been talking about, made possible through our intense love of the Lord. As Pope Benedict XVI has written, a primary role of priests is to be witnesses to Christ: "There is absolutely no need for the priest to know all the latest, changing currents of thought; what the faithful expect from him is that he be a witness to the eternal wisdom contained in the revealed word."[3]

Lastly, the priest has to be transparent to Christ, particularly through his use of the sacrament of penance, in which we experience God as merciful Father. In *Dives in misericordia,* Pope John Paul II described mercy as a love that is eager to forgive. Our own experience of God's mercy in the sacrament of penance will mark our life with the quality of love eager to forgive.

To live authentically the vocation of spiritual fatherhood as a priest involves detachment, the surrender of oneself, apostolic asceticism, the investing of oneself passionately while being able to move on when the mission calls us elsewhere. This ascetical practice also preserves spiritual fatherhood from becoming a suffocating paternalism. Every good father, following the pattern of our Heavenly Father, wants his children to be free; and priestly ministry, therefore, is never a form of manipulation.

Conclusion

I have tried to sum up briefly the qualities of priestly life under the rubrics of integrity, integration, and transparency in order to indicate how priests are to live their identification with Jesus Christ in his paschal mystery; how they are to function as spiritual Fathers in the Church; how they are to participate in the divine mystery of self-gift in generative love and to continue Jesus' mission to reveal the Father. In their words, their actions, their very lives, priests echo the words of Jesus: "The One who sent me is true and what I heard from him, I tell the world" (John 8:26). Priests now tell the world urgent truths at a moment of great danger for the Church: when in this country, which prides itself on religious freedom, our freedoms are being restricted through courts and legislatures; when our life will probably be more and more controlled, and we do not really know what dangers await us in the future. This is, therefore, a wonderful moment to be a priest, called to live in self-sacrifice, to love the Church as Christ loves the Church, and to model in this love the Father's will for the world's salvation and joy.

Chapter 13

Worship in the Church

Questions That Test Ecclesial Renewal

T HE CHURCH DISCOVERS HER IDENTITY when she worships the Lord as He wants to be worshiped. The Second Vatican Council's Decree on the Sacred Liturgy, *Sacrosanctum concilium* (1963), remains a document of keen interest because of the central and crucial role of liturgy in the life of the Church. Putting the Latin liturgy into the world's vernacular languages has been an ongoing challenge, and the greater accessibility of the extraordinary form of the Roman Rite has occasioned new debate about the conciliar reform of the liturgy.

Because the subject is broad, vast, and difficult to summarize, I would like to consider a number of areas of research that remain to be explored even after many decades of such liturgical scholarship. These areas are the relationships between: "creativity and fidelity; spiritual worship and life; catechesis and the celebration of the Mystery; presiding at the liturgy and the role of the congregation; and seminary formation and the continuing formation of priests."[1] There remains yet another aspect of the liturgical reform that requires further study: its philosophical and anthropological foundations. I will sketch out some of the main questions relating to these areas, and it is my hope that the questions thus formulated might spark investigations that are more scholarly and in-depth in an area that requires interdisciplinary collaboration. This approach also brings to the fore many pastoral considerations that have arisen because of liturgical change.

My own belief is that liturgical renewal after the Council was treated as a program or movement for change, without enough thought being given to what happens in any community when its symbol system is disrupted. The liturgical calendar, for example, is the place where time and eternity meet, when our experience of duration transcends itself through contact with the Creator of time and history. To change the liturgical calendar means to change our way of relating to God. Since we are not pure intellects but embodied spirits whose reasoning involves imagination, space, and time, changing liturgical time also means that the doctrines expressing the Church's faith, the thinking of the Church, will be affected. Every bishop has been asked: "Since we no longer recognize certain saints on the Church's calendar, why can't the Church change her teaching on sexual morality, on women's ordination, and on other contested doctrines?" A change in space, in architecture, and in the placement of altars and other liturgical furnishings has a similar effect, as has a change in language, which carries and conditions our thinking and evaluating. A change in liturgy changes the context of the Church's life. When the archdiocese of Chicago was introducing the changes mandated by the new *General Instruction of the Roman Missal* (third typical edition), I remarked that the changes were "minor." A lay woman in my diocese replied: "Cardinal, there are no minor changes in liturgy." She was entirely correct!

I raise some questions here in order to clarify the presuppositions of liturgical change and so to advance the liturgical renewal with self-conscious attention to pastoral context as well as to liturgical theory. My points are raised not to bring the renewal itself into question, but to strengthen its call to the Church and its effects in the Church. Since the reform took participation as its hallmark, there are two lines of inquiry: (1) Who is the subject of the liturgy? and (2) How does that subject participate in the liturgy? I will look at the subject from three different angles — theological, philosophical, and anthropological — in each case asking what has yet to be explored.

A Theological Approach

The Subject of the Liturgy

Who is the subject of the liturgy? *Sacrosanctum concilium* (*SC*) 7, continuing in the line of Pope Pius XII's 1947 encyclical letter *Mediator Dei*, defines the liturgy as "an exercise of the priestly office of Jesus Christ." Hence it is the whole Christ, head and members, who is the subject of the liturgy. The text goes on to say that the earthly liturgy is a participation in heavenly worship (*SC* 8): This affirmation expands the subject of the liturgy to include the heavenly host of angels and saints. Since the first section of *SC* ("The Nature of the Liturgy and Its Significance in the Life of the Church") is deliberately brief, these important points are not further developed. Aspects of the theology of the liturgy were taken up again in *Lumen gentium* and *Dei Verbum*, and this area of liturgical theology has been the subject of serious reflection in the last forty years.

The greatest magisterial development of this issue, however, can be found in the *Catechism of the Catholic Church* (*CCC*). This surely fits under the category of development of doctrine, because the *Catechism*'s treatment of the subject of the liturgy takes a significant step forward that is at once disarmingly simple and wonderfully profound. The liturgy is *Opus Trinitatis*, the work of the Holy Trinity (*CCC* 1077, title).[2] While *SC* focuses on the Christological aspect of the liturgy, the new Catechism meditates at length on the role of the Father and of the Holy Spirit as well. In fact, it is the relatively lengthy section on the Holy Spirit (*CCC* 1091–1109) that makes a remarkable contribution to a new Trinitarian understanding of the liturgy.

While the Catechism cites *SC* 8 verbatim on the heavenly liturgy (*CCC* 1090), it also goes a step further by devoting nine paragraphs (*CCC* 1136–1144) to the question "Who celebrates the liturgy?" First of all, there are the celebrants of the heavenly liturgy — the Father, Son, and Holy Spirit; the persons of the Trinity are the primary actors in the liturgy. Then come the all-holy Mother of God, the heavenly powers, all creation, biblical saints, the martyrs, and the great multitude of the elect. The earthly liturgy exists not by itself, but in relation to the heavenly liturgy. The celebrants of the sacramental liturgy include the entire body of Christ extending through time and space, and then the local celebrating assembly, ordered hierarchically in such a way that each person has his or her proper role.

Clarity about the theological subject of the liturgy is crucial. In the postconciliar period, a limited understanding of the "People of God" has often led to a limited, horizontal concept of the subject of the liturgy. It is important that this wonderfully complete vision of the liturgy, earthly united to heavenly, become better known and then internalized and lived.

Participation in the Liturgy

Theologically, how does the earthly liturgy participate in the heavenly liturgy? The question of participation is the overriding preoccupation of *SC.* The text refers over and over to a participation that is *sciens, actuosa, fructuosa, conscia, plena, pia, facilis, interna, externa,* and so on. But *how* does that participation take place?[3] Here the conciliar document is rather reticent. Here also the last forty years have given us examples of participation that range from the sublime to the ridiculous. Once again, it is the Catechism that makes significant strides in this area. The Church participates in the liturgy by *synergy.* This idea comes from the fruitful synthesis of Father Jean Corbon, whose insights in his book *Wellspring of Worship*[4] appear later in the Catechism. Participation is the common work or synergy between divine initiative and human response. The agent who makes participation possible is the Holy Spirit: "When the Spirit encounters in us the response of faith which he has aroused in us, he brings about genuine cooperation. Through it, the liturgy becomes the common work of the Holy Spirit and the Church" (*CCC* 1091). The Holy Spirit prepares the faithful to receive Christ (*CCC* 1093–98), recalls the mystery of Christ (*CCC* 1099–1103), makes present the mystery of Christ (*CCC* 1104–7), and brings about that communion which is an anticipation of the fullness of communion with the Holy Trinity (*CCC* 1107–9). In fact, the most intimate cooperation, or synergy, of the Holy Spirit and the Church is achieved in the liturgy (*CCC* 1108). Without insistent reference to the Holy Spirit, the Holy Eucharist might easily come to be imagined as a re-creation of the Last Supper, a sort of memorial tableau, rather than a re-presentation in unbloody, symbolic forms of the sacrifice of Calvary.

In the magisterium of the Church—in particular in *SC* and the Catechism of the Catholic Church—the liturgical subject is clearly delineated from a theological point of view, and the question of participation at its most profound theological level is wonderfully elaborated. Much remains to be done to communicate this teaching more effectively and to internalize it, but the teaching itself is clear.

What is less clear is its philosophical underpinnings. Under this rubric we will consider the nature of the human person who celebrates the liturgy.

A Philosophical Approach

The Human Subject of the Liturgy

Who is the human subject of the liturgy? The human person as the subject of the liturgy can be considered philosophically from three points of view. First, *SC* refers to the subject of the liturgy simply as *homo*. It is clear that the text is referring to man as such in a generic sense. The fields of study here are the philosophy of man and epistemology. The questions are: What is the nature of the human person and how does he know? These are areas that the Council did not have explicitly on its agenda. Second, *SC* also uses the term *fidelis*, or man as a Christian believer. The discipline here is theological anthropology; the conciliar constitution, *Gaudium et spes*, took some first steps, but its use of terms such as "modern man" and "the modern world" lack a clearly defined framework for their interpretation, a lack that has had unfortunate effect for the development of liturgical forms in postmodern mass culture.[5] In this situation, the question becomes more specific: How does the believer know divine realities? Third, anthropologists have coined the phrase *homo liturgicus*, since we are dealing with human beings as they live and act in a liturgical and sacramental context. This is a new category of philosophical investigation, unknown to the Council Fathers, where the waters are not yet completely charted. The philosophical question then becomes: How does the human person who believes come to know divine realities as communicated in the liturgy?[6]

These questions point to vast and complex fields of study, the investigation of which is needed in order to be in a better position to address contemporary questions of liturgical reform. We can do no more than give a brief historical sketch here of some of the main themes in these areas of philosophical anthropology and note the questions they raise.

I. PAULINE ANTHROPOLOGY

St. Paul's letters reveal a sophisticated anthropology, difficult to put into a system. He speaks of the various constitutive elements of the human person as *soma* (body), *sarx* (flesh), *psyche* (soul), *pneuma* (spirit), *nous* (mind), and *kardia* (heart). How does the Christian, in these polyvalent aspects, know the world around him? How does faith use these elements to help the human person to grasp the things of God?

2. PATRISTIC ANTHROPOLOGY

In patristic ascetical theology, one frequently finds a description of the soul as tripartite: the *logikon,* or rational part; the *thumikon,* or irascible part; and the *epithumikon,* or concupiscible part. How does the human person, understood in this way, respond to the exterior world? How does the human person apprehend reality in liturgical prayer by means of reason, emotion, and sense perception? This is a classic synthesis that has remained a constant point of reference for theological reflection throughout the centuries. The reflection of the Greek Fathers and the Eastern Churches should become a more familiar source for Latin Catholics.

3. THOMISTIC ANTHROPOLOGY

When St. Thomas asks the question of the specific powers of the soul (ST Ia, q. 78, a. 1), he takes the triple distinction of the tradition (the soul described as rational, sensitive, and vegetative) and develops it with extraordinary subtlety and insight. At the risk of grossly oversimplifying, we can say that the vegetative part includes nutritive, augmentative, and generative elements; the sensitive part includes the five exterior senses as well as five interior senses (common sense, fantasy, imagination, and the estimative and memorative senses); and the intellectual part includes aspects such as memory, understanding, and will.

It would be worthwhile for his tightly ordered reasoning to be unpacked and explained again for the sake of the nonspecialist as well as for liturgical scholars, for here is a very sophisticated analysis of how human beings know, how they perceive both interior realities and the exterior world in which they live. This kind of philosophical reasoning could be more helpful in trying to understand how *homo liturgicus* perceives natural and supernatural realities.[7]

4. ENLIGHTENMENT ANTHROPOLOGY

In terms of epistemology, the Enlightenment rationalist position affirms that reason alone is the source of knowledge and the ultimate test of truth. Revelation is not a specific source of knowledge. Human powers other than reason, such as sense perception, imagination, and intuition, are less sources of knowledge than distractions from thinking. While positive elements of rationalist thought can be seen in a rejection of prejudice, ignorance, and superstition, the logical consequence of the rationalist narrowing of our cognitive abilities sooner or later leads to the profound secularization and intellectual impoverishment experienced in the Western world today.

A moderate Enlightenment position would grant worship some role in human life, since religion has as its purpose, according to this point of view, the inculcation of moral virtue. When religious instruction, not the worship of God, was seen as the central point of Church services, the liturgy was more or less reduced to a pedagogical aid.

There are studies today in German[8] and English[9] that argue that the roots of the twentieth-century liturgical movement, and hence of the post-conciliar liturgical reforms, lie in the Enlightenment, with all the attendant positive and negative consequences. These studies merit serious attention.

For our purposes, the question here is how man, understood in this rationalistic sense, interacts with the world and understands supernatural realities. Has he lost the capacity for worship?

5. ROMANTIC ANTHROPOLOGY

It is not surprising that the extraordinary force of Enlightenment thought would provoke an equal and opposite reaction. The Romantic response was to emphasize all those things that rationalism denied: sense experience, imagination, intuition, sentiment. This experiential emphasis became the hallmark of a new movement in art and literature. In the life of the Church, the positive aspects of this movement were a rediscovery of the medieval period, a new God-centeredness, and a high theology of the Church as the mystical body of Christ. Romanticism is not without its negative consequences, however, such as piety without dogma, subjectivism, an exaggerated emphasis on feeling, and a kind of deification of "cosmic nature." How does man know? The Romantic answer is usually: He feels. The Church has usually allowed for a greater expanse of emotional display in public devotions other than sacramental worship.

6. CONTEMPORARY PERIOD

The contemporary period seems to be heir to this dichotomy between the Enlightenment and Romantic movements. The dominant view is still a rationalist one, but the vigor of the Romantic reaction is striking. It is ironic that in his encyclical *Fides et ratio,* John Paul II would have to defend reason itself in the face of a massive movement of popular culture toward New Age spiritualism. In the area of the liturgy, this same dichotomy finds expression in a multitude of ways. The reality is a complex one, different in different places, but liturgical polarization between a rationalist and a Romantic position is common, and few people seem to have the tools necessary to move beyond the present impasse.[10]

A curious concept that seems to be pervasive, an idea born of evolutionary theories and the experience of scientific progress in the nineteenth and twentieth centuries, is that the human race is always progressing, getting better and better. The myth of human progress replaces salvation history. Since modern people are more advanced than in ages past, they cannot be understood using categories of earlier times. While it is true that technological changes have revolutionized the way we live, how true is it that human *nature* has changed? *SC* gives an impression of ambiguity in this regard, referring frequently to the need to adapt liturgical structures and forms to the needs of our time (*SC* 1), to contemporary needs and circumstances (*SC* 4). It is necessary to explore the question of how every age needs to adapt to the demands of liturgical worship, as well as how liturgy adapts to contemporary demands.

Participation in the Liturgy

How does the personal human subject participate in the liturgy? Given the polyvalent reality that is the human person and the difficulties of formulating how the individual subject knows, it is with some caution that we approach the topic of participation philosophically. *SC* appears to set up a dual approach. First of all, the Christian people must understand; then they will be able to participate.

To foster understanding, the Council places a heavy emphasis on catechesis and instruction (see *SC* 35/3). Our understanding of liturgy should be readily accessible or easy (*facile*) (see *SC* 21, 50, 59, 79, etc.). If we apply the tripartite anthropology discussed above, it seems that the conciliar text emphasizes a rational understanding of *ritus et preces* (rites and prayers). Intuition and imagination are not discussed, nor the apprehension of reality by sense experience explored. In all fairness, it should be said that *SC* does not pretend to give an exhaustive treatment of liturgical epistemology, nor could the Council Fathers have possibly imagined the diverse cultural and pastoral situations that would arise in subsequent years, which would require a more nuanced and sophisticated treatment of this topic.

By understanding the liturgy more easily, so the reasoning goes, the Christian believer is better able to participate in it. While the conciliar text mentions interior as well as exterior participation (SC 19), and states that sacred silence is also a form of participation (SC 30), the emphasis is on verbal response and physical gesture (SC 30) In fact, the postconciliar experience is one of an extremely verbal liturgy with much activity going on. The more profound understanding of participation, not in the external, visible sense, but in the sacramental, internal, and invisible dimension,[11] is not elaborated by *SC*. What is needed, therefore, is a more unified vision of the human person and a more profound understanding of liturgical participation. The human person understands the liturgy by means of reason, without a doubt. The best and brightest intellect has ample material for reflection in the rich complex of truths that the liturgy expresses. At the same time, the human person experiences the liturgy through emotion and feeling, through an aesthetic appreciation of beauty, through the intuitive making of connections, through associations that take place on the subliminal level. This kind of human knowing should not be undervalued. And finally, the human person experiences the liturgy through the five senses, the human foundation of the sacramental system. This sensory experience has the capacity to open up spiritual realities, as the famous text of Tertullian says:

> The body is washed so that the soul may be freed from its stains; the body is anointed, so that the soul too may be consecrated; the body is signed, so that the soul too may be strengthened.[12]

In addition to a renewed philosophical investigation of human nature and how human subjects participate in the liturgy, a third field of needed study is that of cultural anthropology.

A Cultural Anthropological Approach

The Subject of the Liturgy

The cultural anthropologist examines not only the individual subject, but also the communal subject of the liturgy, that is, the ritual assembly. In the liturgy, the celebrating community is usually a heterogeneous gathering of people: old and young, rich and poor, "male and female, slave and free, Jew and Gentile" (as St. Paul says), from every level of society, gathered together not because of some common human element, but because God, who transcends every human category, calls them together. For such an unlikely combination of people to act together as one, something extraordinary must take place. From the theological point of view, what happens is the synergy between the Holy Spirit and the Church that we spoke about earlier. From an anthropological and sociological point of view, what happens is a specific kind of ritual behavior.

Participation in the Liturgy

The ritual assembly participates in the liturgy according to a complex set of rules and roles. The activity is ceremonious, formal, repetitive. What happens this Sunday is the same as what happened last Sunday, for authentic ritual functions according to disciplined patterns of habit and continuity. This kind of participation avoids spontaneity and on-the-spot adaptation in favor of the predictable and the familiar. The vehicle of expression includes words, but relies more heavily on symbols and symbolic actions. The more profound symbols, including words as verbal symbols, have many levels of meaning. They are "opaque," not susceptible to superficial or easy understanding. Symbols are always self-involving, objective in a way that incorporates the subjective. The qualities of beauty and holiness are communicated by signs that are the product of the highest cultural achievement. Immersion in the ritual action takes the participants out of themselves and transforms them. Numerous and rapid changes in ritual forms can produce estrangement and *anomie,* an experience reported by many of the faithful in the postconciliar years.

In recent decades, ritual activity has been the object of study by the relatively new discipline of social anthropology. This discipline began to come into its own a decade or so after the promulgation of *SC,* and thus the valuable insights of social anthropology were not available at the time of the drafting of the conciliar text and the implementation of liturgical reforms, although we can see perhaps an oblique reference in the assertion that liturgical change must respect the general laws of the structure and *mens* of the liturgy (*SC* 23). Aidan Nichols observes:

> The postconciliar *Consilium ad exsequendam Constitutionem de Sacra Liturgia* was wound up in 1975 through absorption into the Congregation for Divine Worship, that year coinciding more or less with a real turning point in the anthropology of religion as new schools of thought began to emphasize meaning, not explanation, the non-rational as well as the rational, and ritual's transformative power: all of which led to a new respect for the formal, ceremonious ordering of rite.[13]

From the point of view of social anthropology, it is not self-evident that simplicity in ritual form is more effective than complexity. It is not clear that a sign that is immediately intelligible will be more effective than a multifaceted symbol that reveals its meaning only over time. In short, simplifying ritual action will not necessarily bring about the greater understanding and more active participation desired by the Council.[14]

Further work in the area of social anthropology, then, could provide insight into the many open questions concerning liturgical participation.

Conclusion

We must hope that over forty years of experience since the promulgation of *SC* will lead us from a kind of naïve innocence to a wisdom shaped by pastoral shrewdness. The difference between the two, of course, is the knowledge of what advances holiness and what does not. Experience teaches us that in this area, which is absolutely central to the Church's life, an interdisciplinary approach can bear much fruit. While much work has been done in the area of liturgical theology, not enough has been done in the fields of philosophy, epistemology, and cultural anthropology. In addition to wise pastoral action in liturgical matters, what is also necessary is renewed, serious, and in-depth study of the open questions I have tried to delineate. This work has to be part of a critical rereading of the constitutions and other documents of Vatican II, so that liturgical renewal contributes more integrally to the renewal of the Church.

Chapter 14

A True Home Everywhere

John Paul II and Liturgical Inculturation

INCULTURATION OF THE LITURGY is less frequently developed in Pope John Paul II's writing than is inculturation of the faith, as we explored elsewhere.[1] John Paul II often spoke about inculturation because his own interest in philosophical anthropology moved him to make culture a necessary term for theological discourse. His reflections built on a few paragraphs in *Gaudium et spes*, to which he had contributed as a young bishop at Vatican II. About inculturating the liturgy, however, we have to look less at his personal writings than at some of the instructions issued over his signature, particularly the fourth General Instruction on the implementation of *Sacrosanctum concilium*, published by the Congregation for Divine Worship in 1994.

John Paul's encyclicals, especially on the Eucharist, and his instructions on liturgical discipline offer theoretical insights; but these do not address inculturation as fully as he addressed it in practice in the World Youth Day liturgies, in the liturgies at the conclusion of the continental synods, and on various other liturgical occasions when the pope met people in different countries and adjusted his style of liturgical celebration to their cultures. There, one saw his pastoral concern and theological understanding of inculturation working itself out in liturgy, sometimes in a very ad hoc way that wasn't to be so much a model as a response to the immediate occasion. His style of liturgical celebration, however, had an impact beyond the immediate celebration over which he was presiding.

Inculturation in the Church's Life

Behind the pope's concern for inculturation in all aspects of the Church's life lay his faith in the incarnation of the eternal Word of God, who took flesh among a particular people, speaking a particular language, at a particular time. The incarnational principle is the foundation for inculturation. Missiologists used to use "adaptation" and several other terms to describe the encounter between Christian faith and a particular culture, but they began in the 1960s to use "inculturate" to express the dialogue between faith and culture that challenges every evangelizer.

When the Eternal Word was made flesh, when the Son of God became man, born of the Blessed Virgin Mary, a new conversation between God and his human creatures took place. This conversation is always rooted in a particular culture because, precisely as humans, we are products of a culture to which, generation after generation, we in turn contribute. John Paul II used to talk about culture as "the realm of the human as such." As properly human creatures, we are not first of all products of biology, although our genes obviously contribute to who we are; but precisely as humans we are cultural beings: Nigerian, French, Chinese. The conversation between God and his human creatures is necessary because the human race created by God and the cultures created by human beings are good but fallen. Cooperation between God and his human creatures is possible because our nature, although fallen, is not totally corrupt, and neither are our cultures, wounded by sin though they are. Because grace is received as pure gift from God, it can transform us from within and it can also transform human cultures from within.

The late pope was convinced that not only was transformation or conversion of culture possible, but that it must happen if faith is to be faith. He often said that if faith is authentic, it must become culture, as the Word became man for our salvation. He was sensitive to cultural realities as he traveled, always meeting with cultural representatives from universities and the media world in a way that was novel in papal travels. He spoke to them about their own culture, often in their own words, he spoke to them of their history and what shaped their sense of identity as a particular human group, a people. In this, he was developing Vatican II's concern that the mission of the Church is to make Christ incarnate everywhere in the world, known and loved by all peoples who can find themselves in him, able to receive their identity purified and transformed in the person and work of their redeemer.

The purpose for calling the Second Vatican Council was to unite the entire world, all of nature and all nations, around Jesus Christ, the world's redeemer. The Council told the Church to look for events where God is at work in the world, although at work different from the way he works explicitly in salvation history, in the sacramental action of the Church, and in the proclamation of the Gospel itself. The evangelical conviction is that there is always something for faith to build on, that faith does not face a culture that has to be totally rejected because it is unable to be transformed. The Council taught the need to look for the signs of the times in historical events and to look for the *semina verbi,* the seeds of the Word in cultures and in the various religions of peoples to be introduced to Christ. The Church also looks for the *vestigia ecclesiae* in other Christian communities. Ours cannot be a religion withdrawn from the world. Faith trusts that the world can be reordered, that we can find something to build on as we proclaim who Christ is and introduce peoples with their diverse backgrounds and histories and cultures to their Redeemer.

This looking entails investigation and research. It entails projects for incorporating cultural elements into the faith in fresh ways in order to transform a culture. And it entails converting those elements of a culture that are resistant to the faith and that cannot be used for liturgy, for catechesis, or for expressing the faith in any way, elements of a culture that do have to be rejected. How to "investigate" a culture and the rules for inculturating faith and evangelizing culture in liturgical matters are to be found in the fourth General Instruction for the renewal of the liturgy, *Varietates legitimae* (1994). That Instruction presupposed *Vicesimus quintus annus* (1988), written for the twenty-fifth anniversary of the conciliar decree on the sacred liturgy.

Inculturation in the Church's Liturgy

Inculturating the liturgy entails approaching culture as a symbol system that is carried first of all by language. Inculturation allows liturgical gestures of the Roman Rite to remain uniform, at least in the beginnings of inculturation, but it encourages using the vernacular language. The use of the vernacular language for liturgical ceremonies, even though the gestures are to remain the same from language group to language group, presupposes that language, while in itself a symbol system, can change and yet meaning would remain the same. In other words, there could be a change of expression and yet the basic meaning would remain unaffected.

That was, I would argue, a rationalist presupposition on the part of Pope John XXIII and others over forty years ago. We have discovered since that time, through linguistic studies and through the experience of trying to keep a united liturgy bearing witness to the unity of faith, that a symbol system is always self-involving, involving the self in different ways depending upon the culture that is carried. The form of a language carries a message that qualifies the meaning of the words, and a vernacular language involves the native speaker in ways that a code, which liturgical Latin had become, does not. Latin was a highly useful instrument for keeping us involved in the history of the liturgy and for the transmission of the faith as it had come to us in many documents through the centuries, but something happens when prayer is put into the vernacular. There were so many wonderful devotions before the Second Vatican Council because the people, while appreciative of the liturgy and able to be united to the Lord through it, nonetheless wanted that self-involvement that only their own native tongue could bring them. Even people who are quite multilingual generally pray or go to confession in their first language. That is the language that involves them more intimately, involves their very selfhood in a way that other languages, while known, nonetheless do not.

Inculturating the liturgy through the use of contemporary English has to face the fact that English now is expressive of a society that sees itself as a collection of individuals; it is a language that has to some extent lost touch with its own history and therefore makes community across generations problematic. Using contemporary English in liturgical celebrations that presuppose and then strengthen a community of faith is even more problematic because the language has been so developed as a vehicle for individual self-expression. Just as our contemporary culture and its expressions make family life fragile and the society contentious so also, in the liturgy, contemporary English has to be stretched to transcend its own symbolic proclivities. I say that as introductory to what I'm going to write about the Fourth Instruction, because reflection on what has happened since the Second Vatican Council has shown that some of the presuppositions of forty years ago were naïve or even misguided.

The basic principle for beginning a process of inculturating the liturgy is that the unity of faith expressed in liturgy must be secure. If the faith itself is not firmly held, if it is not deeply understood and loved, then any move can be a false move. The Fourth Instruction's rules for inculturation involve legislation by the bishops' conferences in ways that may seem to reduce spontaneity. All suggestions for change can be explored, but they cannot be acted on without approval by the principle that keeps the visible community together, episcopal authority.

Legitimate Variations in Liturgical Expression

The Fourth Instruction starts out by acknowledging that there are different situations around the world. There are situations where the liturgy is celebrated only in the last decade or in the last generation, by peoples new to the faith and the Church. The newly converted faithful are carriers of a culture that has never been influenced or shaped or transformed by the Catholic faith, this by contrast to cultures that at one point were created in conversation with the Catholic faith but have now become more secularized. Because the Instruction points out that there are different situations around the world that have to be taken into account, the conversation on inculturation contains many topics and cannot be submitted to a single set of procedures. The Instruction privileges as normative: the language and culture of God's self-revelation. The memory of the first language of revelation and prayer should be carried by later translations from the scriptural and liturgical texts. There is no "essence" of faith devoid of any kind of linguistic expression in any human community. There is always in the later communities of faith the living memory of God's revelatory action in history:

> making promises to Abraham,
>
> calling his chosen people out of Egypt into slavery,
>
> giving commandments to Moses,
>
> reprimanding and encouraging through the prophets,
>
> and finally, in God's own time, revealing himself in Jesus, born of the Virgin Mary, crucified, died, and risen for our salvation.

In those cultures that first received God's self-revelation, there are elements that have to be echoed, that have to be carried along until Christ returns in glory. There is no public faith except as a response to historical events. In celebrating liturgy in Arabic in the Maronite Rite, the words of consecration in the canon of the Mass are sung in Aramaic with everyone, including the presiding priest, on their knees. The question of what has to be carried along in its original form and what can be transformed through translation is one object of inquiry when we begin raising questions about liturgical inculturation.

The requirements for inculturation of the liturgy, the document continues, are qualified not only by the fact that there are many different cultures and situations and that there are privileged cultures in this project; there is also the nature of the liturgy itself as the worship of the Church making present the paschal mystery of Jesus Christ, celebrated in local churches in a particular language but in universal communion. The transcendence of liturgical action to any particular culture or its forms must be evident. Any inculturation or experiment that does not respect these three facts will be destructive of liturgy and faith.

This instruction, given us under Pope John Paul II, reaches back to *Sacrosanctum concilium,* which also discusses, at least in passing, norms for adapting the liturgy to the temperaments and the traditions of peoples. In a very few paragraphs, the Second Vatican Council document talks about the culture of nations contributing to the liturgy, provided always that cultural contributions are free from superstition and error and harmonize with the authentic spirit of the liturgy. The spirit of the liturgy has been a much controverted topic ever since. In all cases, the substantial unity of the Roman Rite is to be preserved, but there can be variations in its use. Adaptations are to be made by the ecclesiastical authorities, especially in mission countries.

These adaptations are to be considered when the liturgical books are being revised, as the Council mandated. A first goal would be adaptation within the limits set by the editions of liturgical books for the administration of the sacraments, for sacramentals, processions, and sacred music and the arts. But there could also be a more radical inculturation. The Council Fathers spoke about an inculturation of the liturgy that would allow elements from particular cultures and traditions to be introduced into divine worship. In other words, gestures and elements of celebration, like diverse languages, would not be universal. This observation raises the possibility about separate rituals within the present Roman Rite. Any such development, however, has to be organic, fostered carefully in collaboration with local ecclesiastical authority, with the Holy See, and with the help of experts. Any such development will take a considerable amount of time and will never be merely the decision of a particular parish or a particular diocese at a particular time. It was the hope of the Council, as it had been the hope of the prior liturgical movement, that new practices in the liturgy would enable the Church to transform contemporary cultures, so that the faith may find a true home everywhere and elements of any culture may be used to worship God in spirit and in truth.

There was precedent for such a hope. The great historian of cultures Christopher Dawson pointed out that it was through the liturgy, more than through any other means, that the whole Christian world — Roman, Byzantine, and barbarian — found an inner principle of unity. "After the fall of the Roman Empire," wrote Dawson, "the Church possessed in the liturgy a rich tradition of Christian culture as an order of worship, a structure of thought, and a principle of life."[2]

In the nineteenth century, this vision inspired the beginnings of the modern liturgical movement, which appeared to find its fulfillment in the Vatican II Constitution on the Sacred Liturgy.

Msgr. Francis Mannion, the distinguished founder of the Liturgical Institute at Mundelein Seminary, commented in a comprehensive article, "The Crisis of Cultures": "The relationship between liturgy and culture continues to be one of the most complex and troublesome issues for the Church as she seeks to advance the reforms proposed by the Council." This observation explains why it has been easier to talk about inculturation of the faith before speaking about inculturation of liturgy. Inculturation of the liturgy is not possible unless the faith itself is firm in the hearts of people in a particular culture.

Modernity and Liturgy

Mannion suggested that the impact of modern culture in the United States is not mentioned in liturgical matters. The Council and Pope John Paul II talked about culture in the anthropological sense, that is, as ways of living that are the result of hundreds of years and, in the case of Catholic cultures, of particular ways of living inspired by the faith, building up ways of speech and of looking at things and celebrating feasts. But culture in the anthropological sense has been partly replaced by a more ideological culture that is developed not as a way of living but with a particular purpose. In modern times, these ideological cultures have a primary source in the French Revolution. Entire cultures have been reshaped quite deliberately — intentionally, not organically — in order to privilege certain values and to change the course of history itself.

The culture of modernity carries elements that are inimical to Catholic liturgy. Tracey Rowland observes, "The tendency towards lowest common denominator cultural standards, the instrumentalist account of language, the project of a thoroughly rationalistic 'Christianity,' the disjunction of form and substance, and hence symbol and meaning, the severance of the relationship between memory, tradition, and transcendence, the lop-sided emphasis on the immanence of God, at the expense of His transcendence" support an unwaveringly subjective view of beauty, goodness, and truth. Where negative cultural dynamics such as these are allowed to shape liturgy, the outcome is not only problematic, but dysfunctional.[3]

When the massive efforts toward renewal generated by the Second Vatican Council were interpreted by too many as an accommodation to modernity, the outcome could only be problematic for an authentic inculturation of worship and liturgy. Mannion mentions three negative cultural dynamics affecting the liturgy in this country. The first he calls the "subjectification of reality." This occurs when the individual person rather than institutions or traditions are made the center and origin of meaning and values. America regards individuals as the primary reality, and society and community and family are second-order realities. Many Americans will claim a personal rather than an ecclesial or social source for their religious beliefs. God is an inner voice or their personal conscience, rather than the voice that comes to us from community or from a historical revelation. Religion becomes a matter of personal choice, and personal conscience determines not just actions but the principles of morality. The institutions of Christian faith and practice — Holy Scripture, worship, preaching, ministry, received doctrines, ecclesiastical structures — are useful to the extent that they serve one's experience of inner truth and personal encounter with the divine. In such a perspective, the serious, the solemn, the dignified too easily give way to the trivial, the self-centered, the pragmatic. Pope John Paul II referred to this in his encyclical on the Eucharist (*Ecclesia de Eucharistica*, 52) where he said, "A certain reaction against 'formalism' has led some, especially in certain regions, to consider the 'forms' chosen by the Church's great liturgical tradition and her magisterium as non-binding."

When the sense of the sacred is localized in the self rather than in the ritual of the liturgy itself, liturgy becomes a resource for getting in touch with God in one's heart. The focus shifts from the transcendent God to God known in one's very self. Liturgy is perceived as the context in which to experience the divine presence and not the sacramental mediation of God's presence to us. Forms of the liturgy necessarily take on a certain experimental character as expressions of the interior dispositions of those taking an "active part" in the liturgy. The traditional and the official are easily replaced by forms made up and considered more consonant with the experience of the individuals or groups participating in the worship service. Another variation of this is to celebrate the liturgy, not following a calendar of saints given us by the Church's calendar but around chosen themes.

After the subjectification of reality, the second negative dynamic of modernity that affects inculturation confronting modernity and postmodernity is "intimacy." Our culture has come to place ultimate value on bonds of intimacy, personal closeness, and radical familiarity. Closeness among persons becomes a moral good, even the norm of all morality. This ideology of intimacy breaks down traditional customs, manners, and gestures that enable people to relate to larger realities; it leads to a loss of politeness and civility that also has ecclesiastical repercussions.

When I grew up on the streets of Chicago, we sang children's songs — "Ring Around the Rosey" and similar pieces — that came out of fourteenth-century London, although we didn't know their provenance or that they were handed on generation after generation by children to other children. Our parents didn't teach us those songs; we taught each other, older children to younger children. My great-nephews don't know those songs. Their songs come to them from the television programs that teach them something different every TV season. Music has to be applicable to this particular group, at this particular time, in ways that deliberately break our receiving something vital from the past, that interrupt tradition as a source of meaning and value.

In this context, the Church herself has come to be understood by many Catholics as primarily a club for individuals who share a similar religious experience. The Church's goal and purpose are largely to give a sense of belonging, to create small internal communities, even when there are large numbers of believers. We situate altars so that everybody can get a sense of being in close contact with everybody else. The idealization of small groups has tended to make some liturgical celebrations more of a gathering for the like-minded, with a weakened sense of the universal Church's unity and diversity. Religion becomes a personal attitude that hardly impinges on the public world and has no right to speak on public issues, even if they have a moral dimension. The personalities and charismatic qualities of the clergy and liturgical ministers take on an undue importance and become the arbiters of good liturgy. Liturgical rites and truths themselves lose their capacity to engage the Christian community with society, tradition, and history. The power of the liturgy to affect the public culture is diminished.

The third of the negative dynamics of modernity that affect inculturation is the politicization of culture. Liturgy speaks directly to matters of justice, because in liturgy God establishes a right relationship with us and expects us to be rightly related to all others; but liturgy cannot be reshaped to serve directly political goals. When social ideologies manipulate worship for political ends, the transformation of minds and hearts, which is the authentic effect of the liturgy, is reduced to creating motivation for political changes. There is, of course, a clear connection between good liturgy and social justice. Father Virgil Michel pointed out the connections, as does Vatican II; but *liturgy finally is its own goal.* It is not a means or instrument to do something outside itself. Politicization of culture means that the inculturation question becomes moot because liturgy is co-opted for purely political ends.

A Distinctive Ecclesial Culture

These developments have prompted a rethinking of the meaning of inculturation and its application to the liturgy of the Catholic Church. Pope Benedict XVI, inspired as a young priest by the works of Romano Guardini, has rethought the "spirit of the liturgy."[4] Benedict points out that, in modern Europe, a concept of culture has been developed that separates culture from religion and often leaves them in opposition, but it is religion that determines the scale of values and thereby the inner cohesion and hierarchy of values that separate one culture from another. Every culture prizes freedom, every culture prizes security, every culture teaches you to love your parents. The same values are always enshrined, but they are arranged in different cultural hierarchies, and each distinctive order serves to distinguish one culture from another.

Cardinal Ratzinger described the exchange between faith and culture signified by the term "inculturation." There is an exchange not only between God and ourselves in the mystery of the Incarnation, but an exchange between us with our culture and the faith as it comes to us already inculturated historically in other cultures. An exchange of cultures is involved in any authentic project of inculturation. The cardinal introduced a point about the history of culture that John Paul II did not emphasize in his more anthropological approach:

> Culture is the social form of expression, as it has grown up in history, of those experiences and evaluations that have left their mark on a community and have shaped it....Culture is concerned with understanding, which is a perception that opens the way for practical action, that is, a perception of which the dimension of values, of morality, is an indispensable part....In any question concerning man and the world, the question about the Divinity is always included as the preliminary and really basic question. No one can understand the

world at all, no one can live his life rightly, so long as the question about the Divinity remains unanswered. Indeed, the very heart of the great cultures is that they interpret the world by setting in order their relationship to the Divinity.[5]

With this observation, we move beyond the purely anthropological and the ideological to the historical character of culture. People formed in a particular culture not only live out their own experience of God and the world and other human beings but, on their path through history, they necessarily encounter other cultural agents and have to react to quite different experiences, depending on the degree to which a particular culture may be open or closed. These encounters can deepen and purify a culture and they sometimes effect a profound realigning of a culture's previous form. Nineteenth-century Germany's *Kulturkampf* took place because Chancellor Otto von Bismarck wanted to create a Germany that had a single cultural expression. Jews who were international and Catholics who had a Roman connection were suspect in this Prussian Protestant culture. This history and others like it prompted Cardinal Ratzinger to speak less about inculturation and more about a meeting of cultures. He used another technical term, "interculturality." At times "inculturation" seems to have been taken to mean that a culturally naked faith is transferred into a culture that is indifferent to any point of view, so that two agents that are alien to each other begin to synthesize. That is not what happens, because "there is no such thing as culture-free faith and because — outside of modern technical civilization — there is no such thing as a religion-free culture." Culture is more than mere outward form or esthetics or patterns of behavior or values; it is all these within a historic form of life.[6]

For believers, the Church is a distinct cultural entity in her own right. Pope John Paul II affirmed that there is an ecclesiastical culture, but so taken was he with anthropological studies, and so concerned was he that people had to meet Christ in ways that encouraged them to feel welcomed by Christ in his Church, that he did not often stress the Church herself as a distinct cultural entity as well as an object of faith. Even in historically Christianized society, the Church is not conflated with the dominant culture but retains her own cultural form. Faith is not a private path to God. It brings the person into the community of the people of God, preserving its particular history and culture. God has linked himself to this history and culture, in which the incarnation of Christ and his death and resurrection provide the form of personal and communal life. The Church cannot abandon what has been given to her in her founding, which she carries in distinct cultural form until Christ returns in glory. On her historical path, she meets all the great cultures, bringing with her everything she has gained according to God's providential plan in history.

While established in the past, this cultural history, reflected in forms of worship and of living, is always contemporary. Sacred history represents the story of God's constant involvement in and interaction with finite creatures. Sacramentality uses elements that represent a conscious choice on the part of Christ himself to use particular cultural institutions for his own purposes. The personal incarnation of Christ continues in the sacraments of the Church, which are actions of the Risen Christ. Through the sacraments, we claim God in our culture. The sacraments create their own reality and are, therefore, the last word in determining what we can and what we cannot use from the culture. Rationalistic modernity abstracts from the particular and would argue that in the Eucharist, for example, Christ used the "food of the people," and so should we, using crackers and Coke rather than bread and wine. Although persuasive in our culture, what this mind-set ignores is the providential design of God in using certain peoples, certain symbols, with a historical embodiment that we are not free to change. Tensions in the discussions on the nature of marriage, the nature of the sacrament of holy orders, the nature of the sacraments of Eucharist or baptism, arise from abstract rationality attempting to destroy historical particularities. In discussing the liturgy, "interculturality" helps to clarify questions about the limits of inculturating sacramental and other liturgical forms.

Inculturating both the faith and the liturgy is a historical process marked by many encounters, all rooted in the encounter between God and the human race in the Incarnation of the Father's Eternal Word in Jesus of Nazareth. Christ, who promised to be present at every gathering of his disciples, remains always the center, the touchstone of faith and liturgy. He gives his Church the gift and the grace necessary to continue the process of inculturation in every age and every place.

Chapter 15

Too Good to Be True?

The Eucharist in the Church and the World

S OME YEARS AGO, I was visiting an Oblate missionary in
Zambia.[1] He had been living in southern Africa for only a
year before I arrived. An old friend, he told me about the
country and mission and the people he served on the banks of the
Zambezi River. His ministry brought great joy to him, especially
when he was able to celebrate the Eucharist with the people, both
in the small mission church and in the villages. His heart was often
troubled, however, by the problems of the people, not only as individuals or in families, but also in the society as a whole. Zambia had
not adjusted well to the new global economic order. The people he
served lived, for the most part, by subsistence farming. A whole
generation of young parents was dying of AIDS. The increasing
indebtedness of the country meant that spending on education and
health care was being curtailed.

Too Good to Be True

After Mass one morning, he returned to the priest's house, and I
went to the bank of the river to thank God for the natural beauty
of this troubled country. Four men came out of the bush and asked
where they could find the priest. I indicated the house alongside
the chapel, and three of them went to the door. The fourth stayed

with me, and we began to talk. I did not speak his language, but he spoke some English. When I asked about his family and work, he repeated many of the difficulties the priest had already shared with me. Then I asked him why he and his companions had come to speak to the priest. He explained that many stories were heard in his small village, and some of them were about Jesus, the Gospel, and the Church. They had come to ask the priest for information about his religion. I then asked him why he was not with his three companions, talking to the priest. He responded, "Oh, I've thought about what we've heard, even while I was walking here, and I've decided that it makes no sense when I look at my life — that God would love us, that God would sacrifice himself for us, that God is stronger than the spirits who harm us. I don't believe it. It's too good to be true."

I have thought of this man and prayed for him in the years since that conversation. I do not know if he ever came to believe in the God revealed through Jesus Christ, but what he said was correct. It's too good to be true, except for those whose hearts, minds, and souls have been somehow touched and moved by a God who loves us more than we could ever love ourselves, who is closer to us than we are to ourselves.

"The Word became flesh and dwelt among us." The Prologue of the Gospel according to St. John proclaims that the Eternal Logos, the only-begotten Son of God, chose to enter into the very heart of God's temporal creation so that everything can be a sign and invitation to enter into the communal love of God's Trinitarian life. Jesus Christ, our Savior, does not stand apart from creation; he enters into its very life so that all God has accomplished can be seen to exist for the sake of our salvation. Too good to be true? Yes, except for those who, with the eyes of faith, see the world as Christ sees it.

The Scriptures also tell us that the one born of the Virgin Mary suffered, died, and is now risen. Jesus, who was nailed to the cross, has risen from the dead and lives forever. He has overcome the chains of sin and of death, the ultimate barrier, and now lives in total freedom. We notice how the Risen Lord appeared to those who knew him best before he was crucified. It is truly Jesus, with the wounds of his crucifixion still visible in his risen body. Nonetheless, he is so different that his closest companions often fail to recognize him immediately. Yet it is truly Jesus who eats breakfast and supper, although locked doors cannot confine him. He comes and goes at will. He is perfectly free.

The Risen Lord is therefore free to keep his promise to his disciples: "I am with you always, until the end of the world" (Matt. 28:20). The Risen Lord will never abandon his people. Those who find their personal identity in relation to him will never be alone. How could they be? Having assumed human nature as the new Adam, he now fills the cosmos as Risen Lord. Too good to be true? Yes, unless our aspirations have been transformed by the hope of the glory in which the Risen Jesus lives and which he offers to us.

This Jesus has also promised: "Where two or three are gathered in my name, I will be in their midst" (Matt. 18:20). The Risen Lord has established a community of believers to be a sign and instrument of salvation, to be the means for God's saving love to transform all creation. When the Church lives visibly through, with, and in her Risen Lord, she is revealed as his living body in every generation. When the Church gathers to celebrate the sacraments, Christ continues to act among us. The Risen Christ baptizes and forgives sin and sends the Holy Spirit to seal our membership in the Church. It is Christ who comforts and heals the sick, who unites a man and woman together for life, and who ordains pastors for the Church. It is Christ who makes present his own self-sacrifice on the cross, so that we can join to it our very selves. Each of the sacraments is an action of the Risen Christ gathering with his body, the Church.

In a unique fashion, the Eucharist is both the action and the abiding presence of the Lord. In the Eucharist, Christ gives himself as food for our journey, as our daily bread, as a banquet, which brings us together as pilgrims. Christ never comes to us alone. Christ comes to us with the Father and the Holy Spirit. Mary, the mother of Christ and our mother in him, accompanies her Son. All the angels and the saints, who have gone before us in faith, together with the souls in purgatory, join in the great communion. Moreover, all those who are the visible body of Christ throughout the world today are united in the divine gift of love. We never go to Jesus alone. In the Eucharist, we are most clearly members of a body, living stones of a temple, a gathered people of God. Too good to be true? Yes, except for those whose hearts have been turned inside out by the unity given to those who know they are loved by God and who have come to sense their unity with the multitude, who are their brothers and sisters in the Risen Lord.

Eucharist in the Life and Thought of the Church

Today, questions of Eucharistic faith and practice are strongly contested in many areas of ecclesial life. At least in the United States, some have been too neglectful of Eucharistic preaching and teaching. Some have discouraged Eucharistic devotion apart from the celebration of the Mass itself. Liturgical practice sometimes suffers from lack of prayerful preparation and devout attention. Some are confused in knowing and expressing precisely what the Church teaches about the Holy Eucharist. Whatever the reason, there is a growing desire among many Catholics for greater clarity and insight into our Eucharistic faith and practice.

In some ways, contemporary tensions and confusions about the Eucharist should not surprise us. Tension and confusion were there from the beginning: " 'This teaching is difficult; who can accept it?"...Because of this many of his disciples turned back and no longer went about with him" (John 6:60, 66). The tension became unbearable when Jesus began to use realistic language about eating his flesh and drinking his blood. In the face of his disciples' confusion, Jesus only intensified his language;[2] he made no attempt to soften or dilute its meaning.

This Eucharistic realism was clearly understood and accepted by the apostolic Church. By sharing in the real, sacrificed, and risen flesh of Christ and in his blood shed on the cross, the Church becomes a living body, brought into existence by the Eucharist (1 Cor. 10:16 ff.).[3] In the words of St. Cyril of Alexandria, precisely through the Eucharist, through "eating the flesh of Christ," we are made into "living flesh." Cyril's realism even compares the union between Christ and the recipient of the Eucharist to a "fusion of two globs of sealing wax."[4] Christ desires to be as close to us as nourishment is to our bones.

In the Eucharist, the Life of Christ is poured into our lives so that we may have new life as living members of a new body in the world, the body of Christ. St. Ignatius of Antioch (d. c. A.D. 110) emphasizes this ecclesial, corporate context of the Eucharist and its attendant gifts. He exhorts the community "animated by one faith and in union with Jesus Christ...to show obedience with undivided mind to the bishop and the presbytery, and to break the same Bread, which is the medicine of immortality, the antidote against death, and everlasting life in Jesus Christ" (*To the Ephesians* 20, 2).[5] In fact, for Ignatius, the Eucharist is inseparable from the ministry that gathers people visibly together and is responsible for maintaining Christ's sacramental presence in the Church (*To the Philadelphians* 4). No one, Ignatius of Antioch says, can (validly) celebrate the Eucharist apart from the bishop, "or anyone to whom he has committed it" (*To the Smyrnaeans* 8, 1).[6]

This inseparable link between Eucharistic realism and ecclesial union gives rise to the great patristic vision of the Eucharist as the

bond of charity, unity, and peace, signs of an authentic civilization of love. St. Augustine, in particular, placed strong emphasis
on this "social" function of the Eucharist, "social" in the sense that
the bond of love, unity, and peace among the baptized is a participation in the divine *communio* of the Trinitarian life of God.
The Eucharist is the secret of the Church's heart and is her comfort in every generation. In this most blessed sacrament, the divine
communio is disclosed. The Holy Spirit, who works through the
Church, makes the Eucharistic elements holy. In the Eucharist, the
sacrificial death of Christ is truly present, and its saving power is
alive and life-giving. In the Eucharist, the Father is worshiped in
spirit and in truth. In the Eucharist, Christ's sacrificial death and
resurrection restores us to the bonds of unity and peace with the
Father (justification), and makes possible the outpouring of the
Holy Spirit's love into our lives (sanctification).

St. Augustine's central idea is this: through eating Christ's body
and drinking his blood, we become one with him and with each
other. In Eucharistic *communio,* the City of God, God's great civilization of love, is visible on the earth; for "in what [the Church]
offers, she herself is offered" (*De civitate Dei,* X, 6). All of this is
possible because Christ is risen from the dead. The Eucharist is his
glorified Body and Blood which, having suffered and died, now
shares in the eternity of the celestial Eucharist, "the glory given to
the Father by the Son who redeemed the world."[7] In Catholic consciousness, faith in the Eucharist as embodying and presenting the
Risen Christ, who suffered and died for us, must be seen against the
background of creation, specifically, a creation leading to Incarnation (John 1:1–14; Col. 1:15–20). The Creator God enters into
his creation and becomes part of it. This presence continues in a
Eucharistic and sacramental manner. It is this intrusion of eternity
and transcendence into the created world that establishes both the
time and the space of the Eucharist.[8] The Eucharist discloses the
divine *communio* of Trinitarian love and invites our participation.

In this sense, it is a perpetual proclamation of God's transcendence and power, manifest most fully in the life, death, and resurrection of Jesus Christ the Lord (Phil. 2:6–11).

This is true both when the Eucharistic liturgy is being celebrated and breaks the limits of time and history and also when the Eucharist is in the tabernacle, where the drama of salvation is not immediately being reenacted, but where Christ is still present for our contemplation and prayer. St. Thomas expresses this contemplative dimension of the Eucharist in a phrase redolent of Aristotle: "It is the law of friendship that friends should live together" (*Summa theologiae* III q. 75, a. 1). This is why devotion to the Eucharist, apart from the Eucharistic liturgy itself, is an indispensable element of Catholic spirituality. It is also why all devotional life should, in some way, be linked to the Eucharist.

In Christ Jesus, the Father desires to dwell in the heart of reality, down to the very depths of our being. The Real Presence of Christ in the Eucharist is "the presence of the full mystery of God's being and work."[9] Christ accomplishes two things in this sacrament: he glorifies his Father and he shares his life with us.

The Eucharistic Liturgy as the Locus for Evangelization[10]

The Risen Jesus is the Eucharistic Lord. Free himself, he wants us to be free. Free to do what? We are made free to worship and to glorify God. We are given the freedom to evangelize and convert human hearts and thus to transform the world. The very structure of the Eucharistic liturgy discloses the dynamics of a new culture.

The Second Vatican Council reminds us that "the Eucharist is the source and summit of all evangelization" (*Presbyterorum ordinis*, II, 5). I would suggest that one way of understanding this profound, evangelical depth in the Eucharistic liturgy is to "track" the presence of the Holy Spirit in the liturgy. It is the Holy Spirit who groans to set us free and who is present in all the decisive moments of Christ's life. In our Savior's incarnation, life in the world, death, and resurrection, Jesus is seen as doing the Father's will under the guidance, direction, prompting, and assistance of the Holy Spirit.

The New Testament word for invoking the Holy Spirit is *epikalein,* "to call upon/to call down." "Calling upon" or "calling down" is an *epiklesis.* Imagine ourselves now at Mass. During the celebration, there are at least eight moments when we explicitly or implicitly call upon the Holy Spirit of God, the Spirit who sets us free and who renews the face of the earth.

The Epiklesis of Forgiveness

The first moment is the *Epiklesis of Forgiveness.* The Penitential Rite is always an implicit invocation of the Holy Spirit because it is a prayer for forgiveness. The Spirit is sent among us for the forgiveness of sins (John 20:22–23). This moment of forgiveness is essential to the new culture of Christian life and, at Jesus' express command, it is essential to liturgy (Matt. 5:23–24).

We must constantly remind ourselves that we are sinners in need of forgiveness. If, as individuals and as community, we are unaware of our faults, or if we simply ignore them, invariably, we cast them into the lives of others, and we have no true claim on God's mercy and forgiveness. Then, the true drama of God's salvation revealed in Jesus Christ is muted; the humility necessary for authentic worship "in Spirit and truth" (John 4:23) is undermined. Reconciling love is, thus, the first fruit of the divine *communio.*

The Epiklesis of Word

The second moment is the *Epiklesis of Word.* This refers to the point in the liturgy when we proclaim directly from the Sacred Scriptures, "inspired and useful for instruction and for growth in holiness" (2 Tim. 3:16). Our profession of faith describes the work of the Spirit: "He has spoken through the prophets." We respond to the inspired Scriptures and conform our lives to the teaching of Jesus, but, in doing so, we are in fact encountering Jesus through the Spirit that breathes through the Scriptures. The Holy Spirit conforms our lives to the Word of God in human words. The homily, which expounds the Scriptures and relates them directly to the lives of the people in the assembly, is a word integral to Eucharistic worship.

The Epiklesis of Intercession

The third moment is the *Epiklesis of Intercession,* which encompasses the reading of Scripture. It begins with the opening prayer of the Mass and concludes with the General Intercessions. This is another implicit invocation of the Holy Spirit, for the Holy Spirit carries all prayer into the sight of God (Rom. 8:26–27). To pray is to accept the grace that changes us. Our spirit, united with the Holy Spirit, enters into the drama revealed in Jesus Christ. We are taken into God's saving action in history, where the Holy Spirit transforms our personal and social history.

Prayer itself is a form of instruction and evangelization. Prayer purifies our desires; it opens the world to God's transforming action, which waits upon our human freedom. God does not impose himself upon us; we have to ask. Our prayer must therefore constantly reach out to the farthest corners of God's creation. It must mourn in every human misery and rejoice in every human joy.

The Epiklesis of Offering

The next moment is the *Epiklesis of Offering.* We take two material gifts — bread and wine — and, through the power of the Spirit, we ask that they may become "the bread of life" and "our spiritual drink."

On the one hand, these gifts represent ourselves, as we long for ever greater Eucharistic transformation. The bread represents all our united human efforts that contribute to the building up of a civilization of love on this earth in preparation for the final coming of God's kingdom. The wine represents all the pain, suffering, and death involved in the discharge of this holy task, all once again embraced by the Eucharistic body of the Lord.

On the other hand, the bread and wine represent material creation itself, which awaits its own Eucharistic transformation, "a share in the glorious freedom of the children of God" (Rom. 8:19–23). The Spirit's presence in this moment of offering is often made explicit in the Prayer over the Gifts, which concludes the preparation of the altar and the gifts.

The Epiklesis of Consecration

The Epiklesis of Offering points directly to the next invocation, the *Epiklesis of Consecration.* The Holy Spirit effects the transformation of the bread and wine into the Body and Blood of the Lord. The word *consecratio,* which means "to be holy together with," carries the most profound sense of the experience of the Holy Spirit in the individual person, in the Church, and in the world. The Holy Spirit is the Sanctifier, the one who makes us holy in the sight of God. The mission of the Holy Spirit in the world is to sanctify, to consecrate each person and community for worship "in Spirit and truth" (John 4:24). In the transforming power of consecration, the outpouring of the divine *communio* reveals the clear form of the new culture, a life and world suitable for the indwelling of the Trinitarian life of God.

The Epiklesis of Memorial

Next, there is the *Epiklesis of Memorial:* "Do this in remembrance of me." We do not simply live out of the present; we live with an acute awareness of the past, of all that the Father has done for us in Jesus Christ. When we celebrate this memorial of God's saving action, that saving reality is encountered again through the presence of the Spirit, who brings us into the life of the Risen Lord. In this memorial, the future of the world is anticipated, and the new culture of life is received.

The Epiklesis of Communion

The consecration, sanctification, and memorial effected by the Holy Spirit prepare us for the *Epiklesis of Communion.* Before receiving the Body and Blood of the Lord we pray:

> Lord, I am not worthy to receive you,
> but only say the word and I shall be healed.
> (Roman Liturgy, Communion Rite)

This short prayer sums up all the previous moments of *epiklesis:* forgiveness, word, intercession, offering, and consecration. Communion with the dying and rising Jesus is also communion with the Spirit who gives life (Rom. 8:9–11).

The Epiklesis of Mission

The final invocation is the *Epiklesis of Mission.* The Spirit of God is the energy and dynamism of all *mission* in the world. "Mission" is the way we live out our baptismal consecration in the world: as married persons; as bishops, priests, or deacons; as single persons; as those consecrated by religious vows, with the energy and prompting of the Holy Spirit.

Having been prepared by the persistent invocation of the Holy Spirit of God and having been nourished with the Body and Blood of the Lord, the baptized are now sent out, by the power of this same Holy Spirit, to evangelize and to transform society itself. The People of God *dwell* in this "evangelical form." Together as pilgrims gathered in the Eucharist, we walk every day the journey of forgiveness, word, intercession, offering, consecration, communion, and now of mission. What is the context of this mission today? What world is the Eucharist to inform and to transform?

The Eucharist in the World

In a world always in search of freedom, we live more and more in a globalized society. In economics and in politics, in culture and in communication, the human race is more connected than ever before. But a connection is not necessarily a personal relationship. The scope of economic and political activity today brings with it the opportunity of uniting the human family in justice and love. It brings with it as well the danger of an order in which the poor are cut off from participation in the goods of the earth and are unable to enjoy the freedom that God desires for all. Globalization will not be globalization with solidarity, unless the Church evangelizes in a new way. It is the Eucharist that gives us the courage to evangelize, because the goal of our human unity is already present in the Eucharist itself. Because of the Eucharist, the Church can be the "sacrament of the unity of the human race" (*Lumen gentium*).

In giving himself freely for our salvation and in sending the Holy Spirit, Christ makes us free; but Gospel freedom is greater than the freedom this world understands. In Christ, we are free to act, to do what we need to do, what we should do. The world understands this freedom to act. But if freedom is reduced to actions willed by each of us alone, the world becomes a brittle place. Each one's freedom is limited by the action of others; and each action is then negotiated, often in a court of law, with the consequence that life becomes a contest of wills. On the streets, this contest is often violent.

Freedom in Christ is more than freedom to do. It is also freedom to give totally, even to the point of self-sacrifice, as Christ freely gave himself to death on the cross. The world understands generosity and often rewards it. The world has a more difficult time understanding self-sacrifice. The crisis in Christian marriage, consecrated life, and ordained priesthood is a crisis of Christian freedom, the freedom to give oneself totally to God, to a spouse, to the Church.

Gospel freedom is freedom to do, freedom to give, and finally freedom to receive. This dimension of freedom in Christ is even more problematic today, for receiving means admitting we are needy, and no one likes to admit poverty. Yet, if we are not free to receive, we cannot be free in Christ, for in Christ all is gift: the Gospel, the sacraments of the Church, apostolic governance, the Church herself—it is all gift. To be free is to receive the gifts that Christ bestows on us. If we are not free as well to receive all those persons whom Christ loves, we are not free in Christ. Each human difference is a gift for all, and it must be welcomed, desired, received by all. In Christ's body, everyone gives and everyone receives. Everyone has something to share, and everyone is needy.

Freedom to do, freedom to give, freedom to receive—all this is freedom in Christ, who died and rose to set us free and calls us to experience this freedom in each Eucharistic celebration, offered for the salvation of the world. Too good to be true? No, not for those who have been set free by Christ and the action of the Holy Spirit in order to be leaven for the whole world. In proclaiming a Eucharistic Lord, we discover again and again who we are and are called to be. It is all gift, and it is all true. "He who does what is true comes to the light, that it may be clearly seen that his deeds have been wrought in God" (John 3:21).

The Eucharist is the great deed wrought in and by God. It will be clearly seen to be true when the whole world, through the evangelizing mission of the Church, is a Eucharistic assembly, a new culture of grace, composed of all those whom Christ loves and has set free.

Part Three

THE CHURCH'S GOAL
Communion with God

Chapter 16

The Difference God Makes

Deus caritas est

I N THE ARCHDIOCESE OF CHICAGO there is a Curia, a chancery office full of people who supervise various ministries and perform different tasks so that the mission of the Church can be more vital. This is true in any diocese around the world, but Chicago has a particularly large group involved in these tasks. From time to time, as I've sometimes told the tale, I have gone to some offices, one after the other, and asked the question: "Would you do anything differently if God did not exist?" Of course, the people involved in the various ministries — the Respect Life Office, the Justice and Peace Office, the Catechetical Office, the Schools Office — have good answers to that question, even though they are immersed in administration, which can be a distraction from thinking about more important matters. As I move along and talk with the development people, they begin to talk about philanthropy and its motivation in the Gospel and not just in good will for all peoples. As I get to the real estate folk, it becomes less clear. They begin to speak about buildings as part of the patrimony of the Church. Finally, the lawyers, who control quite a few things these days, are prone to chortle and say knowingly, "Why are you bothering to ask?"

"Would we do anything differently if God did not exist?" It is an essential question, especially as we consider not only the Source of love in the Godhead, but also the expression of that love in his Church. Why do we organize ourselves in caritative agencies? Would we do things to help others differently if, in fact, God did not exist?

Theologians speak about God, their field of expertise. But, in answering questions about God, one has to start with the question, "Which God?" This is more urgent than ever in our day because attacks on others, in the name of God — sometimes even in the name of the God of Abraham — make more necessary than before that primordial task of theologians to speak of God and do so, not just from their own ideas or own religious or spiritual experience, but from the sources of God's own self-revelation. We must speak, first, a few brief words about *God himself* from the sources of revelation. Second, I would like to look at the mystery of *gift*, because it is difficult to understand God as love without coming to terms with the nature of a gift, and particularly so with the philosophical objections to pure generosity in the literature today. Then I will consider *love*. There are obstacles to the understanding of love in God's self-revelation that arise from a false understanding of human sexuality, or *eros*.

There are also problems of speaking about love when we separate it from justice. Pope Benedict XVI made reference to this challenge in his encyclical *Deus caritas est*.[1] Marxist analysis would say that one has to choose between love and justice, and that love can be considered the enemy of justice, as love can be considered the enemy of *eros*. There is as well an element of our cultural understanding of love that has to be transformed by God's self-revelation, if the message of the encyclical is to be clearly understood: the distinction between longing and its fulfillment that permeate our literature and song and foster resentment of the personal fulfillment promised by faith. To understand the difference God makes, therefore, we will consider God, gift, love, and finally Church, which is

God's love made visible in sacraments, in word, and also in acts of charity.

God

The basic understanding of God in biblical religion, in the Old and the New Testaments, is that God is one. This is the *Shema* of Israel: "Hear, O Israel, the Lord your God is One"; but God is understood in the New Covenant as one in the unity created by the total self-giving of three divine Persons, each to the others, for the others, in the others. Cardinal Ratzinger once wrote that Trinitarian language has much the same function as incense in a liturgy: to obscure one's vision, precluding the possibility of clear seeing and description of the Mystery itself. God language, however, is not only negative; it also presents positive truths. The notion of God as a Trinity of Persons is rooted in the biblical narratives concerning the dying and rising of Jesus, and the sending of the Holy Spirit into the Church for the salvation of the world. The notion of God as simple is not unique to Christianity, but the doctrine of the Trinity, as we know, is distinctive to the Christian faith. The Christian God is the God who, in the Spirit, sends his divine Son Jesus Christ for the salvation of the world.

While much could be said about the biblical seeds of the Trinitarian doctrine in both Old and New Testaments, the end of the Gospel according to St. Matthew has been particularly significant in developing the doctrine of the Trinity. The Pauline literature makes references to the Trinity in the Letter to the Romans, in which only in the Spirit can we call God *Abba*, or Father, as Jesus called God by that name. In the First Letter to the Corinthians, Paul makes use of many seminal Trinitarian formulas, some of which have come to be incorporated into our liturgies. Finally, and most importantly, there is the Johannine literature. In the First Letter of John, we read: "This is how you can know the Spirit of

God: every spirit that acknowledges Jesus Christ come in the flesh belongs to God."

The entire Gospel according to St. John is a meditation upon the Trinity. Its heart is reflection on the *communio* between the Father and the Son, with the love that binds the Sender and the One Sent. Finally, St. John says simply, "God is love." And if love is not simply an activity in which the one God engages but rather what God essentially *is*, then God must be in his nature the lover, the beloved, and the active love itself. Being for the other, in such a way that the other's very being is completely one with one's own being, is the very "to be," the being, the *esse*, of God himself. The giving of oneself to others constitutes the nature of God. The theological reflection on this nature is carried out differently by Augustine, Anselm, and Aquinas, because the speculative grasp of the mystery in the Godhead varies by using different philosophical sources. But each of these figures, in one way or another, comes back to divine self-revelation. When we, conscious that our own way of being is limited in itself, face limits on the giving of ourselves but can still speak of God as the one who gives being itself, then we see the connection between God and *gift*.

Gift

Connecting God and gift is problematic because the very economy of gift-giving is often inadequately distinguished from, or even confused with, the economy of exchange and indebtedness. Sociological and anthropological analysis shows that the giving of gifts can serve as a cover for an elaborate system of obligation and coercion: one gift compelling the giving of another gift. To avoid such compulsion, a gift must be free on the part of both the giver and the receiver, and the gift must involve the presence of the giver to the receiver. A certain object becomes a gift object only if, in fact, it is accepted by someone else as a *gratuitous* offering. Think of how a starry night or a glowing sunset is analyzed differently as an object of curiosity leading to scientific investigation or as a gift that brings with it the presence of a divine Creator. Jacques Derrida has asked whether freedom and presence, in fact, are mutually exclusive in the way that many assume them to be.[2] He plays on a pun in German, where *Gift* means "poison," and he says that every gift, because it brings with it a giver, is poisonous, that is, incompatible with individual autonomy. Gift-giving, which is at the heart of love, and at the heart of God's self-revelation as love, becomes problematic in this version of things. A gift is poison to both giver and receiver because a gift is a present that brings with it the giver in personal presence. In making giver and receiver present to one another, each becomes involved in an oppressive game of superiority, inferiority, debt, and obligation. Gifts therefore seem to devolve, almost despite themselves, into measurable commodities. The gift cancels itself because, understood as a present, it is never completely free of obligations and entanglements with others.

We cannot make the move from God to love, therefore, without going through a purified understanding of gift. If gift is limited to these debilitating rhythms of exchange, then authentic love becomes an ideal impossible of realization. The gift of being would itself generate resentment against the Creator, the giver of life. Jesus breaks this cycle of mutual obligation in the parable of the prodigal son in the Gospel according to St. Luke. The theme of economic exchange is central to the parable, since the younger son asks for the hard currency, the measurable portion, of his father's estate that is owed to him. The elder son complains that he has been compelled to slave for his father for many years while receiving nothing in recompense. Both sons go wrong spiritually in the measure that they assume an interrelationship of strict economic justice with their father. What the parable demonstrates so effectively is that this attitude leads to the commodification of the father's love and adds to spiritual famine for both sons. The gestures of the father toward both his children reveal that his love does not have to be earned because it simply cannot be earned. Even before the prodigal son can finish his speech of repentance, his father embraces him and puts the ring on his finger; and in response to the desperately economic calculations of the older son, the father says, "Everything I have is yours." The father needs neither repentance nor gratitude. His gifts do not have to be earned or returned. When the sons forget this truth, they exit the circle of grace and enter the far country of exchange, of carefully calculated reciprocal obligation.

St. Thomas Aquinas's doctrine of the simple God who creates the entire universe *ex nihilo* is in some sense the technical theological description of the father in Jesus' parable of the prodigal son. Because God is the sheer act of "to be" itself (*actus purus*), God stands in need of nothing outside of himself. There is no other reality, actuality, or perfection that could in any way complete or add to God's own being, since he himself is the ground and fullness of whatever exists. What follows from this is that God neither creates the universe nor relates to it in order to gain something for himself. Therefore God cannot, even in principle, be involved in an economic exchange with his creatures, an exchange of reciprocal obligation. He cannot give in order to receive, nor can he be gracious in order to be thanked. This kind of reciprocity is possible only among and between beings, that is, created things existing interdependently; but God's "relation" to the world that he creates and sustains can only be one of sheer generosity, of being for the other.

God's grace brings into our experience as creatures the very life of the reciprocal sharing of the Trinitarian persons. The created universe is characterized now by economic exchange, not reciprocity. The fallen universe in which we live is a product of the sinful imagination and of the distorting effects of our own sinful acts. At the center of that fallen milieu is the mere projection of a Supreme Being, one who enters into the mix through domination and manipulation. This idol, the same one exposed through the parable of the prodigal son, is a God somehow in competition with his creatures, a God who is a Supreme Being among other beings rather than a simple act of "to be." As we begin to entertain that inadequate sense of God, inevitably, resentment arises. We can no longer see that God is love. God in his plenitude cannot be increased. As we say in the Roman Rite of the Mass, he does not need any gift we could ever offer, including our praise, because our desire to thank God is itself a gift. It is because God has no need of our praise that our prayer of gratitude is a gift and not a poison to him or to us. The solution to Jacques Derrida's problem about competition and calculation is a God who has no real relation to the world he creates *ex nihilo*. Creation is not an exchange.

Love

Being itself is a gift, from a giver who is present to the gift of being, but in such a way that nothing has to be returned to him. When that is our understanding of God, we can pass to a third point, that love can be a form of gift-giving and is, in fact, a giving in which, no matter what else is given and received, one's self is always central to the gift: not in a poisonous manner, but rather in a totally gratuitous manner. God gives himself totally because of his ontological self-sufficiency. The rest of us give ourselves as best we can, in dribs and drabs, in acts that always fall short of complete self-giving, unless we give ourselves to others in God. Our ability to love others correlates to our ability to be present to ourselves, to be transparent to the fallen-ness of our own nature, and transparent, therefore, to our own motives. Recognition that our own being is a gift, a present from God himself, is a prerequisite for *agape,* for the total self-sacrifice that is the highest form of love. St. Augustine wrote, "I call 'charity' that whereby one loves those things whose work in comparison to the love for oneself must not be thought to be of lesser value, those things being the Eternal himself and what can love the Eternal." Therefore, in its consummate and purest sense, charity is predicated only of God and the soul by which God is loved.

Pope Benedict XVI's first encyclical, *Deus caritas est,* explores this notion of love as *agape* in order to show that elements of it pervade every form of love. In showing how divine love as gift unites God himself with the world and all that is in it, the pope shows also how love is the measure and the source of a truly lasting peace, the condition of our being present to one another without animosity and division. Because we have too often separated what should be united, the world knows little peace, and the pope's desire to be a peacemaker, expressed so poignantly immediately after his election, is one of the driving factors in his writing to the world about love in his first encyclical. Because we have separated love of God from other forms of love, the pope would restore unity to the notion and to the experience of charity. But to do this, he must overcome some cultural presuppositions.

The proclamation of the Gospel of love transforms not only individual hearts but whole cultures. In our culture we presuppose that there must be a separation of *eros,* understood as human desire sexually expressed, from *agape.* That point has created the most interest even in the pope's own prior speeches leading up to the publication of his encyclical. The pope tries to overcome a separation of *eros* from *agape* by pointing to the inner movement of erotic love toward a generosity between a man and a woman based on total self-giving of the one to the other. Using the Canticle of Canticles, Pope Benedict shows that *eros,* when it develops properly, becomes devoted to the good of the other for the sake of the other alone. Love becomes ecstasy when a person attains the freedom to give himself completely to another, when there is, in the loving, a purification of desire. It is at this moment that *agape* inserts itself into *eros* as its fulfillment.

If this fulfillment is frustrated, *eros* decays and loses its attractiveness. This is why pornography is an addiction that never satisfies the self. A careful observer of love between a man and a woman notes that *eros* naturally leads to the point at which lovers cheerfully make sacrifices for one another. Think of how a young man will give up his hard drinking and his laziness when he is enthralled by a woman worthy to be pleased. There is, however, a problem between love understood as spontaneity, which the culture magnifies in song and drama, and love considered as a choice. When love is considered as essentially spontaneous, there is a loss of freedom; there is a kind of delight in determinism: we fell in love, we had to do it, it carried us beyond our own freedom. Dante famously illustrates this process in the words of Paolo and Francesca, who are perpetually blown about by winds of emotion.[3] There is, then, a loss of self in the experience of passion, and love can very easily be reduced to an addiction, to a certain experience in which the person "loved" is lost. If love is seen fundamentally as a free choice, there is loss of self not to the experience but to the person chosen and, finally, a finding of oneself in the reciprocity that arises when a man and a woman love one another fully. The experience is not greater than the person whose object it is, despite the frequent glorification of experience in our culture to the detriment of persons.

When I was growing up, movies were made with this story line: an attraction, a courtship, followed by a commitment to one another, of person to person, and then implicit experience of sexual intercourse. Now, in the few movies I see, especially on planes as I am traveling, the experience is depicted progressively in a different way. There is the attraction, there is a giving of bodies (and to some extent of selves) to one another in a sexual experience, which is its own goal, and then there is, or is not, a commitment. We witness that story as well in the experience of couples coming to the

Church to be married now, at least in the United States, many of whom have lived together as if they were married before making the personal commitment that involves the free choice of one another in the matrimonial covenant. Cohabitation does not encourage the development of the habit of self-sacrifice necessary for married love. It prevents our remembering that we become truly ourselves only in opening our lives completely and without reserve to love.

A second cultural problem in keeping love together in unified fashion so that it might become the basis of social harmony and peace is the division between justice and love. The pope's encyclical attributes this division primarily to Marxist thought. I hope this becomes as great a subject of discussion as the division between and reintegration of *eros* and *agape* in the pope's thinking. The Marxist critique of works of philanthropy for the poor is based upon seeing them as a way of excusing the rich from helping to create a society based on justice. The objection is that one may have a society where rich people help poor people, but injustice continues until the society itself and its structures are reformed to prevent economic inequality. The pope points out that, even if economic equality were truly to be established, love would remain the necessary foundation of any economic and political system truly equal to the dignity of the human person. The commodification of exchange in the analysis of gift, as mentioned above, cannot be overcome by economic justice alone. It can be overcome only by love as self-giving. A distinction of roles in creating such an order for the common good is the concern of Catholic social teaching and is sorted out in that teaching and, to some extent, in the pope's encyclical.

There is however a third division that has to be overcome if the teaching of God as love is to transform our culture: the division between longing and fulfillment. Because of our psychologically trained sensitivities, we are quick to recognize our longings and desires. We are equally quick at times to privilege a longing for the impossible. All the great ideals, including justice and charity, haunt contemporary persons, who then define themselves precisely as haunted and resist any path to a fulfillment that would be ultimately transformative, especially any path marked divine. As Stendhal once put it, "God's only excuse is that he does not exist. If God is just, and there is no justice, then God does not exist. If God is love, and there is little love, then God can hardly exist." When charity presents itself as more than just a hint and a guess about what might be finally possible but is in fact impossible, charity itself will be rejected as a delusion that leads us to believe we can eliminate the longings that define us precisely because they cannot be fulfilled. Ecstasy and joy then become temptations that deprive contemporary man of his self-imposed identity as an essentially unfulfilled, always tragic, hero.

Ecclesial Communion

What remains to be considered, then, is a fourth point: the Church, or ecclesial Communion, enters our analysis of charity as a network of caritative agents, as saints shaped by God's love and eager to share God's gifts with all men and women loved by God. Pope Benedict has spoken of the Holy Spirit as the interior power that moves us to love as Jesus loved on the cross and as Jesus loved when he washed the feet of his disciples. From this divine self-revelation, it must follow that the Church is as committed to the service of charity in the form of Christlike love as she is to the preaching of the word and the celebration of the sacraments. These three tasks together, never separated, define the Church's mission. As Jesus commissioned the apostles to preach, baptize, and make disciples, so the apostles commissioned deacons to serve their brothers and sisters at the table of the common life (Acts 6). The deacons were more than technically competent; they were men full of the spirit and wisdom. As we see immediately in their early preaching, moreover, their service to charity reaches beyond the confines of the Church, as the parable of the good Samaritan reminds us it must. The gifts of God must be shared as universally as possible.

We have often been reminded of those agents of Christ's charity who have shaped the life of the Church, especially in our generation. We have been reminded as well that the Church has no monopoly on work for the poor and for the elimination of economic and political injustice. The work of charity is ecumenical and universal both in its scope and in its workers. On this point, I conclude with three personal experiences.

Let me first mention the existence of an agency that may now have disappeared, but that still existed when I was serving in the General Administration of my own religious congregation, the Missionary Oblates of Mary Immaculate, in Rome. The organization was called Agrimissio. Agrimissio was established by Msgr. Luigi Ligutti when he was the founder of the Catholic Rural Life Conference in the United States. He saw how the expertise that the United Nations had about farming was now Rome-based. By contrast, missionaries, whose General Administrations were also Rome-based, usually had the trust of the people but were without expertise in farming. Agrimissio was created to bring together the United Nations FAO (Food and Agriculture Organization) in Rome with the missionary societies headquartered in Rome for the benefit of subsistence farmers in poor countries around the world. The farmers often did not trust those who came to them from the Rome-based Food and Agricultural Organization of the United Nations. For twelve years, I sat on the board of Agrimissio. While it was not always successful, the model of cooperation was good. What it pointed to was the fact that, if we are to do charity, which is necessary for the doing of justice, trust must be a component of the relationships between people who want to help and those who need to be helped, even when the latter sometimes do not understand themselves how they can be helped.

My second experience was in a rural diocese in the northwestern part of the United States, the diocese of Yakima, Washington. Many of the Catholics there are Mexicans who are farm workers. Their life is quite hard. Because of their difficulties, they decided, while I was bishop there, that they needed to form a farm workers' union. They came to me to see if I could assist them in talking with the growers, in creating a dialogue for the sake of a more just and charitable society. Such a dialogue interested both them and a number of the growers. In the discussions with the farm workers, I expected to hear demands for higher wages; I expected to hear about better working conditions in the fields and in various places where they lived. They did not start with any of those issues. They started with a complaint: "Bishop, they don't respect us." Their response surprised me because, in an economy of commodification, which I wrongly assumed was our common environment, I expected them to think first of all about wages and working conditions. But in their deep faith and sense of who they are as persons loved by God, what they most resented was the lack of dignity that the conditions of their work forced upon them: "They don't respect us." This is something else the Church has to bring to the conversation about society. If, in fact, there is to be charity, if there is to be a loving union of people who might otherwise be divided, it must be totally respectful of the dignity of all those involved, no matter at which end of the exchange — giving or receiving — they find themselves.

My third experience comes from Chicago, which is redoing its public housing in order to reduce the violence in many of the public housing projects and to give a better life to the residents. Violence was a chronic danger, because of drug dealers and gangs arguing over turf. The large public housing projects, where elevators didn't work, where services were often not delivered, where sometimes even the police could not enter, were places of chronic violence. Nonetheless, among the inhabitants of these dilapidated high-rises, there was community. Single mothers with several children, not all of them their own, some of them perhaps their grandchildren, knew where they could go for help. They would know that in one apartment there were drug dealers or gang members, and their children had to be very careful. But they knew that, in another apartment, there was a friend who could be of some assistance, even though everyone was poor and threatened.

In talking to these people who are moving to much better quarters, I was surprised to hear some reluctance. Someone outside that community might imagine that these people should be grateful for finding so much better housing. But the housing meant nothing to them if they could not also find a community. As one lady told me, "Cardinal, if my car breaks down, I'm lost." She was in a new, better apartment, but in order to find help, she would get in her car and return to that violent and crime-ridden neighborhood to people whom she knew could help her. She could not find those people in her new neighborhood. The Church therefore created a program called "Welcoming Your Neighbor." The local Catholic parish would try to reach out to someone, particularly a very poor person, perhaps the first poor person to move into a richer or middle-class neighborhood, in order to begin building a community necessary for them to live a truly human life. If we are to be involved as agents in the work of charity, we must be involved in building community and not just in delivering services, even though the services are desirable improvements in strictly commodified terms.

As caritative agents, would we do things differently if God did not exist? Sometimes we might say, *perhaps not.* There are others, not inspired by faith, who work for the poor and who work for social justice out of a sense of benevolence toward others. Nonetheless, how believers do things should point to God's existence. How we do them differently will mean that we must work first to build trust. Second, we must work in such a way that the dignity of every person is profoundly respected. And third, we must work in such a way that, in the giving of gifts, community is formed and strengthened.

Chapter 17

Godly Humanism

Images of God in the Poetic Writings of
Pope John Paul II

T
HE DIFFERENCE GOD MAKES depends, finally, on who God
is. Karol Wojtyla drew in his teaching not only from
Sacred Scripture but also from Western philosophy, his
own original anthropology, and the focus given by his concerns as
a pastor in order to explain to others who God is. This chapter is
an attempt to look at images he employs, especially images of God,
to come to a fuller understanding of a mind and heart in lifelong
conversation with God.

These considerations of images of God in the writings of John
Paul II seek to discern a spirituality for our day. They are in three
parts. First, I offer a few reflections on the separation of concept
and image in the Enlightenment, the epistemological context of
division between faith and reason that has dominated intellectual
life for several centuries and that the pope strove to resolve. Second, I offer an analysis of the pope's own words and the images
behind them in his plays, poetry, and other sources. Third, I
explore a few ideas about the inner culture of the pope. Why would
Karol Wojtyla use images of God in the way that he used them
throughout his life?

The Synthesis of Reason and Faith

Ever since the Enlightenment, thoughtful people in the West have seemingly had two choices: to swear allegiance to religious faith and so foreswear investment in the human project, or to swear allegiance to reason and so foreswear commitment to religious faith. John Paul II's encyclical *Fides et ratio* (Faith and reason), therefore, occasioned a great deal of comment, much of it, whether supportive or critical, fine commentary of a certain depth. On the lighter side, Andy Rooney, the columnist who offered humorous commentaries for many years on *60 Minutes,* wrote a short piece for the *Chicago Sun-Times* in which he said, quite sincerely, "Why is this pope writing a letter on faith and reason? Everybody knows that faith is feeling and reason is logic and there is no connection between them at all." In popular form, Rooney expressed Western intellectual development since the Enlightenment.

Some modern thinkers have attempted to bridge the gap created between faith and reason by Enlightenment thought. In the twentieth century, Jacques Maritain, the famous French personalist philosopher, proposed a philosophically grounded Christian humanism. Significantly, he wrote about the importance of imagination in the life of the mind. William James took imagination and religious experience seriously, but framed them in the descriptive and analytical categories of the then-emerging science of psychology. In James's work, it could appear that science eclipsed faith; in Maritain's, faith was never in danger of being eclipsed, but his synthesis of faith and reason was itself eclipsed by the collapse in the 1960s of the neo-Scholastic philosophical revival.

At the end of the twentieth century and the second millennium, another figure emerged who claimed a new and practical synthesis of human reason and religious faith: Karol Wojtyla, Pope John Paul II. He was obviously a man of faith; he was trained in philology and philosophy; he was a professor of ethics at Lublin University.

He matured in an environment of struggle with a Marxist regime that put all ideas to work in the service of an atheist anthropology. Although he had extensive theological training, I think it is fair to say that John Paul II often took his intellectual direction from philosophical anthropology; but his was a philosophy honed by his practice as a believer. He was remarkably well-equipped to synthesize the polarities of religious faith and rationalist commitment and to look again at the relation between concepts and images, between reason and religion. He wanted to ground philosophically, rationally, human speech about God and to God.

The search for a synthesis, the hope for a reconciliation between reason and faith in a Godly humanism, was stated programmatically in an encyclical from the early years of Pope John Paul II's pontificate, *Dives in misericordia.* In that 1980 text, the pope talked about God as imaged in his mercy:

> In Jesus Christ, every path to man, as it has been assigned once and for all to the Church in the changing context of the times, is simultaneously an approach to the Father and to his love. The Second Vatican Council has confirmed this truth for our time. The more the Church's mission is centered upon man — the more it is, so to speak, anthropocentric — the more it must be confirmed and actualized theocentrically, that is to say, to be directed through Jesus Christ to God the Father. While the various currents of human thought both in the past and in the present have tended and still tend to separate theocentrism and anthropocentrism, and even to set them into opposition to each other, the Church, following Christ, seeks to link them up in human history in a deep and organic way. And this is also one of the basic principles — perhaps the most important one — of the teaching of the last Council.
>
> (*Dives in misericordia,* 1)

The linkage of the human and the divine in the pope's concerns was already evident in the first encyclical that he wrote, *Redemptor hominis,* in 1979:

> Man cannot live without love. He remains a being that is incomprehensible for himself, his life is senseless, if love is not revealed to him, if he does not encounter love, if he does not experience it, and then make it his own, if he does not participate intimately in it. This is why Christ the Redeemer "fully reveals man to himself...." This is the human dimension of the mystery of the Redemption. In this dimension, man finds again the greatness, dignity, and value that belong to his humanity....In reality, the name for that deep amazement at man's worth and dignity is the Gospel, that is to say: the Good News. It is also called Christianity. This amazement determines the Church's mission in the world and, perhaps even more so, "in the modern world." This amazement, which is also a conviction and a certitude — at its deepest root it is the certainty of faith, but in a hidden and mysterious way it vivifies every aspect of authentic humanism — is closely connected with Christ. It also fixes Christ's place, his particular right of citizenship — in the history of man and mankind.
>
> (*Redemptor hominis,* n. 10)

What emerges with great consistency in the writings and talks of Pope John Paul II is the image of a God who is preoccupied with humanity, who takes his creation to heart, who desires that it be healed, reconciled, and flourish, who acts to save the human race. Insistently, the Holy Father spoke of "God's plan" or "God's will" for the whole human family. In his encyclical letter *Ut unum sint,* on Christian ecumenism, he writes, "The unity of all divided humanity is the will of God" (n. 6).

In John Paul II's writing on the permanent validity of the Church's missionary mandate, he appeals to God's plan for all of humanity as the foundation for his reflections (*Redemptoris missio,* nos. 12–19). A God who is preoccupied with all of humanity is a humanist God. This "picture" or "image" of God does not emerge in the magisterial writings of John Paul II through the use of special images, such as one might find in the Bible. The biblical image of God as shepherd, for example, is a striking image of God focused on the care of humanity. The pope used biblical images, of course, but obviously they were not original with him. Nor does the humanist God emerge in any form of mystical analogy. Although John Paul II wrote with deep insight on St. John of the Cross, the pope, unlike St. John, did not often use the relation between intimate lovers as an image of the relationship between God and the human race. In fact, John Paul II presented the humanist God through an insistent narrative of God's action on behalf of the human race coupled with a vision of humanity's destiny as healed, transformed, and called to happiness. In some sense, he followed the program of his phenomenological work in *The Acting Person* by identifying God's "operative" values through and in his action, especially in sending Jesus Christ as our Savior. In Wojtyla's personalist anthropology, a person "creates" himself and is known through his free and deliberate acts.

If God is a humanist, humans should be Godly. The humanist God and the Godly humanist, the God who is intimately and eternally preoccupied with the human race and human beings who are concerned about their own destiny (and whether or not it promises some dimension of eternity), represent the polarities of theocentrism and anthropocentrism that John Paul II sought to connect and to integrate in his philosophy of act. Authentic human action, according to Pope John Paul II, will inevitably lead the actor back to the foundations of human dignity in transcendence, in a God who reveals to us who we are through his generosity and love for us. In a reversal of Feuerbach, the pope asserts that authentic anthropology must necessarily be theology.

Two examples illustrate this linkage and integration of anthropology and theology in the pope's writings. The first has to do with women and with full respect for them and their identity. He writes in the 1995 *Letter to Women:*

> Such respect must first and foremost be won through an effective and intelligent campaign for the promotion of women, concentrating on all areas of women's life and beginning with a universal recognition of the dignity of women. Our ability to recognize this dignity, in spite of historical conditioning, comes from the use of human reason itself, which is able to understand the law of God written in the heart of every human being. More than anything else, the Word of God, in whose image we came to be, enables us to grasp clearly the ultimate anthropological basis of the dignity of women, making it evident as a part of God's plan for humanity.
>
> (*Letter of Pope John Paul II to Women,* 1995, no. 6)

Another example of how anthropocentric concern leads to theocentric foundations lies in the realm of social justice. In his 1991 encyclical, *Centesimus annus,* celebrating the hundredth anniversary of the first modern social encyclical by Leo XIII, *Rerum novarum,* John Paul II criticizes the anthropology of socialism, but this critique immediately leads him to the theocentric reasons for socialism's errors:

> The fundamental error of socialism is anthropological in nature.... If we then inquire as to the source of this mistaken concept of the nature of the person and the "subjectivity" of society, we must reply that its first cause is atheism. It is by responding to the call of God contained in the being of things that man becomes aware of his transcendent dignity. Every individual must give this response which constitutes the apex of his humanity, and no social mechanism or collective subject

can substitute for it. The denial of God deprives the person of his foundation and consequently leads to a reorganization of the social order without reference to the person's dignity and responsibility. (no. 13)

That diagnosis, of course, was the basis of his constant critique of Marxism, both as a bishop in Poland and as bishop of Rome. One cannot sacrifice personal freedom in order to achieve justice without destroying both freedom and justice. That was the theoretical fault line of historical Marxism. But he directed a parallel critique toward democratic capitalism and said that one cannot sacrifice objective truth and the search for truth in order to protect subjective freedom. The Godly humanist is possessed of an interior culture or spirituality shaped by a generosity and love that are the deepest sign of God's image and likeness in us. If we live generously and lovingly, our actions will disclose to us who we are as created in God's image and likeness. We will, in our very experience of acting freely and responsibly and honestly, close the gap between faith and reason.

Images of Light

What images of God does the pope use in his poetry, and how does he rework the more traditional images in his magisterial statements? Karol Wojtyla originally planned to devote his life to the study of Polish letters, language, and history. He embarked on this career before the Nazi occupation of Poland. He gave special attention to the interplay of word and deed in Polish history, and then, later, to the interplay between word and deed in biblical history. In his own early poetic and dramatic works, his fascination with the word, whether spoken, written, or declaimed on a stage, created what was called the "theater of the living word."

With other students who met secretly when their university was closed by the Nazi occupiers, he formed what was called the Rhapsodic Theater Company. In occupied Poland, this meant a theater company that wrote and produced plays with no scenery or costumes, with no resources but the living word itself. In this theater of the inner self, the action arises out of the meaning of words and the problems they articulate rather than through the impact of event upon character, as is the case in ordinary theater. The pope explains, "The supremacy of word over gesture indirectly restores the supremacy of thought over movement and impulse in man."[1]

The third of his plays provides a case in point. *Our God's Brother* is a study of a Pole named Adam Chmielowski. Born in 1845, Chmielowski as a young man was involved in insurrection against Poland's occupiers. He became a painter, experienced a religious conversion, and led a radically religious life. As Brother Albert, he worked with the poor of Krakow and founded a congregation of religious brothers and then of sisters dedicated to that work. He died among the poor in 1916, and Karol Wojtyla called him "Our God's Brother."

In Wojtyla's play, as expertly analyzed by Professor Kenneth Schmitz, the major topic of conversation concerns the social responsibility of art.[2] Written by an artist for a group of artists at a time when Poland was occupied by a foreign power, the play's conversation about art and society is carried by several voices other than Adam's. One of Adam's colleagues protests against subjectivism in art because it betrays the true nature of artistic creation; the artist is not the only author of his creation. Art is not subjective self-expression so much as the expression of something that the artist serves. Some of the characters in the play consider Adam himself to be a seeker drawn out of himself, but Adam objects to this argument against subjectivism. He sees his painting as his own subjective project, of running away from something or someone still indefinable to him. For him, self-expression serves a personal purpose:

escape from society and its demands and, perhaps, from something greater than society.

Another painter friend then does just the opposite. He defends subjectivism in art. He argues that it is sufficient that an artist explore his own selfhood and give it expression. Whether it interests others is beside the point. This colleague admits that he has a public persona, but he dubs this public persona "the exchangeable man" since it is subject to the commodification and barter of social life. A genuine and inviolable person, he insists, is private, a nonexchangeable man, withdrawn behind the fortress-like façade of inaccessible loneliness.

A fellow artist protests that such an attitude diminishes the meaning of art and its creative power, and Adam also cannot accept the isolated loneliness espoused by his colleague. But neither can he be satisfied with the safe routine of social life. He says in the play, "Yes, we are hiding; we escape to little islands of luxury, to the so-called social life, to so-called social structure, and we feel secure. But, no, this security is a big lie — an illusion. It blinds our eyes and stops up our ears, but it will shatter in the end."

There are other protagonists. One is called "the Stranger," without any personal name. He represents the revolutionary who counts on the anger of the poor to break open the circle of poverty in the name of justice. Nowhere does Adam deny the truth of what this stranger says, but it is not that truth that governs Adam's life. Adam rebukes the stranger for exploiting the just anger of the poor, but he recognizes the justice of that anger. In the name of a yet unnamed love that does keep calling him out of himself, Adam urges the poor: "Be one of us!" He also asks the poor to acknowledge a wider and deeper poverty that lies beyond the lack of material goods. This is the poverty of values, for human beings are meant to aspire to all goods, to the "whole vastness of the values to which man is called." And the greatest good calls not for anger but for love.

Besides these external voices, there are a number of inner voices in the play. It is never clear in this dramatic inner space whether or not these voices speak for Adam. "The Other" seems to represent in some way the mind of the Enlightenment intelligentsia, of that division between theocentrism and anthropocentrism discussed above. The Other calls Adam to human maturity. Adam, however, judges it to be a truncated sort of maturity, because it rests everything upon merely understanding the world as it is, without shouldering the world's burdens, a disengaged intellectualism.

At this point, Adam, like St. Francis of Assisi finding himself in embracing a leper, finds his own salvation when he helps a poor man leaning against a lamppost in the cold dark street. Here again we find a conversation shaped by highly philosophical images which, at a certain point, are broken open by an action that reveals a deeper image, but not an image in the ordinary way that we might look for it.

In this poor man, Adam comes at last to see an image of something more than a cause and more than himself. It is not an easy vision, however, and he struggles against the awareness that he must give himself up generously if he is to identify with this image. He cries out, "How can I cease to be who I am?" Nevertheless, it is through this discovery that at last Adam is able to say at the end of the play, "I am not alone."

The newly discovered image is not, however, the visual image to which Adam's painting has given expression. It's not that art doesn't count. In the play, he has a priest confessor who tells him that his art is religiously very important. It is for other people that God reveals himself using human creativity, and "God regards your art with a father's eye." But Adam has seen a deeper image than art alone can shape: It is a nonpictorial image, "imperceptible," he says, "to my eye, but that preys upon my soul."

It is clear that it is the image of God that is struggling for recognition and realization in his own soul and in that of the poor man.

Calling out to the Other, the voice of Enlightenment, Adam shouts with joy over having given up "the tyranny of intelligence," that is, of an intelligence without love, with "a too clear image of the world." Instead Adam has found a different, deeper, mysterious image. The Other does not or cannot understand him, however, and so Adam expresses an exalted liberation: "You don't know! So there is a sphere in my thought that you do not possess." Exposed here is an incompleteness of the Enlightenment project and, in a sense, the justification for the path that Karol Wojtyla himself took: to give up art and poetry for another vocation.

The plays and early poems he wrote before becoming a priest illustrate Wojtyla's sense of the relationship between word and deed, and of his search in action for images beyond the word and beyond the visual. They also furnish a number of metaphors and images for God that depart from the more traditional or biblical vocabulary he later used as pope in his magisterial teaching and documents. If we go to the encyclicals and official teaching, we find him writing about the first Person of the Trinity as Lawgiver, Judge, Creator. We find him speaking about the second Person of the Trinity as Redeemer, Man of Sorrows, Lamb of God, Master, Good Shepherd, Teacher, King, Head, Spouse. The third Person of the Trinity, the Holy Spirit, is called Counselor, the Breath of Divine Love, the Giver of Gifts, Spirit, Love. Those are marvelous images, but they are not original to Karol Wojtyla; they do not give us insight into his original inner-culture, his unique imagination.

If we go back again to his first play, which was called *Job, the Sufferer,* written shortly after the Nazis took over Poland, we find God compared to harmony, truth, beauty, and, in one line, "the bright one who brings light." It is these images of light that take one by surprise. Light is the image that most consistently permeates his poems. A poem called, "The Shores of Silence," at lines 26–27 says, "the element of light, brightness breathes from every side, your Friend, a single spark, yet Luminosity itself. Like a light filled with green, like green with no shade, an ineffable green that rests on drops of blood."

In the poem "Looking into the Well at Sichar," he coins a phrase that returns in other poems: "Multitudes tremble in you transfixed by the brightness of water." Water and light recur again and again, and they are joined together in this phrase "the brightness of water." In "Later Recollection of a Meeting," he speaks about one participant: "He was a great gathering of perception like the well blowing brightness of water into a face. He had a mirror like the well — shining deep in the brightness of water." And in "The Song of the Brightness of Water," he again talks about brightness like a mirror in the well. In another poem, he puts himself into the voice and the persona of a woman looking in amazement at her only child. The poem is called "Her Amazement at Her Only Child," and he reflects: "The light that lingered in ordinary things like a spark sheltered under the skin of our days, the light was you, you as the fruit of my body, my blood."

The choice of images of light in these works brings us to the deeper question about Karol Wojtyla's own inner culture, as I have called it, a question about his imagination and his own preparation for what developed from his particular inner light.

Imagination and Personal Integration

I would suggest that there were three dimensions of the pope's inner human life and, therefore, of his life with a humanistic God. He was a phenomenologist, a mystic, and a missionary. A phenomenologist is a philosopher who walks around things carefully in order to see their every aspect, their every dimension. He is someone who looks at the phenomena piece by piece in order to see things whole. But the phenomenon appears in consciousness, and so the phenomenologist is a philosopher of consciousness who carefully tracks the way objects appear in human consciousness. In *The Acting Person,* Wojtyla's fundamental philosophical treatise, he strives to put together an objective metaphysical structure with a phenomenological exploration of human consciousness. He invites us to look at consciousness itself, going beyond looking at the object to reflection in which the ego looking becomes object to itself, and finally to a reflexive process, as he calls it, where subjective consciousness becomes aware of itself subjectively as source of light for knowing whatever is to be known In some way, this consideration can be traced back to the Kantian intellectual *a priori* or to Aristotle's agent intellect. If there is no intellectual agent, there cannot be an object known. But the way Wojtyla traces the co-relation between known object and knowing subject until he gets back to the inner light, the subjective grasp of subjective consciousness, is original. It would not have been possible without his study, first of Neo-Scholastic philosophy, and second, of contemporary phenomenology. Consciousness is not ultimate; he is not an idealist. The consciousness analyzed is always that of the human subject who is a human being; and, in analyzing being, Thomistic metaphysical vocabulary comes into play. In *The Acting Person,* however, Wojtyla shows how consciousness in the act of reflecting penetrates and illuminates whatever becomes in any way man's cognitive possession. This literally puts into mind what classical philosophy has called immanence, the interior light that belongs to consciousness as such, the proper sphere of its activity by which the mind appropriates its received contents according to its own immaterial mode.

Here the pope worked out of the Platonic, Augustinian tradition of the metaphysics of light, but he put this tradition into modern, contemporary phenomenological discourse. The pope remarks that consciousness not only reflects but also interiorizes, in its own specific manner, what it mirrors, thus enclosing or capturing it in the person's ego. In mirroring the immanent content generated in cognitive activity, consciousness reaches a certain self-awareness, although this illumination is not the same as cognitive objectification of self. Rather, it is the return to the self and its inner light that makes it possible to know anything at all, including the self. Here are the beginnings of a phenomenological description of consciousness as spirit, even though the full reality of spirit is not completely accessible to such a description. Nevertheless, it is a description that can be drawn from the experience of our own moral causality as we exercise it in the actions we perform. It is not a reflection upon our ideas, but rather a bringing to the light of full self-consciousness the actions that connect us through our own generosity to a world that gives itself to those who love it.

The pope is a phenomenologist who is a mystic. Wojtyla's doctrinal dissertation in theology was written on the act of faith in St. John of the Cross, the Carmelite mystic. He wrote it in Rome at a time when scholastic terminology and methodology were the *lingua franca* of the ecclesiastical faculties. His director was the great Dominican Thomist Reginald Garrigou-Lagrange, who analyzed even John of the Cross in scholastic terms. Furthermore, Wojtyla wrote his dissertation in Latin, a language good for law and for scholastic methodology, but not useful for doing the kind of concrete psychological analyses that mark phenomenological research. His use of phenomenological tools for analyzing the self-awareness that arises in acting would have to wait until he began to study the work of Max Scheler for his postdoctoral thesis.

The consistent content of the pope's contemplation, is, of course, the act of faith and its object in mysteries. He explored the deposit of faith from various angles in weekly audiences, in encyclicals and discourses. He assimilated the objective content of the faith in his own person at the deepest level of human subjectivity. His life was a work of art, a work that exposed an inner light.

His was a contemplative life. He began the day with an hour of contemplation before celebrating the Eucharist, he recited the Liturgy of the Hours, prayed the Rosary and other devotions. The result of this interior life of prayer was a mystic's conviction that God is in all things, and that all things can be seen through a divine prism, that God is a source of light and action with whom we are called to cooperate by our own seeing, our own cognition, and our own action. God is, again, never in competition with his creatures. God is not jealous of our activity; he encourages and blesses it, for it shows how we are made in the image of a God who acts to create us and save us and make us holy. Out of this mystic's conviction came deep courage.

In the third dimension of the pope's personality, the dimension of his being a missionary, courage is evident. As a phenomenologist, the pope saw things whole in the light of human consciousness. As a mystic, he saw God in all things as a universal prism that is accessible to him in contemplation. As a missionary, he saw God active in history as someone who makes our action possible because he calls us into a life of loving others.

In this light, we see and understand the pope's programs for the Church and also his spirituality for the new millennium. Beginning in the mid-1990s, he invited Catholics to prepare for the two thousandth anniversary of the birth of Jesus Christ. Perhaps it is useful to note that Poles make much of anniversaries. In a country that did not have its own government for many years, that could not therefore act collectively, the celebration of anniversaries of past actions helped shape a proper collective consciousness. Action tells us who we are, uncovers how we think and what we love. In their contest with foreign aggression, Poles took to celebrating anniversaries in order to act in their own proper identity.

In 2000, the Church found herself facing a marvelous anniversary, a millennium. It happened only once before in the Christian history of the human race. The year 2000 of what is now the common era was prepared in stages. The pope told Catholics to prepare for the celebration by doing penance, both individual and collective penance, for actions in history that, even though they were not ours today, nonetheless are in moral continuity with the Church's life. We were called to confess and acknowledge the wrongdoing of the Church in the past in order to prepare for a future full of hope. We could not continue to carry into the new millennium the terrible baggage, divisions, and bloodshed of the past thousand years. There needed to be a purification of memory in our collective historical consciousness as the body of Christ.

The call to penance was preparatory to a new encounter with the one whose anniversary we were to celebrate, with Jesus, whom the pope and all Catholics and other Christians accept as the Savior of the entire world. A new encounter with Christ would bring us to change, and so courage was needed to move toward the millennium. The pope repeated, "Be not afraid. Open the doors to Christ." Open the doors of your self-consciousness, open the doors of your heart, open the doors of your streets, your homes, your city, your school, of everything. Open the doors not to an invader but to someone who is closer to us than we are to ourselves, who accompanies us and draws us into a life of love. We are not alone and we are not in the dark, for a loving God is a light to us in our own experience of thinking and acting.

Another element in Pope John Paul's preparation for the year 2000 made the same point. He called the world's bishops together, continent by continent, not nation by nation. Calling the bishops together as heads of churches that share continents rather than nation states, the pope seemed to be indicating that the age of the nation states was receding and that we must not imagine ourselves first of all as Poles and Chinese and Congolese or Brazilians. Rather, the major carriers of culture in the third millennium would be language groups, international law, and global faiths. Human culture will also be carried by academic life, especially in the major universities, and by popular culture in the mass media. Great literature both reflects and shapes culture, as do great faiths. The pope insisted that a faith cannot be itself, it cannot come to full self-consciousness as faith, it cannot act, if it does not shape culture, the theater of collective action.

As we move further into the new millennium, there will be a shift in our self-understanding and in our relationships within the human race. For example, in the Synod for America, the bishops from this hemisphere found themselves at home with one another. There was a relatively simple linguistic problem with only four languages, rather than the dozens of languages on other continents. The goal of the mission of the Church in this hemisphere, our action together, is to strengthen communion among the local churches, fostering relationships among ourselves and our peoples in this hemisphere. Mexico City and Chicago, for example, are exploring ways to cooperate in mission and to live more closely together in spirit, dwelling in one another's self-consciousness. In light of that strengthened communion of churches, there will be an increased solidarity among peoples.

"Solidarity" is a word that the pope used for decades. It means strengthening the preexistent unity of the human race through conscious loving, through generosity, through self-giving. Spirituality for the future has to answer the question: "In this new millennium, what do you see, and by what light do you see it?" He invited us to see anew various dimensions of Christ's life in the luminous mysteries he added to the contemplative recitation of the rosary. I believe Pope John Paul II would have said that we are to see things whole and to be aware of how our self-consciousness is to be universal in intention and in action. He would have said we should see things whole by recognizing God's activity in his creation, especially in the inner dynamics of human persons who are made in God's image. We should see the working of God in human history and in salvation history. A spirituality for the new millennium fosters contemplation and grounds courage because it helps us see ourselves acting in the world as God uses us.

The Power of Words

Shortly after Karol Wojtyla was elected pope in 1978, I spoke to a Polish priest who was a good friend, someone I had known as a student. I asked him: "What was the reputation of Karol Wojtyla in Poland?" I expected him to say that he was a good archbishop of Krakow, and he did. But he added that Wojtyla was known to be very careful with words. He always sought the most exact word for everything he said. As the bishop of Rome, he said millions of words in many languages, but each word was at the service of those who in Christian faith accept that there is a single Word made flesh who is God's perfect image, Jesus Christ.

He said this word most powerfully in his own country the first time he returned to Poland as bishop of Rome. Much against the will of the government, which was powerless to prevent it, John Paul II stood in Victory Square in downtown Warsaw, in a square that was dominated by a huge monument to the heroic, liberating work of the Soviet army, a square where, for an entire generation, no word about God had been allowed to be uttered in public. No sign, no symbol, no image of faith was to be found there until he came back. Preparing to celebrate the Eucharist there, the Polish people had raised a huge cross next to the monument to the Red Army. There, the pope proclaimed that the history of Poland could not be understood without reference to Jesus Christ. Three months later, the Solidarity labor union was born. Wojtyla's personal history, his poetry, his plays, his philosophy, his theology, his pastoral writings, his ministry as successor to Peter, have to be understood in light of that gesture and that word.

They brought faith and reason together in action that tells us who we are by proclaiming who Christ is in human history. They disclose a spirituality, a Godly humanism, for a new millennium.

A Philosophical Epilogue

Being through Others in Christ
"esse per" and Ecclesial Communion

A T THE END OF the Eucharistic Prayer, the priest lifts the consecrated host and the chalice and tells the people that we glorify God the Father "through, with, and in" Christ Jesus, in the unity of the Holy Spirit. These words proclaim the very life of the Blessed Trinity and call believers to a deeper understanding of the Church's own life and nature. To live at the depth necessary to establish ecclesial communion, believers have to live not just with others or in community with them. They must live through others. What this entails has been explored variously in the dialogues and conversations reflected on in the essays gathered into this book.

Living through others in ecclesial communion depends upon our living through Christ. Christ is the difference that God makes, through the mission of the Church, in the world at large. Such an assertion calls for explanation that is philosophical in nature. In the encyclical letter *Caritas in Veritate,* Pope Benedict XVI calls for a "deeper critical evaluation of the category of relation" (53–55), for the sake of exploring both ecclesial communion and Catholic social teaching. What are the resources for such an evaluation?

Philosophy has long been, in Catholic intellectual life, at the service of faith. Unlike theology, philosophy is not formally a science based on faith. In contrast to philosophers, theologians are epistemologically dependent on the Church, the community of faith

which sets their agenda and judges their results.[1] But to understand who they are and what they do, theologians not only live
with believers; they also visit philosophers.

Ecclesial communion is a "social form"[2] that comes into existence when something of Christ is shared. The external gifts that
Christ left his Church and that he continues to give the Church
through the action of the Holy Spirit in every age to protect and
cause the internal gifts to come to be and develop in believers' lives
are: the Gospel and its elaboration in Church doctrine; the sacraments and other means of grace; and apostolic governance and
pastoral care of various sorts and kinds. The Church has received
these gifts from her Lord because Christ is a prophet who shares
with us his truth; Christ is a priest who shares with us his holiness; and Christ is a shepherd and king who shares with us his
governance. The sharing of these gifts among the baptized creates a social reality in which the gifts become the foundations of
a thick and complicated skein of relationships. The unity so created extends from the relation uniting the ecclesial person to God
to the relations establishing small faith communities, parishes, dio-
ceses and beyond, to a Church so universal that all its members
can never come personally into one another's presence. Yet each is
"present," in some sense, to all those with whom they are in ecclesial
communion.

When a Catholic goes to Mass in a foreign country, he or she
discovers a personal unity made visible in the Eucharist among
people with whom interpersonal communication remains impossible. This and similar experiences have led some[3] to speak of
Catholicism as possessed of a "sacramental consciousness," an
awareness visibly expressed in a variety of cultural forms but always
governed by certain foundational sensitivities to the corporeal,
the communal, the universal, the cosmic, and the transforma-
tional possibilities latent in human experience. If our experience

of being Church is justly described by these adjectives, the reflective believer must wonder why and begin to advance hypotheses that might underpin, if not totally explain, the phenomenon of ecclesial self-consciousness.

In probing ecclesial social form and its internal relations, one might begin with categories already developed in scholasticism's reworking of ancient philosophy.[4] The relations of ecclesial communion could be treated simply as another case of the Aristotelian category of relation. Ecclesial relations, like all other accidents, inhere in a subject, in this case a baptized believer, uniting him or her to another subject who has received the same spiritual gifts. *Esse in* (being in another) and *esse ad* (being toward another) suffice for an analysis of a network of categorical relations, even if the foundations of the network are various supernatural gifts that configure all believers to Christ. This framework of interpretation, however, leaves a singularly important datum of ecclesial self-consciousness unexamined.

Configuration to Christ creates a communion in which differences as well as similarities are shared. Christ is always more than I can be, so my configuration to him relates me to those who are also configured to him but who, because they remain different from myself, even in their configuration to Christ, bring otherness, difference, into the relation itself. In ecclesial communion we cherish differences because each difference tells us something about Christ. At this point, we come to a specifying characteristic of these relations which does not fall neatly into the Aristotelian categories. More than existing with Christ and each other in the Church, more than existing in Christ and each other in the Church, we exist, in the Church, through Christ and through each other.

Is this *esse per* (being through another) ontological, real outside our own mental processes? Certainly, because its foundation, configuration to Christ as prophet, priest, and king, is a real gift not dependent on the mind of the recipient. The evident example is infant baptism. Yet, living through another does seem to necessitate consciousness of the other as other. Think again of the example cited in the introduction to this book, of a wife shopping for her husband's clothes, knowing what he would like better than he knows himself, knowing also that her personal choices for him would be different from the ones she will make in order to please him. The couple have come to share their differences: each lives through the other. This type of relation seems impossible without shared self-consciousness, without the other as other contributing to the unity of one's self-consciousness. Aristotle's theory of categorical relations is not enough.

St. Thomas Aquinas broke at two points the Aristotelian category of relation because it proved too narrow to serve the data of faith: in his reflections on the Holy Trinity and in his explanation of the relation of creation in creatures. Relatedness, defined only as a reference to something else, as *esse ad,* really exists in the Godhead, in which Father, Son, and Spirit partake of one and the same divine nature. Aquinas called Trinitarian relations subsistent because, in the divine unity, they are identified with the divine nature or substance and because, as relations, each is a divine subject of the numerically identical and infinitely unique divine nature. Among the three divine persons, each relationship creates distinction, reference to another person as other. Since these distinctions are immanent to the divine nature, Aquinas borrows Gospel names and develops Augustine's teaching to speak of the second person of the Trinity as Word, emitted when God as source understands himself, and of the third person as Spirit, breathed out when God the source and God the word love each other.

Thomistic Trinitarian theory shows how distinction can be introduced into the fullness of being without predicating a fall into un-being, as is the case with many modern social thinkers. It also shows how persons, the highest instance of being, can be gifts. When a divine person is given to another divine person, both donor and recipient exist through each other, delighting in their difference because their very distinction serves to unite them. The delight is unalloyed because the spiritual nature of the divine persons leaves them totally open, transparent each to the other two. In describing relations of origin which create a community of persons who exist through each other, Trinitarian theory would seem to be the source needed for ecclesiology. And so it is, in part. The triune unity of the Godhead is both source and goal of all the diverse riches shared in the Church.

We must also look outside of Trinitarian theory, however, because the analogy between Trinity and Church cannot be extended into imagining the Church as a single substantial nature shared by believers only relationally distinct. God is one "what" and three "who's" in a manner that any created unity of order fails to match. Unlike Trinitarian relations, ecclesial relations unite believers who are substantially distinct. The Triune God exists in a personal unity of shared subjectivities beyond our nature; yet this Triune God is the finality and, analogously, the form of ecclesial communion. The unity of the Church, while not substantial, is rooted in Trinitarian sharing and is therefore ontologically prior to the persons in ecclesial communion. Is this another lead? A relation constitutive of, yet ontologically prior to substantially distinct beings, describes the relation of creation in creatures as Aquinas treats it in the *De potentia Dei* and, more clearly, in the *Summa theologiae.*

As the relation of creation in creatures, *esse ad* becomes *esse ab* (being from another), because the relation enters into the constitution of substance as created. In Christian creation theory, the Greek self-sufficient, self-enclosed cosmic harmony and its categories of explanation are superseded. In Aquinas's creation theory, created beings are harmoniously related among themselves because all are related by their being to *Ipsum esse subsistens,* which is both transcendent to the cosmos and, as creator, at its immanent heart, its being. God the creator is *Causus ipsius esse.* To understand the relation of creation in creatures, therefore, Aquinas strips Aristotle's categorical relation of Aristotle's usual foundations — quality, quantity, and action/passion — and founds the relation of creation in created substance itself.[5] The relation of dependence of created being on the uncreated cause of being is intrinsic and prior to its subject in the same sense that the divine causality is intrinsic and prior to the creature in the order of total efficient causality. The relation establishes, therefore, an opposition or distinction between Creator and creature without a negation or exclusion of one by the other, despite their substantial difference. The relation of creation in creatures unites *esse in* and *esse ad* in a reference to God as both efficient and exemplary cause.

The Thomistic community of participation in being is therefore a community of substantially distinct beings, related by their metaphysical constitutions, related because of common origin and likeness in *esse* to a first cause. The source of their differences is limitation, whether substantial or accidental, such that one being cannot "be" the other nor be "through" the other except in the realm of instrumental or secondary efficient causality. What has been gained here in respect for distinction and difference, however, results in the loss of the Trinitarian *esse per;* and ecclesial communion is therefore not adequately modeled in the community of finite participants in being. We can conceptualize a community of created beings without self-consciousness, without relation to the other as other; but such a community cannot be called Church. Obviously, participation in being, if it were limited to connectedness through the relation of creation in dumb creatures, would still remain blind and mute "evidence" of God's generosity; but *esse ab* can become *esse per* only in self-conscious, free creatures. Ecclesial communion is of its nature a self-conscious social form.

The Church is always aware of her own history and action, and ecclesial unity needs to be defined not only metaphysically but also ethically. Intelligent and loving human beings, made aware in the Church of their being made in God's image and likeness, are free to reject their ontological status. They know, however, that they are not railing against the fates, as in a Greek tragedy, but sinning against an all-knowing and ever-loving God. The transcendent other is immanent to their very self-consciousness, which moves the believer to seek the explication of such consciousness in theories of common purpose and action. American philosophy is replete with these.

Josiah Royce (1855–1916) spent his lifetime pursuing, presenting, and explaining a self-conscious structure that intrinsically relates finite individuals to an infinite community both temporal or historical and ethical or normative. Its biography in his writing is long, with important logical twists and metaphysical turns. Finally, he came to call it the Beloved Community. Is it really the Church, come to more self-conscious awareness of its own structured unity? Could Catholic communion find in this classical American philosopher's thought the makings of a theory adequate to her ancient structure and life?

Royce's thematization of social form begins with conflict experience. The conflict, if considered epistemologically, is error; if considered ontologically, it is particularity or finitude. Its subjective and ethical expression is disloyalty, a disloyalty felt at the core of one's being:

> The individual, brought by his very cultivation to a clearer consciousness of the conflict between his self-will and the social laws which tradition inflicts upon him, finds a war going on in his own members.[6]

How bring peace, create unity out of disunity in a consciousness at war with itself? How resolve the separate tugs of opposing loyalties? By willfully constructing an ideal extension of present experience as part of a postulated future in which the great community is able to include all presently disparate purposes. As this choice of a future more inclusive and universal becomes conceptualized and then institutionalized, the future community becomes a higher cause, one more worthy of our loyalty today. Any society is united and harmonious to the extent that all its members engage in creating this ideal community, which is both the dialectical condition of the possibility of present experience and itself dependent on present individual choice.

This community of reconciliation and inclusion, which commands our present loyalty, is a community of interpretation. In 1901, Royce explained to the YMCA at Harvard that what is vital in Christianity is its power of interpreting experience in ideal terms. Religion is normative in our experience not because it has a distinct ethics but because it constantly reminds us of our unity in the Absolute and gives us the emotional support "to bear the sorrow of our finitude and turn our grief into a source of blessing."[7] The metaphysical structure of this community, which is both interpersonal and temporal, is borrowed from C. S. Peirce's logic of signs. Interpretation is a communitarian activity because it is a joining, a communion, of three poles: the interpreter, the sign or object interpreted, and the person for whom the interpretation is intended, the interpretee.

By way of example, one can imagine an international conference during which speeches are translated simultaneously. The speaker's words are the sign or object interpreted; the translator is the interpreter; and those who do not understand the speaker's language are the interpretees. Together, they form a community of interpretation. Without one of the three, but especially without the interpreter, no community exists, and the conference becomes impossible. To push the example a bit further, one can imagine a particularly abstruse speech that makes little sense even to those who understand the language in which it is delivered. Then another sort of interpreter is called for, perhaps a teacher or clarifier, who creates community between speaker and those spoken to. What might happen should even the speaker not understand his speech? Probably the situation would then call for that sort of interpreter called a counselor or psychiatrist, who can explain the speaker to himself. In any set of circumstances, however, the act of interpreting means that someone interprets something or someone to and for another. The "other" might be the interpreter himself at a different time. Everyone has had the experience of puzzling through a conundrum and finally "interpreting" it to himself; but even in this case there are three logically distinct subjects of the relationship: interpreter, interpreted and interpretee. Interpretation is always a communitarian activity.

Royce's theory has obvious value for explaining the Church's task or mission. The Church is a community that interprets the Gospel anew in each generation. Royce also helps us understand how the Church is necessarily a visible, historical community, since, chronologically, the interpreter is in the present, the interpreted in the past, and the interpretee in the future. The activity of interpreting creates a community of memory and of hope. There is a Christian community, therefore, because in the present we all interpret the past Christ-event in such a way that we look forward to his future coming in glory. Those who do not look back to Jesus of Nazareth as Lord and Savior or do not look forward to the Parousia are not members of the visible Church. There is, between them and us, no common interpretation of past history and no common expectations of a shared future. Individuals in Royce's Beloved Community exist through others to the extent they find conceptual space for the other in an inclusive interpretation of future experience. Does this mean, however, that otherness is something to be overcome rather than something to be cherished? A positive answer to this question would diminish Royce's usefulness in explaining ecclesial communion; and his answer must be sought, I believe, in his theory about how individual self-consciousness is born.

Royce explains that the contrast between ego and non-ego arises when an individual imperfectly imitates another's actions. Insofar as I am able to imitate another's act, that act takes on an inner meaning that I could never have recognized if I had remained content with simply observing what another person is doing.[8] My trying to imitate another makes me self-conscious, however, because I do not fit smoothly into the other's act. It represents a pattern of activity foreign to my usual mode of acting. The other becomes real to me precisely as someone whose activities have meanings that are not usually part of my life. The consciousness of this difference fills in the content of the ego, providing a new perspective or interpretation of the action in question.

Consciousness for Royce is "appropriative," to use William James's term.[9] Consciousness reaches out, groping toward the next experience while tucking the last away in conceptualization. The reflective self-consciousness is the psychological condition of the possibility of interpretation. It is the mediating element or interpreter in the triad of interpretation, but it seems curiously devoid of any appropriation of its own activity or of joy in joining itself to another in common action. Consciousness is predominantly critical. It comes to life by separating itself from nature and from other finite consciousness. It further defines itself by reference to its own possible experience, again negatively conceived as conditional or as a norm contrary to actual fact. "Living through" turns out to be less a relation to the other as other than a relation to the similarities we imagine among us or are able to construct through purposive judgment.

Royce gives us much in our search for the philosophical underpinnings of ecclesial communion: a close unity of finite and distinct persons, each conscious and loyal, intrinsically related and, together, free to fashion their common history, living through each other's similar interpretation of a shared future, transforming the world into a community because the world contains its own interpreter whose processes are infinite in their temporal varieties and their ideal permutations.

What we have gained for our understanding of ecclesial social form does not go far, however, because the original giftedness that founds the Church is not clearly disclosed in Royce's loyalty to an infinite self-sustaining process. Royce is often accused of buying unity at the price of collapsing the real distinction, the absolute otherness, between finite and infinite. For the Christian believer, this is a gap that can be bridged only by infinite graciousness rather than by an ideally infinite series of finite choices and interpretations. If God cannot be found also apart from the finite agents constructing the future, then God is the only one who cannot give original meaning to the universe. Differences among ourselves are then included in the future community only as divisions still to be resolved or possibilities still unattended to and therefore not willed. In social theory, Royce would recognize arguments from a search for common ground, a pragmatic notion, but he has no way to ground the common good as source and criterion for our common action. Royce's ethical community lacks a theory of common action based on the truth about the separateness of things.

Such a theory might well be a marriage between a phenomenology of will and a metaphysics of personal being. This can be found, in a somewhat complex manner, in Karol Wojtyla's theory of personal agency.[10] In the future pope's analysis of the acting person and of the person in community, we find a project designed, first of all, to heal the modern split between subject and object. This split has opened chasms between subjective person and objective society, between subjective faith and public life. To restore to human persons both their subjective wholeness and their concrete totality, Wojtyla begins with the phenomenon of "I-act." In acting, the human subject comes to self-possession through conscious self-determination; and acting in the world reveals the "I," the subject, as related. Self-consciousness becomes deeper and more integrated as action brings a person into ever wider fields of experience.

While Wojtyla makes extensive use of phenomenological analysis, the acting person, not consciousness, is subject of existence and action. In every act there is "co-given" with the action the self's experience of itself as the source of the act. As the inner principle of the human act, will is at least as definitive of subjective existence as is reason. The various dynamisms that occur in consciousness retain a personal concreteness in Wojtyla's analysis, because he recognizes that their appearance in consciousness is always filtered through the will. Self-knowledge is not a shadowy appearance on the fringes of someone's consciousness of an object's essence; it is at the center of an action deliberately willed by an experiencing subject interacting with an object. Individuation, which in classical Aristotelian and Thomistic theory is rooted in matter, is established more personally in Wojtyla's anthropology through responsible action. Action reveals both what and who we are; it shapes us ontologically as well as psychologically.

In acting, persons achieve both self-possession and inter-relationship. Action discloses the "I" wholly engaged, the totality of the subject. The person provides the dynamic unity which explains continuity and responsibility throughout the diversity of acts, but the act also contains or structures the mutual interaction between the interiority of the subject and the exteriority of the body and social context that, taken all together, provide the object and the conditions of the act. We change in acting. We are what we do, but we are infinitely more as well. Analysis of the "I-act" discloses the object of the action, of course, but it also and more importantly bestows reflective insight into the object that each person is for himself while acting. While many modern theories of personal identity stop here, effectively turning the subject into a particular kind of object, Wojtyla's analysis of action also shows the person endowed with reflexive self-consciousness, able to be immediately present to and aware of himself as the subject of action and experience.[11] The total person is disclosed in these three dimensions of an acting subject's awareness: (1) in the subject's awareness of an object of action; (2) in the subject's awareness of the subject reflecting on himself as object in action; and (3) in the subject's awareness of the self reflexively, as subject of action.

How does Wojtyla's understanding of personal subjectivity, which integrates self-knowledge and self-transcendence, openness to other subjects and to the world at large, position the person acting in concert with others? How are the structures of personal consciousness opened up in responsible action carried through history by the human subject acting with other human subjects? A person's right to freedom and identity is ontologically basic because of the personal self-possession that is revealed in responsible action. Action, however, is also open to moral judgment according to whether or not the goals of the action are truly in accord with the full subjectivity which the action brings to self-awareness. This ethical judgment on every individual human action cannot be determined by an isolated self-consciousness. Freedom is rooted in a personal, subjective relationship to objective truth, which is a common value in human community and which remains transcendent to all individuals who come to awareness of it. The process of bringing personal subjectivity to objective self-knowledge and to full subjective self-consciousness involves knowing the objective truth, acting freely and rightly in surrender to it and thus coming to self-awareness as a particular person in a community that both knows what it means to be human and values each person as end or goal.

How does Wojtyla describe social form? What forms of human community do acting persons create? There are two, each summed up under the rubric of participation.[12] Wojtyla's philosophical anthropology analyzes the human person in action, and persons act together. Wojtyla distinguishes two types of participation in action: "we" relations and "I-You" relations. The "we" relation unifies persons who face each other indirectly while acting together for the sake of a value faced directly by all, a common good transcendent to them all:

> The pronoun "we," directly indicates the plurality, while pointing only indirectly to the persons belonging to the plurality. "We" signifies first of all a set; this set is, of course, composed of people or persons. The set, which we may call a society or a social group, does not of itself possess a substantial being. However... it brings to the fore that which results from the accidental relation between people as persons; hence, it provides a basis for predication firstly regarding and only secondly regarding each one in the set. This is precisely what is contained in the pronoun "we."[13]

Wojtyla does not argue to the existence of any quasi-substantial "collective person," nor does he insist that a common good must itself possess some sense of personal identity. People come together as "we" for all sorts of purposes, from trout fishing to the alleviation of hunger in another country. However, if human subjectivity is submerged for the attainment of a common goal which is ontologically inferior to the persons acting together for it, the risk of alienation is real. But the social form itself is valid.

Unlike the "We" relation that creates society, in which the object of self-consciousness is shared by all as a common value, the "I-You" relationship that forms community brings immediately to the fore of consciousness the acting subject's self-consciousness as reflective (the self is conscious of being an object for another person) and reflexive (the self is conscious of being its own subject in its growing awareness, through the course of the action, that the other person is also a subject). The human person, both as the "I" and the "You," is a subject who not only exists but also acts. Wojtyla explains:

> In this action the "You" becomes at every step an object for the "I," and this objectivity relates back to the "I" by virtue of a peculiar interaction: the "I" becomes in a special way an object for itself in the action directed objectively to the "You." This, of course, belongs organically, as it were, to the process of constituting the "I" through the "You." If the "I" ... constitutes its own self through its acts, and in the same way the "You" is also constituted as another "I," then the relation "I-You" and the relative effects of this pattern in both its subjects are similarly constituted. The subject experiences the relation to the "You" in the action whose object is "You," and vice versa. Through the action directed objectively toward the "You," the subject "I" not only experiences himself in the relation to the "You," but also experiences his own self in a new way in his own subjectivity. The objectivity of both action and interaction is the source of the confirmation of the subjectivity of the agent, probably simply because the subject is a subject in itself and represents a personal subjectivity peculiar to himself.[14]

In acting, I return to myself through you, when the "You" is another "I" in our mutual interaction. My usual making of myself an object in reflective consciousness seems to be superseded in the "I-You" relation, with the other taking my place, even in my own reflective consciousness; there then occurs an attendant change in my reflexive consciousness, such that I become more intensely aware that my own subjectivity is shared interiorly and intimately. What is emphasized in this relation that creates community is the unity of "I" and "You," their real interchangeability along with the welcome presence of real differences that are not threats but gifts. Unity is here experienced more strongly than is the multiplicity that characterizes the societal "We" relations.

Is this "passing over" to the other and "coming back to self" dialectical? No, at least not in the Roycean or Hegelian sense. It is not a movement from individual differences to common interpretation to shared inclusive project. Nor is it a movement from potentiality to actuality to necessity, except to the extent that spirit "needs" to be *diffusivum sui* (self-giving). The "other" is not a necessary part of myself but simply an invitation to self-transcendence, not something I need in order to be what I choose to be or must become. When I come back to myself enriched with the other's subjectivity and having given myself to the other, my own subjectivity is intensified in the sharing of reflexive consciousness with the "You" who is, in acting, just as truly me as I am "I" myself.

Rescuing this analysis from what might seem complicated jargon can help clarify the nature of ecclesial communion. The condition of the possibility of the social form called communion is reflexive self-consciousness, an awareness born when, in acting together in Christ, each believer passes over to the other and, in the transcendence of shared self-conscious action, begins to be through the other. The self returns to itself transformed, not necessarily bearing new objects for contemplation but with new subjective strength, a new sense of moral agency, of mission. The ecclesial self receives its subjectivity back as gift, gift first of all from God through Christ in the power of the Spirit, and gift also from and through other believers.

A final word can now be said about the common interiority that is predicated of the Church as such, as social form. If, for the individual believer, knowing in communion takes the form of transparent presence to the other, and loving in communion means surrender of one's subjectivity to the other, then, in the Church as such, in the action of the whole, knowing is dialogue in which the other is discovered as an occasion for mutual conversion and loving is that form of charity that goes out to the other in order to receive the ability to give.

Communion as social form, therefore, "means a stable, immanent dynamism of the community which, from multiplicity and
complexity moves toward the unity proper not only to a people
but also of a body — and, at the same time, with the same power
and efficacy, sustains the complexity and multiplicity in the very
same unity of the people and of the body."[15] This is the definition of
communion offered by Archbishop Wojtyla when he explained the
Second Vatican Council's teaching on the Church to the people of
Cracow. What the people of Cracow might have made of it is perhaps unclear; but, in the light of his philosophical anthropology,
the point itself is clear, and it became ever clearer in his own action
as bishop. The unity of a people, their social form, may be only societal; but the unity of a body, which is a primordial externalization
of personal subjectivity, is necessarily communal.

When writing about bodies in intimate interaction, that is, about
human sexuality, Karol Wojtyla examines a continuum of personal relationships, starting with those based on the sexual urge
and culminating in the relationship of betrothed love.[16] In each
relationship, the subjective experience correlates the person with
an object. As the experience becomes more personal, the object
becomes another subject. At one end of the relationships spectrum,
our sexual urges relate us to the other as body and, while good in
themselves, these urges can become the end of a relationship rather
than its beginning. They can move us toward using another person
merely as an object for our own pleasure.

At a higher level, our emotions relate us to the other as value
for ourselves. Our affections relate us to the other as an ideal; but
they can blind us to the person because all we might see is a noble
abstraction. Our sympathy relates us to another more personally, as
a subject of mutual experience. Sympathy, which can still be easily
distorted by subjectivism, can flower into friendship.

In friendship, each wants what is good for the other person. The
friends move beyond the realm of emotions and sympathy to that

of will, and the wills of the two parties form a moral unity. Each is another "I" for the other, and each calls the other to be more than he or she might be alone. If this relationship is extended to many people, it can be described as comradeship, in which all are morally united for the sake of an objective common good or interest. All then freely participate in common activity, creating a solidarity that overcomes both individualism and collectivism. The highest form of friendship, however, is the relationship of betrothed love. Lovers relate in complete mutual trust. They remain committed to each other permanently and can rely on each other implicitly. They live through each other. In betrothed love, participation in the common good becomes mutual self-surrender.

In this array of relationships, I believe we can characterize the Church's social form as a complex ordered unity, part society and part community. God, as common good of believers, is the basis of a set of "We" relations that take on more and more the qualities of reciprocity characteristic of collective "I-You" relations as the goal, union with God, is attained. We grow in love for each other as we grow in union with God. We cannot face God directly without facing each other, directly as well as indirectly. As we enter more fully into ecclesial life, our participation becomes solidarity, a common self-giving. Ecclesial communion is, at its most developed, its own common good. If the Church is true to her most authentic self, she can gather for the sake of her own gathering, confident that, in her, all are gathered in Christ. Her action transforms the world, but her goals reach beyond this world. Of her nature, the Church is not a party; she is an instrument only of her Lord.

In moving together toward union with God, individuals remain unfused, whether with God or with each other. Each person is always an end and never a means. Believers with a developed ecclesial consciousness, however, live and experience their relations of communion in the Church in an ever more personalized fashion. The Church is a society, a set of "We" relations, whose inner dynamism is to become a community in God. Specifically, the Church is a society whose common good is love, an "I-You" relation personalized in the Holy Spirit given to all believers. In the Spirit, the "We" of the Church becomes the "I" of an "I-You" relationship with God. To the extent their faith is an experience of self-surrender, believers' experience of Church gradually becomes more and more infused with the intimacy of marriage. The transformation in ecclesial communion of group relationships from societal to communal accounts for the use of personal images in Scripture to describe the Church: body, bride, mother, living temple, family.

In the light of this analysis, it is also clear that scriptural images for Church are not mere metaphors. They are names designating the self-consciousness peculiar to ecclesial social form, ecclesial relations.

The Church is aware of herself as vital, and so calls herself a body. The Church is aware of herself as personal, and so calls herself a bride who surrenders herself to Christ. The Church is aware of herself as subject, as an active, abiding presence that mediates a believer's experience, and so calls herself mother. The Church is aware of herself as integrated, and so describes herself as temple of the Holy Spirit, a missionary body, able to communicate Christ's message and life to the whole world. The unity of shared reflexive consciousness among separate entelechies or personal *supposita* living through each other is strong enough, thick enough, to carry realist predicates.[17]

A terribly debilitating weakness of contemporary American Catholic life is the habit of treating even doctrinal questions extrinsically, as matters to be settled politically rather than through deepened insight into revelation. If ecclesial self-consciousness is born of common action, and if action is stymied by lack of insight into the manner in which we each live through Christ and one another in order to be ourselves, then the mission of the Church is paralyzed and the Church forgets who she truly is. Believers are true to themselves when they raise the question of who they are in ecclesial communion and judge all their personal actions in the light of that truth which, when all is said and done, is Christ himself:

"I am the way, the truth and the life; no one comes to the Father but through me." (John 14:6)

Notes

Chapter 1 / Of God and Man

1. This chapter is adapted from an address given June 16, 1999, at the Library of Congress.

2. Robert Sokolowski, *The God of Faith and Reason* (Notre Dame, Ind.: University of Notre Dame Press, 1982), 41–43.

3. Anselm of Canterbury, *Proslogion* in *St. Anselm: Basic Writings* (La Salle, Ill.: Open Court Press, 1962), 7.

4. Thomas Aquinas, *Summa theologiae,* Ia, q. 4, art. 2.

5. Thomas Aquinas, *De potentia,* q. 3, art. 1.

6. John Milbank, *Theology and Social Theory: Beyond Secular Reason* (Oxford: Blackwell Publishing, 1990), 389–90.

7. St. Augustine, *The City of God against the Pagans* (Cambridge: Cambridge University Press, 1998), Books 1 through 10.

8. Milbank, *Theology and Social Theory,* 389.

9. Catherine Pickstock, *After Writing: On the Liturgical Consummation of Philosophy* (Oxford: Blackwell Publishing, 1998), 142–45.

10. Ibid., 121–26.

11. John Milbank, "Only Theology Overcomes Metaphysics" in *The Word Made Strange,* ed. John Milbank (Oxford: Blackwell Publishing, 1997), 40–41.

12. William Placher, *The Domestication of Transcendence* (Louisville: Westminster John Knox Press, 1996), 80.

13. Thomas Hobbes, *Leviathan* (New York: Penguin Books, 1968), 186.

14. Reinhold Niebuhr, "Augustine's Political Realism," in *The Essential Reinhold Niebuhr: Selected Essays and Addresses,* ed. Robert McAfee Brown (New Haven: Yale University Press, 1986), 123.

15. Reinhold Niebuhr, *Moral Man and Immoral Society* (New York: Charles Scribner's Sons, 1932), 257–59.

16. H. Richard Niebuhr, *Christ and Culture* (New York: Harper and Row, 1951), 45–189.

17. John Courtney Murray, *We Hold These Truths* (New York: Sheed and Ward, 1960), 10.

18. Ibid., 28.

19. Ibid., 48–49.

20. Michael Baxter, C.S.C., "Writing History in a World without Ends: An Evangelical Catholic Critique of United States Catholic History," *Pro Ecclesia* 5, no. 4 (Fall 1996): 446.

21. *Dignitatis humanae,* in *The Documents of Vatican II* (New York: Herder and Herder, 1966), 679–82.

22. John Paul II, *Christifideles laici,* 37–45.

23. Josephism refers to the kind of state domination of religious affairs associated at an early date with Emperor Joseph I of Austria (ruled 1705–11).

Chapter 2 / Evangelizing American Culture

1. Avery Dulles, S.J., *The Catholicity of the Church* (New York: Oxford University Press, 1985), 175.

2. Louis J. Luzbetak, S.V.D., *The Church and Cultures: New Perspectives in Missiological Anthropology* (Maryknoll, N.Y.: Orbis, 1988), 223–91.

3. Marcello de Carvalho Azevedo, S.J., *Inculturation and the Challenges of Modernity* (Rome: Gregorian University Press, 1982). Father Azevedo, a Brazilian Jesuit, explores the relations between Catholic faith and modern culture. While American modernity is influenced by our Puritan heritage, it is also the product of the dynamics of capitalist economic development. A capitalist economy can flourish in different political systems, but it has natural affinity for the social contract theories associated with classical liberalism. In this situation, which is the case in the United States, the model for all relations easily becomes the commercial contract.

4. William A. Dyrness, *How Does America Hear the Gospel?* (Grand Rapids: Eerdmans, 1989), 62–64 and 84–86.

5. Alexis de Tocqueville's *Democracy in America* is the starting point for an influential cultural critique by a group under the direction of sociologist Robert N. Bellah, *Habits of the Heart: Individualism and Commitment in American Life* (New York: Harper and Row, 1986).

6. While this chapter traces individualism back to Puritan religious experience, its civil counterpart is usually attributed to the political theories of English philosopher John Locke (1632–1704). Locke retained a sense of natural law that the American founders used to justify their rejection of the social contract with the British Crown. As our legal system has become more positivistic and our society more pluralistic, Locke's defense of the natural rights of individuals has become less

influential and the philosophy of Thomas Hobbes (1588–1677) more so. Hobbes taught that rights are reducible to force, and government acts primarily as a referee among competing interests.

Chapter 3 / Sowing the Gospel on American Soil

1. This chapter is adapted from an address given to the Catholic Theological Society of America, June 7, 2001.

2. John Henry Newman, *Apologia pro vita sua* (New York: Doubleday, 1956), 127.

3. See James William McClendon, *Systematic Theology*, vol. 3: *Witness* (Nashville: Abingdon, 2000), 81–88.

4. Friedrich Schleiermacher, *The Christian Faith* (Edinburgh: T & T Clark, 1989), 40.

5. Thomas Aquinas, *Summa theologiae,* Ia, q. 1, art. 1.

6. Hans Urs von Balthasar, *Theo-drama: Theological Dramatic Theory,* vol. 3, *Dramatis Personae: Persons in Christ* (San Francisco: Ignatius Press, 1992), 26.

7. John Henry Newman, *An Essay on the Development of Christian Doctrine* in *Conscience, Consensus and the Development of Doctrine* (New York: Image, 1992), 101–13.

8. See John Milbank, *Theology and Social Theory: Beyond Secular Reason* (Oxford: Blackwell Publishing, 1990), 302–6.

9. *Planned Parenthood of Southeastern Pennsylvania v. Casey,* 112 Sup. Ct. 2791, at 2807.

10. Pope John Paul II, October 5, 1979, in *U.S.A.: Message of Justice, Peace, and Love* (Boston: St. Paul Editions, 1979), 198.

11. Ibid., 199.

12. Ibid., 200.

13. John Paul II, Homily in Dodger Stadium, September 16, 1987.

14. Address of Pope John Paul II during His Visit to Battery Park, October 3, 1979, in John Paul II, *U.S.A.: Message of Justice, Peace, and Love,* 95.

15. John Paul II, Homily at Logan Circle, Philadelphia, October 3, 1979, ibid., 96.

16. Ibid., 109.

17. This biographical sketch was taken from *L'Osservatore Romano: Weekly Edition in English,* November 21, 1988.

Chapter 4 / Making All Things New

1. This chapter is adapted from an address given to the Kendrick Lecture in St. Louis, March 22, 2000.

Chapter 5 / Ancient Traditions in Contemporary Culture

1. This chapter is adapted from an earlier address given to the First Friday Club of Chicago, October 1, 2004.

2. Ibid.

3. Ibid.

4. Francis Cardinal George, O.M.I., "The Quandary of Being a Catholic and a U.S. Citizen," in *Chicago Studies* 43, no. 2 (Summer 2004): 119–29.

5. Francis E. George, O.M.I., *Inculturation and Ecclesial Communion: Culture and Church in the Teaching of Pope John Paul II* (Rome: Urbaniana University Press, 1990), 107.

6. See John Paul II, "Address to Priests, assembled at the Oratory of St. Joseph, Montreal, Canada, September 11, 1984," *AAS* 77 (1985): 389–97.

7. George Weigel, *Witness to Hope: The Biography of Pope John Paul II* (New York: HarperCollins, 1999), 7.

8. George, *Inculturation and Ecclesial Communion*, 120–21.

9. *Nostra aetate: The Declaration on the Relationship of the Church to Non-Christian Religions,* no. 2, in *The Documents of Vatican II,* ed. Walter M. Abbot, S.J. (New York: American Press, 1966), 662–63.

10. George, *Inculturation and Ecclesial Communion,* 217.

Chapter 6 / A Necessary Conversation

1. This chapter is adapted from an address given as the seventh annual Henri de Lubac Lecture in Historical Theology, delivered at St. Louis University, April 19, 2002.

2. Francis Cardinal George, "Catholic Christianity and the Millennium: Frontiers of the Mind," address at the Library of Congress, June 16, 1999 (unpublished; this talk appears in modified form as chapter 1 of the current book).

3. Gabriel Meyer, "Troubled Beginnings, Hope for Dialogue in Understanding Islam," *Catholic International* (February 2002): 41.

4. Pope John Paul II, *Crossing the Threshold of Hope* ed. Vittorio Messari, trans. Kenny McPhee and Martha McPhee (New York: Knopf, 1994), 93.

5. Ibid., 92.

6. Josef Cardinal Ratzinger, *Salt of the Earth: The Church at the End of the Millennium* (San Francisco: Ignatius Press, 1997), 244.

7. Bernard Lewis: *What Went Wrong? Western Impact and Middle Eastern Responses* (New York: Oxford University Press, 2002), 100.

8. Mohammed Said Al-Ashmari in *Liberal Islam: A Source Book,* ed. Charles Kurzman (New York: Oxford University Press, 1998), 50.

9. Antoine Moussali, *La croix et le croissant: le christianisme face a l'islam* (Paris: Editions de Paris, 1998), 87.

10. Bat Ye'or, *The Decline of Eastern Christianity under Islam: From Jihad to Dhimmitude* (Madison, N.J.: Fairleigh Dickinson University Press, 1996), passim.

11. Lewis, *What Went Wrong?* 106–7.

12. Al Ashmari, *La croix et le croissant,* passim.

13. Lewis, *What Went Wrong?* 100.

14. Walid Saif, "An Assessment of Christian Muslim Dialogue," *Catholic International* (February 2002): 38.

15. Lewis, *What Went Wrong?* 156.

16. Charles Kurzman, "Liberal Islam: And Its Liberal Content," *Liberal Islam: A Source Book,* ed. Charles Kurzman (New York: Oxford University Press, 1998), 6.

17. Mamadiou Dia, quoted in ibid., 13.

18. Ibid., 12.

19. Ibid.

20. Ibid. Commentators describe three ways in which liberal Islam relates to the primary sources of Islam, which are the basis of Islamic law, the Sharia. "The first mode takes liberal positions as being explicitly sanctioned by the Sharia; the second argues that Muslims are free to adopt liberal positions on subjects that the Sharia leaves open to human ingenuity; the third mode suggests that the Sharia, while divinely inspired, is subject to multiple human interpretations" (Lewis, *What Went Wrong?* 14). All three in varying degrees are questioned or opposed by traditional scholars and interpreters of Islamic law. Yet the debate is on, and its impact on Islam cannot be denied. Its significance for dialogue and for the place of Islam in the modern world is considerable. It means that significant numbers of Muslims, and many of those among the most thoughtful, stand against theocracy, for democracy, for the rights of women, for the rights of non-Muslims, for freedom of thought, for some possibility of progress. In all of this, liberal Muslims "seek to ground their interpretation of Islam in a return to the original sources," seeing such causes as "part of proper Islamic practice" (ibid., 25).

In the 1950s and the 1960s these developments were conditioned by the resentment that, at many levels in Muslim countries, began to build up against the colonialism of the West. Western progress in most fields came to be seen as a humiliating criticism of the apparent inability of Muslim countries to adapt and to organize their economies and societies in a way that would benefit them similarly. This led numbers of Muslim thinkers and politicians to look for a solution in socialism. The outcome was a disastrous failure (ibid., 62). A high level of state involvement in national economies had preceded this socialist phase and continues after it — all with the same lack of success. Nor did a strong current toward nationalism offer a remedy; it did ensure that most Muslims now live in independent states, at the expense of dividing and disrupting the wider Islamic community but without effectively bringing Islam into the modern world or to a real share in its advantages (ibid., 158).

21. Ratzinger, *Salt of the Earth,* 245–46.

22. Ibid., 239.

23. Ibid.

24. Eugene Linden, "Showdown in Cairo," *Time,* September 5, 1994: 53.

25. Ibid., 54.

26. Ibid.

27. Muzammil Siddiqi, "How an Islamic Leader Views Dialogue," *Catholic International* (February 2002): 18.

28. Archbishop Alexander Brunett, "What Dialogue Means for Catholics and Muslims," *Catholic International* (February 2002): 12.

29. It is recognized that there must be an openness if there is to be dialogue. The Muslim scholar Dr. Walid Saif says: "It is inherent in religiosity and part of the religious freedom for one to believe that his/her religion is the truest one. But for this belief not to breed exclusion it should never imply that the believer is the truest." He elaborates on this: "The dialogue serves to promote our awareness of so many issues otherwise outside our conceptual gaze.... It motivates us to reconsider ideas and concepts outside our own tradition, certainly without compromising our religious constants and foundational conviction.... Our common grounds and concerns should be defined in positive terms, stemming from our own initiative as faithful Muslims and Christians — from our awareness and moral obligations dictated by our religions," in "Striving Together in Dialogue: Report on Muslim-Christian Dialogue," in Saif, "An Assessment of Christian Muslim Dialogue." 39.

30. *Catholic International* (February 2002), 35.

31. Avery Cardinal Dulles, "Christ among the Religions," lecture at Fordham University, November 7, 2001, 17. In a joint document of the Pontifical Council for Interreligious Dialogue and the Congregation for the Evangelization of Peoples published in 1991, four kinds of dialogue are described: (1) The dialogue of life where people strive to live in an open and neighborly spirit, sharing their joys and sorrows, their human problems and preoccupations. Clearly this goes on already in some places, but it needs to be extended greatly if there is to be a solid foundation for the reception of other kinds of dialogue between the Catholic Church and Muslims. (2) The dialogue of action in which Christians and others collaborate for the integral development and liberation of people. (3) The dialogue of theological exchange where specialists seek to deepen their understanding of their respective religious heritages and to appreciate each other's values. (4) The dialogue of religious experience

where persons, rooted in their own religious traditions, share their spiritual riches, for instance with regard to prayer and contemplation, faith and ways of searching for God. Though prayer together will not be possible, the concern for holiness can be a strong bond (Pontifical Council for Interreligious Dialogue and the Congregation for the Evangelization of Peoples: Dialogue and Proclamation, 1991).

32. The formula that made the Assisi Prayer for Peace in 1986 and 2002.

33. Pontifical Council for Interreligious Dialogue and the Congregation for the Evangelization of Peoples, 48.

34. Henri de Lubac, *Catholicism: A Study of Dogma in Relation to the Corporate Destiny of Mankind* (New York: Longmans, 1950), 107–25.

35. Congregation for the Doctrine of the Faith, *Dominus Jesus* (2000): 16.

36. In the words of Pope John Paul II, it is a matter of asking together "the real questions: the truth about God and the truth about man. God is not at the beck and call of one individual or one people, and no human venture can claim to monopolize him. The children of Abraham know that God cannot be commandeered by anyone: God is to be received." The Pope illustrates this from the perspective of Catholic faith when he says: "Standing before the crib, Christians can better realize that Jesus himself did not impose himself, and he rejected the use of power as a means of promoting his kingdom" (Address to the Diplomatic Corps, January 10, 2002, *Origins* 31, no. 33 [January 31, 2002]: 541–45).

37. Christoph Cardinal Schönborn, "Why the Uniqueness of Christ and the Church Lead to Dialogue," *Origins* 31, no. 37 (February 28, 2002): 623.

38. Address to the Islamic Leaders of Senegal (1991) in *John Paul II and Interreligious Dialogue*, ed. Byron L. Sherwin and Harold Kasimow (Maryknoll, N.Y.: Orbis Books, 1999), 67.

39. Ibid., 68.

40. Address to the Young Muslims of Morocco (1985), in Sherwin and Kasimow, *John Paul II and Interreligious Dialogue*, 62.

41. Address to the Delegation of the World Islamic Call Society (1990), in Sherwin and Kasimow, *John Paul II and Interreligious Dialogue*, 64.

42. Message to the Faithful of Islam, Ramadan (1991), in Sherwin and Kasimow, *John Paul II and Interreligious Dialogue*, 65.

43. Pope John Paul II, apostolic exhortation *Ecclesia in America* (1999): 52.

44. Fazlur Rahman, *Major Themes of the Quran* (Minneapolis: Bibliotheca Islamica, 1980), 62.

45. Moussali, *La croix et le croissant*, 14–15.

46. de Lubac, *The Christian Faith: An Essay on the Structure of the Apostles' Creed* (San Francisco: Ignatius, 1986), 162, 165.

47. Romano Guardini, *Vie de la foi* (Paris: Editions du Cerf, 1968), 23.

48. de Lubac, *The Christian Faith*, 301.

49. Ibid., 82.

50. Christopher Dawson, *Medieval Essays* (New York: Sheed, 1956), 117ff, 135ff.

51. Pope John Paul II, *Novo millennio ineunte* (2000): 55.

52. Ibid.

53. Moussali, *La croix et le croissant*, 95–102.

54. M. Basil Pennington, "Cistercian Martyrs of Algeria" *Review for Religious* 55, no. 6 (1996): 608.

55. Ibid., 611.

Chapter 7 / The Universal Church and the Dynamic of Globalization

1. Pope John Paul II, "From justice of each comes peace for all," *L'Osservatore Romano* (English weekly edition), nos. 51/52 (December 17–24, 1997).

2. Emphasis in the original.

3. April 28, 2007, letter to Professor Mary Ann Glendon, President of the Pontifical Academy of Social Sciences.

4. These sentiments of building up a just and equitable culture were echoed in many of the interventions at the 1997 Synod for America. See especially those of Bishop Morales Reyes of Mexico, Bishop Arancedo of Argentina, and Bishop Collazzi of Uruguay.

Chapter 8 / One Lord and One Church for One World

1. *Redemptor hominis* [*RH*] 1.

2. *Tertio millennio adveniente* (1994).

3. *Redemptoris missio* [*RMis*] 2.

4. Ibid. This is implied in his observation that "in the Church's history, missionary drive has always been a sign of vitality, just as its lessening is a sign of a crisis in faith."

5. "What is man? What is the meaning of suffering, evil, death…? What is the purpose of these [human] achievements, purchased at so high a price? What happens after this earthly life is ended?" (*Gaudium et spes* 10).

6. *Gaudium et spes* 22.

7. *RMis* 8; cf. *Gaudium et spes* 22 and *Ad gentes* 8.

8. *RH* 9.

9. *RH* 13 and 14.

10. *Redemptoris missio* also commemorates that of the publication of the Decree on the Church's Missionary Activity, *Ad gentes*.

11. *Evangelii nuntiandi* [*EN*] 4.

12. *EN* 14.

13. *EN* 18. "Evangelization is a complex process made up of varied elements: the renewal of humanity, witness, explicit proclamation, inner adherence, entry into the community, acceptance of signs, apostolic initiative" (*EN* 24).

14. *EN* 9.

15. *EN* 30–32.

16. Cf. *RMis* 32.

17. *EN* 35.

18. *EN* 22.

19. *EN* 27.

20. *EN* 80.

21. Ibid.

22. *EN* 5.

23. *EN* 78–79.

24. *RMis* 2.

25. *RMis* 4.

26. The position that defends religious pluralism in principle argues that: (1) since every belief system is historically and culturally conditioned, none has the right to make universal claims and to judge other religions; (2) it is impossible to know God ("Ultimate Reality") in a definitive way; and (3) it is unethical and oppressive to claim normativity for any religion, for this implies a depreciation of other religions. See K. W. Brewer, "The Uniqueness of Christ and the Challenge of the Pluralistic Theology of Religion," in H. Häring and K.-J. Kuschel, eds., *Hans Küng: New Horizons for Faith and Thought* (London: SCM Press, 1993), 198–215, at 201.

27. *RMis* 44.

28. *RMis* 46.

29. *RMis* 48. He continues: "This is a central and determining goal of missionary activity, so much so that the mission is not completed until it succeeds in building a new particular church which functions normally in its local setting."

30. *RMis* 34.

31. *RMis* 33.

32. *RMis* 32. Some positive features are (1) the restoration of "the missions" into the mission of the Church, (2) the inclusion of missiology in ecclesiology, and (3) the integration of mission theology into the Trinitarian plan of salvation.

33. The deeper response concerns faith in Jesus Christ, the topic of the next section.

34. *RMis* 39 and 7.

35. *RMis* 10–11; 36.

36. *RMis* 60.

37. *RMis* 11.

38. For a presentation of these objections, along with a Catholic response, see Paul Griffiths, "The One Jesus and the Many Christs," *Pro Ecclesia* 7 (1998): 152–71.

39. *RHMis* 11.

40. *RH* 1.

41. Ibid.

42. *RMis* 4.

43. *RMis* 5.

44. Ibid.

45. *Dominus Iesus* [*DI*] 6.

46. *DI* 9–10.

47. See John P. Galvin, "From the Humanity of Christ to the Jesus of History: A Paradigm Shift in Catholic Christology," *Theological Studies* 55 (1994): 252–73. Galvin notes that the "Jesus of history" does not name the human nature, just as the "Christ of faith" does not name the divine nature (at 256). The apparent correspondence, however, suggests to some authors that Jesus is only human and Christ is only divine. In traditional usage, these are two concrete names for one and the same Person.

48. See St. Augustine, Sermon 186 ("On Christmas Day"), 3.

49. *RMis* 7.

50. *RH* 10.

51. *RMis* 17–18.

52. *RMis* 17.

53. *RMis* 28–29.

54. *RMis* 29.

55. *DI* 12.

56. *Ad gentes* 2.

57. *Ad gentes* 2–4; see *RMis* 1.

58. *RMis* 7.

59. *RMis* 12.

60. *RH* 9.

61. *RMis* 23.

62. *RMis* 28.

63. *RMis* 12.

Chapter 9 / The Crisis of Liberal Catholicism

1. This chapter is adapted from an address given to the Commonweal Forum, Loyola University Chicago, October 6, 1999.

2. Nominalism is the philosophical view that the names (Latin: *nomina*) we give things that seem to belong in groups are merely conventions that are notional with no actual existence in reality. E.g., there are individual human beings, but no real human nature that describes them all.

3. *Christus Dominus* 13.

Chapter 10 / Lay Catholics

1. This chapter is adapted from an address given to the Spring Assembly of the United States Conference of Catholic Bishops, June 20, 2003.

Chapter 11 / Receiving Identity from the Risen Christ

1. This chapter is adapted from an address given at Loras College, April 27, 2004.

2. "It is a great suffering for the Church in the United States and for the Church in general, for me personally, that this could happen. If I read the history of these events, it is difficult for me to understand how it was possible for priests to fail in this way in the mission to give healing, to give God's love to these children. I am ashamed and we will do everything possible to ensure that this does not happen in future. I think we have to act on three levels: the first is at the level of justice and the political level. I will not speak at this moment about homosexuality: this is another thing. We will absolutely exclude paedophiles from the sacred ministry; it is absolutely incompatible, and whoever is really guilty of being a paedophile cannot be a priest. So at this first level we can do justice and help the victims, because they are deeply affected; these are the two sides of justice: one, that paedophiles cannot be priests and the other, to help in any possible way the victims. Then there is a pastoral level. The victims will need healing and help and assistance and reconciliation: this is a big pastoral engagement and I know that the Bishops and the priests and all Catholic people in the United States will do whatever possible to help, to assist, to heal. We have made a visitation of the seminaries and we will do all that is possible in the education of seminarians for a deep spiritual, human and intellectual formation for the students. Only sound persons can be admitted to the priesthood and only persons with a deep personal life in Christ and who have a deep sacramental life. So, I know that the Bishops and directors of seminarians will do all possible to have a strong, strong discernment because it is more important to have good priests than to have many priests. This is also our third level, and we hope that we can do, and

have done and will do in the future, all that is possible to heal these wounds." From his in-flight interview, April 15, 2008.

3. Peter Steinfels, *A People Adrift: The Crisis of the Roman Catholic Church in America* (New York: Simon & Schuster, 2003), 307.

4. Ibid., 327.

5. Ibid., 330.

6. Ibid., 330–31.

7. Ibid., 338.

8. Ibid., 339.

9. *Pastores gregis,* para. 6.

10. See for instance *Co-workers in the Vineyard of the Lord* (U.S. Conference of Catholic Bishops, 2005).

Chapter 12 / To Reveal the Father's Love:

1. This chapter is adapted from an address to seminarians on March 14, 2003.

2. Jean Laplace, *The Direction of Conscience* (London: G. Chapman, 1967), 70ff.

3. Pope Benedict XVI, address at the Cathedral of St. John the Baptist in Poland, May 25, 2006.

Chapter 13 / Ongoing Liturgical Renewal

1. See Angelo Sodano, "For the Celebration of Italian National Liturgy Week," *L'Osservatore Romano,* English edition 39 (September 24, 2003): 4.

2. Father Jeremy Driscoll throws light on this with his comment that the Christian taking part in the liturgy is "a person who can participate in the community of Divine Persons," indeed, who is "created for this in the image of the Divine Persons" (Jeremy Driscoll, "Liturgy and Fundamental Theology," *Ecclesia Orans* 11, no. 1 [1994]: 79).

3. Contrary to popular, and sometimes academic, misconceptions, active participation in the liturgy is not first of all saying, reading, or taking part in rites. It is primarily, essentially, and indispensably the devotion of mind, heart, and will elicited and brought into vital contact with Christ through the rites. The Latin word *devotio* signifies consecration to God (Odo Casel, *The Mystery of Christian Worship* [New York: Crossroad, 1999], 36). For the liturgy to be fruitful in a person's life there has to be a subjective dimension; those taking part must cooperate with and accept inwardly the act of Jesus the Priest by their devotion (see Pope Pius XII, *Mediator Dei,* 28, 29; CCC 2563).

4. Jean Corbon, *The Wellspring of Worship* (New York: Paulist Press, 1988).

5. Tracey Rowland, *Culture and the Thomist Tradition: After Vatican II* (London: Routledge, 2003), 18–21, 168.

6. The implications of this question, though not as yet fully taken account of by many liturgists, have begun to be spelled out by anthropologists such as Victor Turner, who writes, "If ritual is not to be merely a reflection of secular social life, if its function is partly to protect and partly to express truths which make men free from the exigencies of their status-incumbencies, free to contemplate and pray as well as to speculate and invent, then its repertoire of liturgical actions should not be limited to a direct reflection of the contemporary scene" (Victor Turner, "Passages, Margins and Poverty: Symbols of Communitas," *Worship* 46 [1972]: 391). Traditional liturgy, precisely because of its archaic quality, has power to modify and even reverse the assumptions made in secular living; the archaic is not the obsolete.

7. See Jeremy Driscoll, "Deepening the Theological Dimensions of Liturgical Studies," *Communio* 23 (Fall 1996): 513–14. This article shows how prerational instincts and rhythms make possible an expression of God's Word in human words.

8. Waldemar Trapp, *Vorgeschichte und Ursprung der liturgischen Bewegung: vorwiegend in Hinsicht auf das deutsche Sprachgebiet* (Regensburg, 1940).

9. Aidan Nichols, *Looking at the Liturgy: A Critical View of Its Contemporary Form* (San Francisco: Ignatius, 1996).

10. A noteworthy exception to this is the paper delivered by Stratford Caldecott at the Fontgombault Liturgical Conference in July 2001, titled: "Liturgy and Trinity: Towards an Anthropology of the Liturgy," in *Looking Again at the Question of the Liturgy with Cardinal Ratzinger* (Farnborough, 2003), 36–48.

11. See the masterful analysis of St. Cyril of Jerusalem's theology of sacramental participation by Enrico Mazza, *Mystagogy: A Theology of Liturgy in the Patristic Age* (New York: Pueblo Publishing Co., 1989), 150–64.

12. Tertullian, *De resurrectione carnis* 8.

13. Nichols, *Looking at the Liturgy*, 57.

14. Further and well-documented evidence for this is given by Dr. Tracey Rowland (*Culture and the Thomistic Tradition*, 27–29, 168, n. 69, 175), where she outlines the dilemma created when, in the wake of Vatican II and because of some assumptions of the architects of *Sacrosanctum concilium*, the forms of the liturgy come to be dominated by postmodern mass culture.

Chapter 14 / A True Home Everywhere

1. This chapter is adapted from an address given to the Liturgical Institute Conference, April 5, 2006.

2. *Religion and the Rise of Western Culture* (New York: Doubleday Image, 1991), 43.

3. Tracey Rowland, *Culture and the Thomist Tradition: After Vatican II* (London: Routledge, 2003), 48–49.

4. Romano Guardini, *The Spirit of the Liturgy*, trans. Ada Lane (London: Sheed & Ward, 1937); Joseph Ratzinger, *The Spirit of the Liturgy*, trans. John Saward (San Francisco: Ignatius Press, 2000).

5. Joseph Cardinal Ratzinger, *Truth and Tolerance: Christian Belief and World Religions* (San Francisco: Ignatius Press, 2004), 60–61.

6. Ibid., 64.

Chapter 15 / Too Good to Be True?

1. This chapter is adapted from an earlier address given to the International Eucharistic Congress, Rome, Italy, June 20, 2000.

2. Note the movement from John 6:44–51 to John 6:53–58. The intensification of language may be seen in the Greek verbs used: first *phagein*, to eat; but then, *trogein*, to chew or gnaw.

3. Hans Urs von Balthasar, *Gottbereites Leben* (Freiburg: Johannes Verlag, 1994), 10.

4. Christoph Schönborn, *God's Human Face* (Ignatius: San Francisco, 1994), 93; Cyril of Alexandria, *In Iohannis evangelium*, X, 863: *Patrologia Graeca* 74, 341D.

5. Ignatius of Antioch, *To the Ephesians*, 20, 2, in J. A. Kleist, *The Epistles of St. Clement of Rome and St. Ignatius of Antioch*, Ancient Christian Writers (Westminster, Md.: Newman, 1946), 68.

6. Ibid., 86 and 93.

7. Robert Sokolowski, "The Eucharist and Transubstantiation," *Communio* 24, no. 4 (1997): 870, 869. See Thomas Aquinas, *Summa theologiae*, III, 76, q. 5, where Thomas argues that Christ's body is not in the sacrament in the normal way an extended body exists; not as in a place, but purely in the way *substance* is, in the way that substance *is contained* by the dimensions, wherever that substance might be. This is Thomas's understanding of presence *per modum substantiae*.

8. Ibid., 873–74.

9. Ibid., 873.

10. The material in this section was first developed by Rev. Lawrence Hennessey. See "The Eucharistic Liturgy As Our Expression of Caring for the Church and the World," *Seminary Journal* 5, no. 3 (1999): 21–33.

Chapter 16 / The Difference God Makes

1. This encyclical can be read online or purchased in several different editions, such as the Pauline Books edition (2006).

2. See Jacques Derrida, *Given Time: I. Counterfeit Money*, trans. Peggy Kamuf (Chicago: University of Chicago Press, 1992), 36.

3. Dante Alighieri, *Divine Comedy, Inferno*, V.

Chapter 17 / Godly Humanism

1. Drama of Word and Gesture, in *The Collected Plays and Writings in Theater* (Berkeley: University of California Press, 1987), 380–82.

2. The following analysis is heavily indebted to Kenneth L. Schmitz, *At the Center of the Human Drama: The Philosophical Anthropology of Karol Wojtyła/Pope John Paul II* (Washington, D.C.: Catholic University of America Press, 1993), 8–12.

Epilogue

1. See Aidan Nichols, O.P., *The Shape of Catholic Theology* (Collegeville, Minn.: Liturgical Press, 1991), 41–54.

2. The term is borrowed from Prof. Kenneth Schmitz. See Schmitz, "Community: The Elusive Unity," *Review of Metaphysics* 37 (1983): 243–64.

3. Avery Dulles, S.J., uses these headings from Robert P. Imbelli ("Vatican II: Twenty Years Later," *Commonweal* 109 [October 8, 1982]: 522–26) to begin his discussion of Roman Catholic communion in *The Catholicity of the Church* (Oxford: Clarendon Press, 1985), 4–5.

4. See Mark G. Henninger, S.J., *Relations: Medieval Theories, 1250–1325* (Oxford: Clarendon Press, 1989), 3–10.

5. *Summa theologiae* I, 45, 3, c; *De potentia Dei* VII, 9, c ad 4.

6. Josiah Royce, *The Hope of the Great Community* (New York: Macmillan, 1916), 47.

7. Josiah Royce, "What Is Vital in Christianity," *William James and Other Essays* (New York: Macmillan, 1912), 182.

8. Josiah Royce, *The World and the Individual*, vol. 2 (New York: Macmillan, 1901), 170–72; also "Self-consciousness, Social Consciousness and Nature," in *Studies in Good and Evil* (New York: Appleton, 1906), 218–19.

9. William James, *Principles of Psychology*, vol. 1 (New York: Henry Holt, 1890), 401.

10. In discussion of this point, Father Frank Oppenheim, S.J., has pointed out that the awareness of persons as gifts and the explicit use by Royce of St. Paul's vocabulary of grace grew more evident in his later philosophy, in particular in the four

years between the publication of *The Problem of Christianity* and Royce's death. See Oppenheim, *Royce's Mature Philosophy of Religion* (Notre Dame, Ind.: University of Notre Dame Press, 1987), and Oppenheim, "A Roycean Response to Individualism," in *Beyond Individualism* ed. Donald Gelpi (Notre Dame, Ind.: University of Notre Dame Press, 1989), 87–119. Stuart Gerry Brown, however, argues that Royce's main concern is the protection of the individual as such; see Brown, ed., *The Social Philosophy of Josiah Royce* (Syracuse: Syracuse University Press, 1950), 6. At least, one's interpretation of passages such as the fourth chapter ("The Realm of Grace") in *The Problem of Christianity* depends on whether one sees Royce's work primarily as a philosophy of religion or basically as a philosophy of human experience expressed in religious terms.

11. "Reflective" and "reflexive" are technical terms in Wojtyla's writing, but their separate meanings have to be carefully sought in the many passages of *The Acting Person* (Dordrecht, Holland: D. Reidel Publishing Co., 1979) where the English terms are not fixed consistently with the terminology of the Polish original (*Osoba i Czyn,* 1969).

12. Karol Wojtyla, "The Person: Subject and Community," *Review of Metaphysics* 33 (1979): 305.

13. Ibid., 297.

14. Ibid., 295.

15. Karol Wojtyla, *Alle fonti del rinnovamento: Studio sull' attuazione del Concilio Vaticano Secondo* (Rome: Libreria Editrice Vaticana, 1981; Polish original, 1972), 127. The translation from the Italian is my own.

16. Karol Wojtyla, *Love and Responsibility* (New York: Farrar, Strauss, Giroux, 1981).

17. This solution delivers predication about the Church from reduction to poetic metaphor while resisting any temptation to make the Church a *Gesamtsperson* in Max Scheler's sense of collective person. For a similar but more explicitly theological solution, see Yves Congar, O.P., *I Believe in the Holy Spirit,* vol. 2 (New York: Seabury Press, 1983), 19–20.

Index

Permissions

We gratefully acknowledge the following for permission to reprint material that appears in this book. Citations here indicate the titles of the original works. Please see copyright page for additional information.

Libreria Editrice Vaticana, for *Lecture Commemorating Sacrosanctum Concilium.*

L'Osservatore Romano, for "One Church and One World."

Tulane University, Philosophy and Theology in the New Millennium series, for public lecture "Images of God in the Writings of Pope John Paul II Spirituality for a New Millennium."

The USCCB, for "The Eucharist in the Church and the World," first published in *Book of Readings on the Eucharist.*

Archdiocese of Chicago: Liturgy Training Publications, for reprint of "Cardinal Reflections: Active Participation and the Liturgy" and for "John Paul and Liturgical Inculturation," in *The Liturgical Legacy of John Paul II,* the latter forthcoming from Hillenbrand Books. © LTP, 2005, 1-800-933-1800 *www.LTP.org.* All rights reserved.

Cor Unum, for the address at the World Conference of Charity (2006).

Adoremus and the *Adoremus Bulletin,* for *Sacrosanctum Concilium* anniversary address, "The Foundations of Liturgical Reform," March 2004.

The *Proceedings of the American Catholic Philosophical Association,* for "Being Through Others in Christ: Esse Per and Ecclesial Communion," vol. 66 (1992): 29–44.

Commonweal Foundation, for "The Crisis of Liberal Catholicism," © 1999, Commonweal Foundation. Reprinted with permission. For subscriptions, *www.commonwealmagazine.org.*

Origins (For further information on Origins and the CNS documentary service, visit *www.CatholicNews.com* or *www.OriginsOnline.com*).

Theology Digest, Winter 2000 and Winter 2002 issues.

Paulist Press, for excerpts from *The New Catholic Evangelization,* edited by Kenneth Boyack, C.S.P., and for excerpts from "The Catholic World, Evangelizing American Culture," copyright © 1992 by The Missionary Society of St. Paul the Apostle in the State of New York, Paulist Press, Inc., New York and Mahwah, N.J. Reprinted by permission of Paulist Press, Inc. *www.paulistpress.com.*

The Crossroad Publishing Company is honored to present the finest works on Catholic thought.

Joseph Cardinal Ratzinger (Pope Benedict XVI)

Values in a Time of Upheaval

The Yes of Jesus Christ
Spiritual Exercises in Faith, Hope, and Love

Journey to Easter
Spiritual Reflections for the Lenten Season

A New Song for the Lord
Faith in Christ and Liturgy Today

Christoph Cardinal Schonborn

The Source of Life
Exploring the Mystery of the Eucharist

With Jesus Every Day
How Believing Transforms Living

Walter Cardinal Kasper

The God of Jesus Christ

A Celebration of Priestly Ministry
Challenge, Renewal, and Joy in the Catholic Priesthood

Sacrament of Unity
The Eucharist and the Church

Leadership in the Church
How Traditional Roles Can Help Serve the Christian Community Today